International Liquidity and the Financial Crisis

Most policy-makers did not anticipate the financial crisis of 2008. Nevertheless, in contrast to their performance during the Great Depression, central banks around the world, led by the Federal Reserve, acted decisively following the collapse of Lehman Brothers and provided huge injections of liquidity into the financial markets, thereby preventing a far worse outcome. *International Liquidity and the Financial Crisis* compares the 2008 crisis with the disaster of 1931 and explores the similarities and differences. It considers the lasting effects of the crisis on international liquidity, the possibilities for an international lender of last resort, and the enlargement of the International Monetary Fund after the crisis. It shows that there is no clear demarcation between monetary and macro-prudential policies, and discusses how central banks need to adapt to a new environment in which global liquidity is much scarcer.

WILLIAM A. ALLEN worked in the Bank of England from 1972 to 2004, where he was Head of the Money Market Operations Division, Head of the Foreign Exchange Division and Director for Europe. Since 2004 he has been an honorary senior visiting fellow of Cass Business School in London and has published widely on central banking and international finance. He is a specialist adviser to the House of Commons Treasury Committee and a consultant to the International Monetary Fund.

International Liquidity and the Financial Crisis

WILLIAM A. ALLEN

CAMBRIDGE
UNIVERSITY PRESS

CAMBRIDGE
UNIVERSITY PRESS

University Printing House, Cambridge CB2 8BS, United Kingdom

Published in the United States of America by Cambridge University Press, New York

Cambridge University Press is part of the University of Cambridge.

It furthers the University's mission by disseminating knowledge in the pursuit of education, learning and research at the highest international levels of excellence.

www.cambridge.org
Information on this title: www.cambridge.org/9781107420328

First published 2013
First paperback edition 2014

A catalogue record for this publication is available from the British Library

Library of Congress Cataloguing in Publication data
Allen, Bill, 1949–
 International liquidity and the financial crisis / William A. Allen.
  p. cm.
 Includes bibliographical references and index.
 ISBN 978-1-107-03004-6 (hardback)
 1. International liquidity. 2. Financial crises. 3. Global Financial Crisis,
 2008–2009. I. Title.
 HG3893.A45 2012
 332´.042–dc23
 2012024503

ISBN 978-1-107-03004-6 Hardback
ISBN 978-1-107-42032-8 Paperback

Contents

Figures

Tables

Preface

This book draws very heavily on a programme of work which Dr Richhild Moessner of the Bank for International Settlements and I embarked on in late 2008, to explore the effects of the financial crisis on international liquidity flows and the ways in which central banks and governments were responding to the crisis. Our work has been released in articles in economics journals and working papers, details of which can be found in the references at the end of the book.

The purpose of the book is to provide a coherent account of the effects of the crisis on international liquidity. Dr Moessner and I have been equal partners in the research on which the book is largely based. She has very generously allowed me to draw freely on our joint work and has been characteristically supportive of the book project. I therefore owe her a great deal. The book also contains some material and expresses some views which are mine alone and for which Dr Moessner bears no responsibility.

I am very grateful to the Bank for International Settlements for its hospitality, and for allowing me to use material which it has published. The views I express in the book are mine and do not necessarily reflect those of the BIS. The book also draws on papers published in *Central Banking*, the *Financial History Review*, the *Journal of Financial Transformation*, *Revista de Economia Institucional* and *World Economics*. I am grateful to the publishers for permission to use this material.

Many other people have assisted the work programme by means of comments on papers, discussions at seminars, statistical advice and conversations on the subject matter. They include Bob Aliber, Edmund Allen, Lucy Allen, Rosalind Allen, Naohiko Baba, Peter Bernholz, Bilyana Bogdanova, Claudio Borio, Maria Canelli, Matt Canzoneri, Forrest Capie, Stephen Cecchetti, Jae-Hyun Choi and other officials of the Bank of Korea, Henning Dalgaard, Petra Gerlach, Homero

Goncalves, Charles Goodhart, Jacob Gyntelberg, Dale Henderson, Takamasa Hisada, Corinne Ho, Toshio Idesawa, Harold James, Anders Jorgensen, Andrew Levin, Ivo Maes, Istvan Mak, Bill Martin, Bob McCauley, Patrick McGuire, Dubravko Mihaljek, Shinobu Nagakawa, Ed Nelson, Tim Ng, Jacek Osinski, Judit Pales, Jong Seok Park, Zoltan Pozsar, Swapan Pradhan, Catherine Schenk, Gert Schnabel, Peter Stella, Agne Subelyte, Camilo Tovar, Ted Truman, Philip Turner, Christian Upper, Lorant Varga, Anders Vredin and Geoffrey Wood. I am grateful to them all. None of them bears any responsibility for errors and misinterpretations in the book, and the views expressed are my responsibility alone.

I owe a very great debt to the late Michael Dealtry, who spent much time in teaching me about the international monetary system.

My greatest debt is to my wife Rosemary, for her steadfast support through thick and thin and for tolerating my frequent physical and mental absences. The book is dedicated to her.

1 | *Introduction*

The world financial crisis of 2008 threatened to destroy the international monetary system, and would have done so if governments and central banks had not prevented it. There had been several financial crises in the previous forty years, including the Latin American debt crisis of the early 1980s, the Nordic banking crises of the early 1990s and the Asian crisis of 1997–98. However, the crisis of 2007–09 was on a different scale. Its essential difference was that it endangered the continued existence of many of the largest financial companies in the world, and consequently threatened to do devastating damage to much of the world economy. It was a global systemic crisis rather than a serious regional crisis. In that respect, the only comparably serious event in the previous century was the banking crisis of 1931, which not only threatened but actually destroyed the international monetary system of that time. When the crisis struck in 1931, governments and central banks could not prevent the severe recession that had begun in 1929 from turning into the global Great Depression.

At the time of writing in early 2012, the global economic outlook is overshadowed by the euro-area sovereign debt crisis, which has remained unresolved since it emerged in the spring of 2010. That crisis may in some part be regarded as a consequence of the crisis of 2008, in that the public finance problems of Ireland and Spain have arisen from the need to support commercial banks, and the public finance problems of other euro-area countries have been aggravated by the recession that followed the 2008 crisis. Nevertheless, the euro-area crisis largely reflects problems within the euro area, notably payments imbalances among the member countries and persistent public finance problems in some of them. It can be regarded as an event separate from the 2008 crisis. This book is confined to the 2008 crisis, and a comparison with 1931; a comparable analysis of the euro-area crisis would be premature.

The book describes how the 2008 crisis was propagated from country to country, and how it was contained by the actions of central banks, led by the Federal Reserve, and governments. It compares the two crises, and argues that the crisis of 2008 was much better managed than that of 1931, largely because the gold standard, which was still in operation in 1931, prevented any adequate response to the earlier crisis. The fact that global economic growth resumed in 2009 testifies to the success of governments and central banks in short-term crisis management. Nevertheless, the crisis management of international liquidity in 2008 relied heavily on ad hoc action by the Federal Reserve, and the crisis exposed inadequacies in the normal management of international liquidity. These inadequacies are now being addressed, both by individual countries and by international bodies such as the G20 and the International Monetary Fund. The book discusses possible solutions, and explores the ways in which the crisis may affect macroeconomic policies.

The world financial crisis broke surface in 2007, when it became clear that defaults on mortgages in the United States were rising alarmingly and that many securities backed by mortgages were worth nothing like what the market had previously assumed. There was a contagious reaction, as Chapter 2 describes. It became very difficult to use US mortgages to raise funds, either by selling them or by using them as collateral for borrowing. The wholesale financial markets in which banks and other financial companies borrowed money to finance their lending dried up.[1] In the United Kingdom, too, banks were unable to sell UK mortgage-backed securities, and Northern Rock, whose business model depended on doing just that, had to be provided with emergency liquidity by the Bank of England and subsequently nationalised, even though, according to the UK Financial Services Authority, it was solvent, exceeded its regulatory capital requirement and had a good quality loan book.[2] The difference between the eurodollar interest rates (the cost of borrowing to banks) and US Treasury yields widened sharply in August 2007 (see Figure 1.1).

In all, the household mortgage losses of banks in the United States and Europe in the years 2007–10 were about $560 billion, or 4.7 per cent of their total mortgage assets.[3] The losses were the equivalent of

---

[1] See FCIC (2011a), ch. 13.
[2] Cited in Bank of England statement of 14 September 2007 (www. bankofengland.co.uk/publications/news/2007/090.htm).
[3] IMF (2010a), table 1.2.

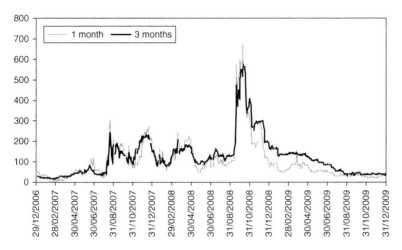

Figure 1.1 The 'TED spread': difference between eurodollar interest rates and US Treasury yields (basis points).
Source: Federal Reserve Table H15, author's calculations.

about 1 per cent of the world's annual gross product. This is a large amount, but not nearly as large as the amounts lost as a result of the ensuing financial crisis, which caused the largest recession since the Great Depression of the 1930s. World output, which had grown at 5.2% in 2007, decelerated to 2.8% in 2008 and contracted by 0.6% in 2009. Even if world output returns very quickly to its former growth path, which would require extremely rapid growth in the next few years, there will have been a permanent loss equivalent to a multiple of the original mortgage losses. The losses will therefore be quite disproportionate to the shock which was their immediate cause, which is prima facie evidence that the financial system was in an unstable condition when the shock occurred. Nevertheless, this book will argue that the outcome would have been much worse had it not been for the prompt emergency provision of international liquidity by the Fed.

Central banks responded to the events of August 2007 by providing additional liquidity in massive amounts, and by accepting a wider range of assets as collateral than hitherto. Governments extended deposit insurance schemes. In most cases these measures were sufficient, and were adopted quickly enough, to contain the crisis, though the United Kingdom experienced its first bank run since the nineteenth

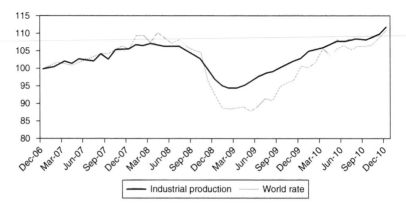

Figure 1.2 World activity indicators (indexes, December 2006 = 100, seasonally adjusted).
Source: CPB Netherlands Bureau for Economic Policy Analysis.

century when depositors queued to withdraw money from Northern Rock.

With the passage of time it became increasingly clear that, for some financial companies, the problem was not just one of liquidity but that there was also a threat to their solvency. Bear Stearns, a New York broker-dealer, was taken over by J.P.Morgan in March 2008, in an operation managed by the Federal Reserve, which was concerned about the risk of financial instability if Bear Stearns failed. In order to facilitate the transaction, the Fed accepted considerable financial risk: it lent $28.8 billion to the buyer, J.P.Morgan, against the collateral of Bear Stearns' mortgage assets and without recourse to J.P.Morgan. The news that Bear Stearns had needed to be rescued caused additional problems for banks in borrowing money to finance their lending (see Figure 1.1). During this period, the problems of the financial industry had no dramatic effects on the economy at large. World trade continued to increase from August 2007 to April 2008 (see Figure 1.2). After April 2008, it fell, but only moderately.

The crisis became acute when Lehman Brothers filed for bankruptcy on Monday 15 September 2008, after attempts to find a private buyer for it had failed. On the same day, Bank of America announced that it would take over Merrill Lynch, whose survival had been in doubt. On Tuesday 16 September, the Fed rescued American International Group. Interest rate spreads blew out to their widest levels yet (Figure 1.1).

There was extensive financial contagion in US financial markets, as uncertainty about the scale of the exposures to the now-insolvent Lehman Brothers caused doubts about the solvency of a wide range of other financial companies.

A run on money market mutual funds began when the net asset value of shares in the Reserve Primary Money Market Fund, which had lent to Lehmans, fell below $1 ('broke the buck') on Tuesday 16 September. On Friday 19th, the Fed announced that it would finance commercial banks' purchases of high-quality asset-backed commercial paper from money market mutual funds, and the Treasury announced a temporary guarantee programme for money market mutual funds.

Noting that Lehman Brothers, a non-bank broker-dealer, had been allowed to fail despite its systemic importance, hedge funds withdrew massive quantities of cash and unsecured assets from other non-bank broker-dealer companies that had been providing them with prime brokerage services. Securities markets dried up. Banks knew that they would have to meet pre-arranged commitments to lend to borrowers who could no longer borrow in commercial paper and other markets. To protect themselves against unforeseeable contingencies, they added massively to their cash assets, mainly in the form of deposits with the Fed. The pressures thus created led to a 'collateral squeeze'. There was a general surge in demand for cash and liquid assets or assets which could be turned into cash even in the stressed market environment of the time.[4] This had the effect of sucking dollar funds from abroad into the United States. It was in this acute phase that the crisis caused major problems for international liquidity and began to do serious damage to the world economy.

The flow of dollars home to the United States meant that banks in other countries were unable to roll over the short-term wholesale dollar borrowing with which they had been financing longer-term dollar assets, many of which were claims on US borrowers. They could either sell the assets, or find other financing. The first option was difficult in the prevailing illiquid markets and would have depressed asset prices further and compounded the existing stresses in US financial markets. The second option was also difficult and unattractive. Non-US banks

---

[4] For accounts of these events, see Paulson (2010), FCIC (2011a), chs 18–20 and the timeline available on the Federal Reserve Bank of St Louis website (http://timeline.stlouisfed.org/index.cfm?p=timeline).

were able to borrow from their home central banks in their home currencies, but the markets in which they could swap their home currencies for dollars quickly became stressed and illiquid.

Central banks outside the US had the option of using their own foreign exchange reserves to provide dollar liquidity to their domestic commercial banks, but few were both willing and able to do so. The Fed itself solved the international liquidity problem by greatly extending the size and geographical scope of the swap lines that it had set up in 2007, and providing dollars for foreign central banks to on-lend to local commercial banks to replace the dollars that had been pulled back to the United States. In doing so, it took both financial and political risks; nevertheless, it acted promptly and decisively.

International liquidity stresses were not confined to dollars. There were also large homeward flows of yen to Japan and of Swiss francs to Switzerland. The yen flows were the result of the unwinding of some of the yen carry trades that had been established after Japanese interest rates fell to very low levels in the late 1990s. The unwinding of these carry trades had serious macroeconomic effects in the countries, such as New Zealand, which had earlier received large capital inflows from Japan. The Swiss franc flows were largely from Hungary, Poland and Austria, where many mortgages had been denominated in Swiss francs, on account of the low level of interest rates in that currency.

Amid these vast flows of funds caused by distress within the financial system, the credit needs of many bank customers were not met, and many credit lines were abruptly curtailed. According to the Fed's quarterly Senior Loan Officer Survey, credit conditions for commercial and industrial borrowers in the fourth quarter of 2008 were at their tightest since the survey was first published in 1990. Surveys conducted by the European Central Bank and the Bank of England also showed very tight credit conditions at that time.[5] Trade credit insurance suddenly became very expensive and hard to get. The volume of world trade fell by 7.8% (seasonally adjusted) between October and November, and by February 2009 it had fallen by 15.4%. World industrial production

---

[5] These surveys are available on the websites of the sponsoring central banks. See www.federalreserve.gov/boarddocs/SnLoanSurvey/default.htm, www.ecb.int/stats/money/surveys/lend/html/index.en.html and www.bankofengland.co.uk/publications/other/monetary/creditconditions.htm.

fell by 8.1% between October 2008 and February 2009 (see Figure 1.2).

The swap lines that were provided, particularly those provided by the Fed, were provided promptly. They prevented bank failures that would have made the global recession much more serious, and thereby prevented the financial crisis from having far worse consequences than it actually had. They demonstrated enlightened self-interest on the part of the United States. However, in different circumstances, they might not have been forthcoming. For example, the Fed might have been less sensitive to market developments, or less conscious of the need to respond to them. Or if political sentiment in the United States had been more isolationist, it might have been impossible for the Fed to provide funds to other financially important countries, even though it was clearly in the interests of the United States for it to do so.

Problems of bank liquidity within a single currency area can be managed if the local central bank is able and willing to act as 'lender of last resort' by providing emergency liquidity promptly and in as large amounts as are needed, at high interest rates and against good collateral, as recommended by Bagehot in 1873, and as practised by the Bank of England in various nineteenth-century banking crises. International liquidity problems are inherently more difficult to manage because there is no acknowledged international lender of last resort. Nevertheless, the globalisation of finance has brought with it the globalisation of liquidity problems. The Fed acted decisively as an ad hoc international lender of last resort in 2008, but it cannot be assumed that a future international liquidity crisis could be managed in the same way as the recent one.

For a period in 2008 and early 2009, the spectre of the Great Depression of the 1930s hung over the global economy, and there were serious concerns about 'tail risks'. If the crisis had been badly managed, the tail risks might have materialised, and a comparison of the recent crisis with the one which happened eighty years earlier is therefore pertinent. The economic boom of the 1920s ended in June 1929, when world output reached its peak. The equity market famously collapsed in October. The United States was affected more quickly and more severely than countries in western Europe, and the monetary policies of the Federal Reserve have been widely blamed for failing to combat the depression effectively.[6] Bank failures had been fairly widespread in the United States during the 1920s,[7] but they increased sharply in 1930 and 1931. In the absence of effective deposit insurance, they played an important role in aggravating the depression.[8] In Europe, the initial economic downturn was less severe, but the collapse of Creditanstalt, the largest bank in Austria, in May 1931, set off banking crises in Hungary and Germany, as well as Austria itself. Those countries' gold and foreign exchange reserves were quickly exhausted by the support provided to distressed domestic commercial banks, and they imposed restrictions on foreign payments. London banks had large short-term claims on borrowers in central Europe, which suddenly became illiquid. As a result, the financial stress was transmitted to London, the financial centre of Europe. The international liquidity position of the UK was already fragile, in that the Bank of England's gold reserves were much smaller than the UK's short-term external liabilities. There were large withdrawals of funds from the UK and associated sales of sterling. The Bank of England tried vainly to support sterling by foreign official borrowing but eventually abandoned the gold standard in September 1931. This marked the end of the attempt to recreate the pre-war international monetary system in post-war conditions. Other countries, notably France, maintained the gold standard for several more years, but were ultimately forced to abandon it, against a background of high unemployment, weak output and growing political instability in Europe.

It is obviously of the highest importance to understand the reasons why so many bank assets went bad, and why banks incurred such enormous losses, so that the necessary institutional changes can be considered and put into effect. However, this book is concerned with first aid rather than diagnosis and cure. Much research has been done on diagnosis and cure. For example, Acharya, Carpenter, Gabaix *et al.* (2009) discuss the corporate governance of large complex financial institutions (LCFIs), many of which came under severe stress during 2008. They distinguish between 'equity governance', which is the responsibility of corporate boards, and 'debt and regulatory

---

[6] See Almunia, Bénétrix, Eichengreen, O'Rourke and Rua (2010), Maddison (2010) for information on output. On the role of the Federal Reserve, see for example Meltzer (2003).

[7] See Board of Governors of the Federal Reserve System (1976), p. 281.

[8] See e.g. Friedman and Schwartz (1963), Bernanke (2000).

governance', which is at least partly the responsibility of regulators. As regards equity governance, they comment that:

It is hard to say how many of the large losses we have seen were the result of inefficient risk choices and how many were simply bets gone awry. But there are several reasons why even a strong equity governance system could have given rise to risky strategies with the outcomes that we have observed. Gaming of TBTF [too big to fail] guarantees, priced deposit insurance, and coarse capital requirements would all have led to similar strategies even if equity governance was effective.[9]

However, Acharya *et al.* also identify three reasons why equity governance may have been weak, namely:

i.   Some LCFIs are so enormous that even the largest investors hold only a small fraction of the equity, which is not enough to make it worthwhile for them to incur the costs of becoming activist investors.
ii. LCFIs are so complex that it is difficult for board members, or potential acquirers, to exert discipline on the management.
iii. Entry into the banking industry is difficult, owing to high fixed costs and to capital requirements, so that competition is unable to exert discipline on managements.

Acharya *et al.* suggest that the second of these reasons also made it difficult for regulators to ask relevant hard questions.[10]

Just as this book does not attempt to analyse the causes of the crisis, nor is it primarily concerned with the development of the crisis in the year between August 2007, when sub-prime mortgage concerns caused liquidity in financial markets to dry up, and September 2008, when Lehman Brothers failed. Its focus is on how the crisis developed and was propagated internationally, and how it was managed, in its acute phase after Lehman Brothers failed. It describes why liquidity conditions became critical in the United States, and how the shortage of liquidity in the United States created localised shortages of dollar liquidity in other countries, and how the prompt emergency actions of the Federal Reserve relieved the shortages and thereby prevented

---

[9] P. 191.
[10] For more information on diagnosis and cure, see Shiller (2005), Reinhart and Rogoff (2009) and Davies (2010).

the crisis from having far graver consequences. It also describes how localised shortages of other currencies emerged outside their home countries, and what measures were taken by central banks to relieve them. In other words, it is about crisis management rather than crisis prevention.

This book compares the acute phase of the recent crisis with that of 1931. It finds parallels in the way in which the two crises were propagated from country to country. As regards the management of the two crises, it concludes, consistently with the currently prevailing consensus, that the gold standard exerted a malign influence in the 1930s by preventing central banks from pursuing policies that might have alleviated the depression.[11] The management of the recent crisis was certainly not perfect, but it was decisively better than that of the 1930s.

Some might say that the recent crisis was fundamentally about the solvency of banks, that the liquidity crisis was just a symptom of that fundamental problem, and that the overriding priority is therefore to reduce the risks to bank solvency in future. Reducing the risks to bank solvency is certainly extremely important, but the example of Northern Rock shows that a bank judged to be solvent can nevertheless be destroyed if it has inadequate liquidity. The main official response to the crisis has been the Basel 3 programme, which intensifies the stringency of bank regulation by increasing minimum capital requirements and imposing for the first time internationally agreed minimum liquidity requirements. Whatever the merits of the programme, it would surely be unwise to assume that it will eliminate the risk of future crises.

The crisis has exposed the need for new thinking, not only about financial regulation but also about international liquidity. Many central banks simply did not have enough foreign exchange reserves to provide foreign currency liquidity support to commercial banks in their territories during the recent crisis. The book therefore reviews the development of international liquidity over the past four decades, since the collapse of the Bretton Woods structure. It discusses the main influences on reserve-holding behaviour, which have varied enormously among countries; so much so that a single country (China) held on its own 26.6 per cent of global foreign exchange reserves

[11] See Eichengreen (1992).

at the end of 2009. Global foreign exchange reserves had risen by a very large amount since the collapse of the Bretton Woods system in 1971, and were $6.7 trillion at the end of 2007. Those reserves would have been amply sufficient to manage the flows of funds set off by the Lehman failure if they had been appropriately distributed. However, the reserves were mostly in the wrong place. By and large, the countries which needed foreign currency liquidity the most had the least reserves, and vice versa. The crisis and its aftermath showed that countries needed more assurance that they could get access to international liquidity in an emergency, as they might do if there were an institutionalised international lender of last resort. Current indications are that the role of lender of last resort will be assigned to the International Monetary Fund. The resources available to the Fund have been greatly enlarged since the crisis, and a debate is in progress about the future management of international liquidity risks. While the debate has continued, countries have in any case been self-insuring against international liquidity risks in the aftermath of the crisis by adding to their foreign exchange reserves. These actions are likely to have significant macroeconomic consequences. The book reviews the debate and discusses the implications of the IMF being designated as the international lender of last resort, and its likely effectiveness.

The increased demand for foreign exchange reserves is just one aspect of a post-crisis surge in demand for liquid assets, resulting partly from intensified bank regulation and partly from the natural caution of banks and others. This is likely to have macroeconomic effects, and macroeconomic policy will have to take the supply and demand for liquid assets much more seriously in the future than it has done in the past. Policies which affect the balance between supply and demand for liquid assets, such as public debt management, are likely to have much more macroeconomic significance than in the past. These issues are discussed in the concluding chapter of the book.

2 | *The domestic liquidity crisis in the USA*

1. The flight to liquidity and safety

The global liquidity crisis began in the US mortgage market. It became clear during 2007 that delinquencies on non-prime mortgages that had been originated in 2006 were very much higher than on similar mortgages originated in previous years.[1] This development caused serious doubts about the true value of mortgage-backed securities. Holders of mortgage-backed securities were not able to find out precisely which mortgages were supporting their particular securities, so all mortgage-backed securities were stigmatised.[2] Market participants were unsure of the value of mortgage assets, of other market participants' exposures to mortgage assets, and of other market participants' exposures to market participants who were exposed to mortgage assets. A flight to liquidity and safety accordingly began.

This development had profound consequences for the 'shadow banking system', which consisted of financial companies which were not banks, but which performed maturity transformation by holding inventories of longer-term assets, in many cases including mortgage-backed securities, financed by shorter-term liabilities such as asset-backed commercial paper. Investors became unwilling to roll over asset-backed commercial paper when it matured, and became suspicious of companies and funds which held asset-backed commercial paper. The shadow banking system began to contract. Many shadow banks had back-up liquidity guarantees from commercial banks, so that the doubts about the assets of the shadow banks, as well as about the assets of commercial banks themselves, led inevitably in turn to doubts about the soundness of commercial banks.[3] After the failure

---

[1] See International Monetary Fund (2007), p. 7, fig. 1.6.
[2] The securitisation of sub-prime mortgages and their lack of transparency are described by Gorton (2010), ch. 3.
[3] See for example Pozsar, Adrian, Ashcraft and Boesky (2010).

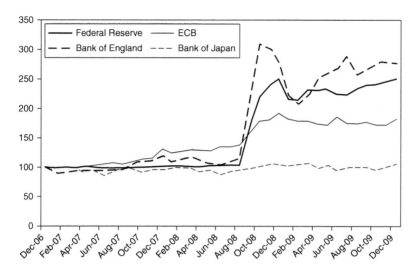

Figure 2.1 Central banks' total assets, 2007–09 (in national currencies, December 2006 = 100).
Sources: Central banks.

of Lehman Brothers on 15 September 2008, the flight intensified and turned into a full-blown crisis, as is described below.

The liabilities of governments and central banks in countries with stable public finances were regarded as liquid and safe, and the demand for them surged. Above all, the demand for US government securities was very strong, as was the demand for deposits with Federal Reserve banks. Central bankers had learned the lessons of the Great Depression, and none had learned it better than Federal Reserve Chairman Ben Bernanke who had done extensive research on the Great Depression while at Princeton University, and had published a book on the subject.[4] They generally recognised this surge for what it was and supplied deposits and other liabilities in large quantities, using the proceeds to acquire additional assets, thus acting as 'lender of last resort' in defence of financial stability. The balance sheets of some central banks, not only the Fed but also those of the European Central Bank and the Bank of England, ballooned in size, as Figure 2.1 shows, and budget deficits widened massively as incomes and employment fell.

[4] See Bernanke (2000).

The flight to liquidity and safety was manifested in many ways. For example, the 'TED spread', the yield differential between eurodollar deposits and US government securities, widened sharply after August 2007 (see Figure 1.1). This reflected the growing doubts about the security of commercial banks (not just US-owned ones), the strength of commercial banks' demand to borrow and the strength of demand for US government securities. This chapter aims to describe how the crisis developed in the United States after Lehman Brothers failed, and to explain how domestic developments in the United States pulled in dollar funds from abroad and thereby propagated the crisis to the rest of the world.

2. The collateral squeeze

The contraction of the shadow banking system was accompanied by, and accelerated by, a collateral squeeze, which may be defined as a surge in demand for cash and collateral assets which can be turned into cash. The squeeze became particularly intense after Lehman Brothers failed in September 2008, and had powerful effects on the many shadow banks which routinely financed their assets by collateralised borrowing, using the assets as collateral. This section describes how a collateral squeeze can develop and what its effects on the balance sheets of banks and shadow banks can be. The heavy inflow of funds to the United States after the failure of Lehman Brothers can be partly explained as one of the side-effects of the collateral squeeze.

A collateral squeeze affects leveraged companies which use their assets as collateral for their borrowings. For present purposes such companies are defined as 'shadow banks'. This definition of shadow banks therefore includes many broker-dealers and hedge funds, but it excludes most money market mutual funds, which are strictly speaking not leveraged, because investors buy shares which have no guarantee of capital value.[5] Table 2.1 shows the essential features of the balance sheet of a shadow bank as thus defined.

---

[5] Nevertheless, the Fed went to great lengths in 2008 to prevent money market mutual funds from 'breaking the buck', by establishing the Asset-backed Commercial Paper Money Market Mutual Fund Liquidity Facility and the Money Market Investor Funding Facility. The Fed commented that: 'Without additional liquidity in the money markets, forced sales of ABCP could have depressed the price of ABCP and other short-term instruments, resulting in

Table 2.1 *The balance sheet of a shadow bank*

Assets	Liabilities
Liquid assets (L)	Capital (K)
Securities (S)	Unsecured liabilities (U)
	Collateralised liabilities (C)

We assume that the shadow bank holds securities (S), which it uses to collateralise borrowings, and a precautionary reserve (L) of liquid assets which are in the form of cash and securities which are unencumbered but which could be used in an emergency to obtain cash quickly, e.g. by selling them to the central bank, or using them as collateral for borrowing from the central bank. When using its securities (S) to collateralise its borrowing, the shadow bank has to pledge a surplus margin of securities in excess of the value of the loan. This is known as a haircut. For the purposes of exposition, we assume that the fractional haircut is h. The amount of securities that the company has to pledge as collateral for its liabilities is therefore (1 + h) C. Since the shadow bank's securities holdings are S in total, it follows that:

$$S \geq (1 + h) \, C, \text{ i.e.} \qquad (2.1)$$

$$S \leq (1 + h) \, (K + U - L) \, / \, h \qquad (2.2)$$

One kind of collateral squeeze can be represented as an increase in h, i.e. an increase in the surplus margin of collateral that the shadow bank has to pledge to secure a loan. If h were to increase to, say, h^*, there would be no necessary consequences for the balance sheet if its leverage is not too great, i.e. if

$$S \leq (1 + h^*) \, (K + U - L) \, / \, h^* \qquad (2.3)$$

In that situation, the shadow bank would have enough unpledged securities to be able simply to provide the additional required collateral out of its assets.

a cycle of losses to MMMFs and even higher levels of redemptions and a weakening of investor confidence in MMMFs and the financial markets' (see www.federalreserve.gov/newsevents/reform_amlf.htm).

If however the shadow bank has insufficient unpledged securities to accommodate the increase in h, then it must reduce its holdings of securities to S*, increase capital to K*, increase unsecured liabilities to U*, or reduce its precautionary liquid assets to L*, where

$$S^* \leq (1 + h^*) \, (K^* + U^* - L^*) \, / \, h^* \qquad (2.4)$$

In practice, it is likely to try to do all four: reduce securities holdings, try to increase capital, try to increase unsecured liabilities, and use liquid assets.

For the purpose of exposition, we assume first that the shadow bank is unable to increase capital or unsecured liabilities, and that it decides not to use its liquid assets (or that it has none), and that the entire adjustment is therefore accomplished by sales of securities. In that case, the volume of sales must be at least

$$S - S^* = ((1/h) - (1/h^*))(K + U - L) \qquad (2.5)$$

If h increases from, say 0.1 to 0.2 – in other words, if the firm's trading counterparties require it to pledge 1.2 units of assets to secure 1 unit of borrowing, rather than 1.1 – then the firm might have to reduce its securities holdings by up to half.

Another kind of collateral squeeze can be represented as a fall in U – i.e. a reduction in the amount of unsecured funding available to the shadow bank. This might happen for example if trading counterparties which had previously been willing to tolerate unsecured exposures to the shadow bank suddenly begin to demand collateral, or cut their exposures.

Again for the purposes of exposition, we assume that the entire adjustment is accomplished by the sale of securities. If U falls to U', then S will have to fall to S', where

$$S' - S = ((1 + h)/h)(U' - U) \qquad (2.6)$$

If h is, say, 0.1, then the required fall in securities holdings is eleven times as large as the fall in unsecured funding. Thus both an increase in haircuts and a fall in unsecured funding can threaten to force a shadow bank to make extremely large asset sales.

Shadow banks hold liquid assets precisely to protect them against the risk of being forced to sell large amounts of assets in a short time. However, if the firm has used its liquid assets to meet additional collateral demands, it is likely to want to rebuild them as protection against future contingencies (unless it is confident that the risk has passed). Therefore liquid assets enable the firm to spread its asset sales over time, but not to avoid them altogether.

If the collateral squeeze is a general market phenomenon, rather than specific to one firm or a few firms, then all shadow banks which finance themselves in this way will be subject to the same pressure. It is therefore unlikely that the buyers of securities sold by shadow banks will be other shadow banks. They are much more likely to be unleveraged 'real-money investors', who will pay for the securities they buy from shadow banks by drawing down commercial bank deposits. The funds withdrawn by real-money investors from banks will be transferred to shadow banks in payment for securities. The shadow banks will use the proceeds to repay collateralised loans to the commercial banks. Thus the assets and liabilities of the commercial banks fall in parallel. The deleveraging of the shadow banking system is matched by deleveraging of the commercial banking system.

The problems of the shadow banks are likely to be greatly aggravated by falls in securities prices caused by the additional supply. These price falls will cause equal reductions in S and K, making it harder for shadow banks to meet collateral requirements and causing a positive feedback loop between securities prices and supply of securities.

The positive feedback loop generates a downward spiral of securities prices, which may fall to levels which look extremely cheap when valued by reference to 'fundamentals'. As prices fall, shadow banks have an increasingly powerful incentive to interrupt the positive feedback loop by increasing capital or unsecured liabilities (K or U), or by using liquid assets (reducing L), and real-money investors have an increasingly powerful incentive to interrupt it by buying securities for cash.

The deleveraging of the shadow banking system began in the summer of 2007, but it became much more intense after the Lehman failure in September 2008. Lehman Brothers' failure shocked the market by showing that a large, systemically important broker-dealer might be allowed to fail. After that, not only did collateral margins (h) increase, but the market trading counterparties of the remaining large broker-dealers, mainly hedge funds to which the broker-dealers provided prime brokerage services, became more anxious about their stability and became much less tolerant of unsecured exposures to them. In the terms of Table 2.1, U fell sharply (and K was falling at the same time as a result of trading losses), as Section 4 will show in one important case. This greatly magnified the pressure to find new sources of capital and unsecured liabilities.

3. Commercial bank balance sheets after the Lehman Brothers failure

As noted above, the post-Lehman crisis in the United States drew in massive amounts of funds from abroad. Between 3 September and 31 December 2008, the net debt of commercial banks located in the United States to their foreign offices increased by $575 billion, of which $165 billion was accounted for by US-chartered banks and the remainder, $410 billion, by foreign-related banks. Table 2.2 shows how other items in the commercial banks' balance sheets changed over the same period.

The increase in bank assets, other than cash, is not hard to explain. Commercial banks had provided liquidity guarantees to issuers of commercial paper, particularly shadow banks issuing asset-backed commercial paper, and as the asset-backed commercial paper market dried up, the guarantees were called.[6] It is also likely that lending facilities provided to other borrowers were heavily drawn on. The increase arising from these sources appears to have outweighed the decrease that will have arisen from debt repayments by shadow banks. On the liabilities side, it seems at first sight remarkable that the deposits of US-chartered commercial banks increased at all during this turbulent period. The phenomenon may be attributed to two factors. The first is the generous terms of federal deposit insurance (100 per cent of deposits up to $250,000 were insured, the limit having been temporarily increased from $100,000 in the Emergency Economic Stabilization Act of 2008, signed by President Bush on 3 October), together with the fact that the Prompt Corrective Action procedure mandated under the Federal Deposit Insurance Corporation Improvement Act of 1991 for resolving distressed banks creates confidence that bank assets will be liquidated sufficiently promptly for depositors to be repaid. The

[6] The total of commercial paper outstanding fell by just $142 billion
between 3 September and 31 December 2008 (source: Federal Reserve),
but if commercial banks fulfilled their liquidity guarantees by taking unsold
commercial paper onto their own balance sheets, no fall in the amount
outstanding would have been recorded.

Table 2.2 *US commercial banks: changes in selected balance sheet items from 3 September 2008 to end-December 2008 (US dollar billions)*

	Domestically char-tered banks	Foreign-related institutions	All commercial banks
Total assets	+1,093 (+11.2%)	+225 (+17.3%)	+1,319 (+11.9%)
Cash assets	+515 (+187.6%)	+236 (+432.7%)	+751 (+228.3%)
Deposits	+653 (+11.2%)	−258 (−21.1%)	+415 (+6.0%)
'Borrowings from others'	+161	+73	+235
'Net due to related foreign offices'	+165	+410	+575
Ratio of cash assets to total assets (percentage points)	+4.5	+14.9	+5.7
Deposits with Federal Reserve Banks			+850

Source: Federal Reserve tables H8, H4.1.

second is the flight to liquidity and safety described in Section 1, which was accompanied after 16 September 2008 by a flight from money market mutual funds, when the Reserve Fund announced that two of its funds were worth less than 100 cents in the dollar (see Baba, McCauley and Ramaswamy 2009).[7] The funds coming out of the commercial paper market, money market mutual funds and other markets similarly affected had to be placed somewhere, and Treasury securities were in fixed supply (though the supply was expanding, owing to the Federal budget deficit). Investors who did not roll over their holdings of commercial paper on maturity, or who redeemed their money market mutual fund shares, left the money in the bank. There was nowhere else for them to go, except perhaps to banknotes or real assets, and the outlook for bank deposits was not bad enough for that (though the

---

[7] Of course, some of the sales of ABCP were made by money market mutual funds that had experienced heavy redemptions.

price of gold rose very sharply). The increase in bank deposits caused by the flight from the shadow banking system and money market mutual funds appears to have outweighed the reduction arising from purchases of securities by real-money investors from shadow banks.

The contraction of the shadow banking system led to changes in bank balance sheets but it did not in itself have any effect on aggregate commercial bank liquidity. The acquisition of additional assets by commercial banks as the shadow banking system contracted did not affect their aggregate cash flow, because the contraction of the shadow banking system also provided them with additional deposit funding; in other words it involved no pressure at all on the liquidity of the banking system in aggregate. The enforced deleveraging of some shadow banks will have led to a fall in the bank deposits of real-money investors, as described in Section 2 above, but the funds withdrawn by real-money investors will have been used by the shadow banks to repay commercial bank loans, so that the effect on the commercial banks' aggregate cash flow will again have been zero. Individual banks, however, cannot have been sure that the amounts of money that they had to find to finance additional assets on their balance sheets would all come back to them in additional deposits, or that lost deposits would all come back to them in the form of loan repayments. In the turmoil, they must have become much more uncertain about their future cash flows. The increase of $751 billion in cash assets recorded in Table 2.2 can therefore be interpreted as additional precautionary demand for liquid assets.

4. Secured funding and the liquidity management of large broker-dealers

The failure of Lehman Brothers shocked the market because it had been widely thought that no systemically important financial institution would be allowed to fail. After Lehman Brothers had failed, market participants did not know how large were other financial companies' exposures to Lehman, e.g. through outstanding over-the-counter transactions, and they became much more anxious about credit exposures to their own trading counterparties. They became much less tolerant of unsecured exposures and demanded additional collateral against existing secured exposures, e.g. on repos or derivative positions. Gorton and Metrick (2009) provide data obtained from dealers showing how 'haircuts', i.e. margins of surplus collateral demanded from borrowers of cash under bilateral repurchase agreements, increased very sharply, especially after Lehman Brothers failed. The IMF (2010b) reports these data in fuller form.

Copeland, Martin and Walker (2010) report that in the tri-party repo market, haircuts did not increase much, and suggest reasons for the difference in behaviour between the bilateral and tri-party markets. They comment that some lenders of cash in the tri-party repo market were mainly concerned in their risk management about the identity and credit standing of the counterparty, while others were mainly concerned about the nature of the collateral.[8] This suggests that haircuts would have depended not only on the nature of the collateral offered but also on who was offering it, i.e. on the credit standing of the counterparty. They also suggest that some of the lenders in the bilateral repo market were prime brokers lending cash to their hedge fund clients, who may have had no other source of funds. Some of the prime brokers will have been broker-dealers which were themselves experiencing large outflows of liquidity, and they may have increased the collateral margins they demanded from their clients in order to ease their own liquidity situations. The Financial Crisis Inquiry Commission (FCIC 2011a, p. 361) say that, after Lehman Brothers failed, the two clearing banks in the tri-party market became concerned about their intra-day exposures to broker-dealers and demanded more collateral.

Whatever pressures the tri-party repo market put on the broker-dealers, of which by far the largest were Goldman Sachs, Merrill Lynch and Morgan Stanley, the failure of Lehman Brothers affected them profoundly, as it cast serious doubt on their ability to survive.[9] On the day that Lehman Brothers filed for bankruptcy, Bank of America announced that it would take over Merrill Lynch. The fortunes of Goldman Sachs and Morgan Stanley in the immediate

---

[8] Copeland *et al.* (2010), p. 59, suggest that lenders in the tri-party repo market therefore adjusted quantities, rather than haircuts: 'This unresponsiveness of haircuts could reflect cash investors' strategy of considering counterparty risk first and collateral risk second. Hence, rather than raise haircuts, cash investors may have simply refused to lend to Lehman Brothers.'

[9] Goldman Sachs and Morgan Stanley became bank holding companies on 23 September 2008, which enabled them to improve their access to Federal Reserve financing and thereby improve their market credibility.

post-Lehman period are vividly related in the report of the FCIC (2011a, ch. 20).

An impression of the nature and scale of the resulting collateral squeeze on broker-dealers can be obtained from the 10-K and 10-Q reports that Morgan Stanley submitted to the Securities Exchange Commission. A condensed version of Morgan Stanley's balance sheet, as at its 10-K and 10-Q reporting dates, is shown in Table 2.3. Between September and November 2008, the period in which Lehman Brothers failed, Morgan Stanley experienced a massive withdrawal of unsecured funding. The main element in this was an outflow of $203 billion on account of 'payables', which we surmise included reductions in collateral provided by trading counterparties to Morgan Stanley, and notably by the hedge funds to which Morgan Stanley provided prime brokerage services.[10] Prime brokerage clients also exercised their contractual rights to borrow from Morgan Stanley. The FCIC reports that cash and securities withdrawn from non-bank prime brokers were transferred to prime brokers which were in bank holding companies, and to custodian banks (see FCIC, 2011a, p. 360).

Of course, Morgan Stanley, like any prudent financial company, had liquidity reserves which it could draw on in an emergency. It maintained a Contingency Funding Plan (CFP), which it described as follows in its 10-Q report for end-August 2008 (p. 93):

The Company's CFP model is designed to be dynamic and scenarios incorporate a wide range of potential cash outflows during a liquidity stress event, including, but not limited to, the following: (i) repayment of all unsecured debt maturing within one year and no incremental unsecured debt issuance; (ii) maturity roll-off of outstanding letters of credit with no further issuance and replacement with cash collateral; (iii) return of unsecured securities borrowed and any cash raised against these securities; (iv) additional collateral that would be required by counterparties in the event of a two-notch long-term credit ratings downgrade; (v) higher haircuts on or lower availability of secured funding; (vi) client cash withdrawals; (vii) drawdowns on unfunded commitments provided to third parties; and (viii) discretionary unsecured debt buybacks.

[10] Singh and Aitken (2009) suggest that the withdrawals by hedge funds were motivated by fears of rehypothecation, that is, the fear that their assets would be pledged by the prime broker as collateral for the prime broker's own borrowing, and that they would be hard or impossible to disentangle if the prime broker became insolvent.

Table 2.3 *Condensed balance sheet of Morgan Stanley, 2007–08 (US dollar billions)*

	End-Nov 2007	End-May 2008	End-Aug 2008	29 Sept 2008[a]	End-Nov 2008	End-Dec 2008
Assets						
Liquidity reserves	118	169	179	55[b]	130	147
Other assets	927	862	808		529	530
(of which pledged to Fed as collateral for PDCF and TSLF loans)		*20*	*8*	*225*	*36*	*15*
Total assets	1,045	1,031	987		659	677
Liabilities						
Capital	31	34	36		52	49
Deposits and uncollat-eralised securitised liabilities	256	270	253		217	241
Payables	216	304	325		121	129
Other liabilities, including collateral-ised borrowing	542	423	373		270	258
Total liabilities	1,045	1,031	987		659	677
(Borrowings from PDCF and TSLF)		*3*	*2*	*100*	*20*	*11*

Notes: [a] Date of peak usage of the PDCF and TSLF; see text for more details. [b] End of September (Source FCIC 2011a, p. 363).
Sources: 10-K and 10-Q reports, information released by Federal Reserve about use of credit and liquidity facilities (see www.federalreserve.gov/newsevents/reform_transaction.htm).

It held liquidity reserves, which it described as follows (end-August 10-Q report, p. 93):

These liquidity reserves are held in the form of cash deposits with banks and pools of unencumbered securities. The parent company liquidity reserve is managed globally and consists of overnight cash deposits and unencumbered US and European government bonds and other high-quality collateral. All of the unencumbered securities are central bank eligible.

In the same report (p. 93), Morgan Stanley disclosed that

During the month of September 2008, the credit markets experienced significant disruption. In response to the market disruption, the Company implemented certain CFP actions to further support its liquidity position. These actions included, but were not limited to: (i) hypothecation of previously unencumbered collateral; (ii) selective reduction in certain funding and balance sheet intensive businesses; (iii) selective asset reduction through sales; and (iv) pledging collateral to federal government-sponsored lending programs. The Company's total liquidity reserve levels subsequent to August 31, 2008 declined, but remain at levels well in excess of those observed on average for 2007.

Morgan Stanley's total unsecured funding fell by $239 billion in September–November 2008 (see Table 2.3). The company drew down $49 billion of liquid assets, so that its liquid assets met about a fifth of the loss of unsecured funding. The company reduced its other assets by $279 billion, or 35 per cent, in the three months, so that its total assets decreased by $328 billion.[11] It also raised new capital from investors. The company used its liquid assets to buy time, while making large reductions in total assets. The reduction in total assets in September–November was about 1½ times the reduction in capital and unsecured borrowing – much less than the maximum multipliers indicated by the analysis in Section 2 above. This suggests that Morgan Stanley had surplus collateral at the beginning of the crisis, in addition to its liquidity reserve, which it was able to deploy with the help of the facilities provided by the Fed.

Despite the deployment of liquidity reserves by Morgan Stanley and, no doubt, other firms, the drying-up of unsecured funding, combined with increasing collateral demands from trading counterparties, led to a collateral squeeze.[12] Information from the 10-K and

[11] The reported decreases in asset holdings in September–November will include the effects of falls in the prices of assets held at the end of August, as well as of transactions during the three months.

[12] American International Group (AIG) was also subject to additional collateral demands in the summer of 2008. AIG was not able to meet the additional demands and was rescued on 16 September by a loan from the Federal Reserve Bank of New York. The 10-Q report that AIG submitted to the SEC in November 2008 contains an interesting account of how collateral demands put pressure on the company's liquidity, and how the company's attempts to find a market solution to the problems failed (see American International Group 2008, pp. 49–51).

Table 2.4 *Morgan Stanley's identified net collateral position, 2008–09 (US dollar billions)*

End of	May 2008	Aug 2008	29 September 2008[a]	Nov 2008	Dec 2008	Mar 2009
Collateral received	424	421		192	211	213
Collateral pledged	183	157		117	107	89
of which pledged to Fed (PDCF and TSLF)	20	8	225	36	15	0
Net collateral position	+241	+264		+75	+104	+124

Notes: The data are calculated from the published data as follows: Collateral received equals securities purchased under agreements to resell plus securities borrowed; Collateral pledged equals securities sold under agreements to repurchase plus securities lent; [a] Date of peak usage of PDCF and TSLF.
Source: 10-K and 10-Q reports, information released by Federal Reserve about use of credit and liquidity facilities (see www.federalreserve.gov/newsevents/reform_transaction.htm).

10-Q reports about Morgan Stanley's collateral position is summarised in Table 2.4. These data show the balance of the firm's identified collateralised financing transactions. They show that up to the end of August 2008, before Lehman Brothers failed, the firm held a large surplus of collateral received over collateral provided in repo and securities lending transactions.[13] At the end of August 2008, the surplus was $264 billion. After Lehman Brothers failed, the surplus fell heavily and it was down by $189 billion to $75 billion at the end of November 2008.

The large array of emergency financial support facilities supplied by the Federal Reserve provided considerable relief, even to broker dealers. The facilities that were most relevant to the collateral squeeze were:

a. The Primary Dealer Credit Facility (PDCF), which was an overnight loan facility for primary dealers in US government securities,

---

[13] They do not show the balance of collateral received and collateral provided on secured lending transactions; the 10-Q reports disclose collateral provided but not collateral received.

intended to support the tri-party repo market at a time when it was under severe strain, so that broker-dealers were experiencing difficulties in financing their securities inventories. PDCF credit extended by the Federal Reserve was fully collateralised. Initially, eligible collateral was restricted to investment grade securities. In September 2008, the set of eligible collateral was expanded to match closely all of the types of instruments that could be pledged in the tri-party repurchase agreement systems of the two major clearing banks. The total amount borrowed through the PDCF peaked at $155.8 billion on 29 September 2008.

b. The Term Securities Lending Facility (TSLF) was established in March 2008 as a means of addressing the pressures faced by primary dealers in their access to term funding and collateral. Primary dealers normally obtain funding by pledging securities as collateral. When the markets for the collateral became illiquid, primary dealers had increased difficulty obtaining funding. Under this programme, the Federal Reserve loaned relatively liquid Treasury securities for a fee to primary dealers for one month in exchange for eligible collateral consisting of other, less liquid securities. Loans were allocated through auctions. The TSLF enabled broker-dealers to convert low-quality collateral into high-quality collateral, which they could repo for cash. The total value of Treasury securities borrowed under the TSLF peaked at $270.0 billion from 26 September to 1 October 2008.

c. The Commercial Paper Funding Facility (CPFF). Under the programme, the Federal Reserve Bank of New York purchased commercial paper directly from eligible issuers. The commercial paper that was eligible for purchase was highly rated, US dollar-denominated, unsecured and asset-backed commercial paper with a three-month maturity. To manage its risk, the Federal Reserve required issuers to pay fees to use the facility. The CPFF was used by broker-dealers, among other firms, and provided them with extremely valuable access to unsecured funds.

Morgan Stanley borrowed from all these facilities. Its borrowings from the PDCF and TSLF taken together peaked at $100.5 billion on

29 September.[14] By the end of November, the date of its 10-Q reports, these borrowings had fallen to $20.1 billion. The fact that the firm used these facilities in large amounts suggests that it was unable to finance its securities inventories in the market; in other words that it did not have sufficient unencumbered assets which, in the prevailing environment, were perceived to be of sufficiently high quality that they could be used to secure market borrowing. And the fact that the firm's use of the facilities had fallen by four-fifths between 29 September and 30 November suggests that the liquidity pressures on the firm had eased considerably by the time of its end-November 10-Q report. As well as using the PDCF and TSLF, Morgan Stanley also borrowed from the Fed by issuing commercial paper which the Fed purchased under the CPFF; the amount outstanding peaked at $4.3 billion from 4 December 2008 to 25 January 2009.

In addition to the credit facilities provided by the Fed to Morgan Stanley and other broker-dealers, the rescue of AIG on Tuesday 16 September (the day after Lehmans failed) prevented the contagion that would certainly have resulted if AIG had failed, and thus provided massive indirect assistance to surviving market participants.

5. Central bank reserve management

In the middle of 2008, global foreign exchange reserves were $7.4 trillion. Foreign exchange reserves were, and are, generally managed by central banks separately from domestic market operations. While central banks generally try to maximise returns on their reserves, the pursuit of returns is subject to a low tolerance for the risk of losses and lack of liquidity. In this respect, the operations of central banks are very similar to those of many commercial asset managers. However, quite extensive information is available about the reserve management behaviour of central banks, thanks to the data released under the IMF Special Data Dissemination Standard, to the BIS international banking statistics and to US sources.[15]

---

[14] The amounts quoted include borrowings from the Fed by the London office of Morgan Stanley. The collateral pledged by Morgan Stanley on 29 September was valued at $224.5 billion.

[15] McCauley and Rigaudy (2011) provide a comprehensive and interesting analysis of central bank reserve management during and after the crisis.

Pihlmann and van der Hoorn (2010) show that, after a period in which they appeared willing to take increasing amounts of risk in pursuit of additional returns, reserve managers withdrew large amounts of unsecured deposits from banks between August 2007 and August 2008 (before Lehman Brothers failed), and further large amounts between September and December 2008.

Total foreign exchange reserves were $5,937 billion at the end of June 2007 (source: IMF). There are no comprehensive data on the asset classes in which foreign exchange reserves were invested, but there is quite a bit of partial information. Specifically:

- The BIS locational banking statistics show reporting banks' cross-border assets and liabilities vis-à-vis official monetary authorities, classified by currency of denomination.[16]
- Countries which adhere to the IMF Special Data Dissemination Standard report the distribution of their international reserves among asset classes (securities, deposits in foreign central banks, deposits in commercial banks, SDRs, gold). There is no currency breakdown by asset class, however.[17]

As at the end of June 2007, SDDS-reporting countries' total foreign exchange reserves were $3,172 billion, or 53% of the world total. The most important non-SDDS reporter is China, which on its own held 23% of the world total. SDDS-reporting countries' bank deposits were 47.8% of the world total. Table 2.5 illustrates the withdrawal of deposits in 2007–09.

The main points are:

- On the most comprehensive measure available, namely BIS reporting banks' liabilities to official monetary authorities, central bank deposit holdings fell from $1,357 billion at the end of June 2007 to $903 billion two years later. The exchange rate-adjusted fall was $458 billion, or 33.8 per cent.
- Countries reporting under the SDDS withdrew proportionately more deposits than other countries: their deposits fell from $649 billion to $311 billion (52.0 per cent, ignoring exchange rate adjustments).

---

[16] See BIS international banking statistics, table 5C.
[17] Some countries report the currency composition of their foreign exchange reserves under the IMF's COFER programme.

Table 2.5 *Bank deposits in foreign exchange reserves, 2007–09 (US dollar billions)*

	Jun 2007	Jul 2007	Jun 2008	Aug 2008	Dec 2008	Apr 2009	Jun 2009
World foreign exchange reserves[a]	5,937		7,434		7,322		7,544
Bank deposits in foreign exchange reserves[b]	1,357		1,281		1,141		903
Bank deposits of SDDS countries[c]	649	664	516	532	343	313	311
of which							
Australia	45	44	9	7	7	9	9
Brazil	20	11	3	4	2	3	6
Euro area	37	42	38	38	11	6	9
Japan	118	118	108	103	88	74	67
Korea	33	42	25	34	21	30	23
Russia	129	130	82	84	19	17	14
South Africa	21	22	26	26	26	26	27
Bank deposits of non-SDDS countries[d]	708		766		798		592

Notes: [a] Source: IMF. [b] Source: BIS international banking statistics, table 5C.
[c] Source: IMF SDDS data. [d] Derived by subtraction.

Assuming that the BIS data are comprehensive, other countries' deposits fell from $708 billion to $592 billion (16.4 per cent, ignoring exchange rate adjustments).

• Nearly all of the largest holders of bank deposits among the SDDS-reporting countries (those which had more than $20 billion at the end of June 2007 are separately identified in Table 2.5) made large withdrawals in the following two years. South Africa is the only exception. The six other countries listed in Table 2.5 between them withdrew $255 billion; Russia alone withdrew $116 billion.

On plausible assumptions, the unsecured deposits that central bank reserve managers withdrew from commercial banks will have been replaced by collateralised loans extended to the commercial banks concerned by their home central banks. Thus the net effect of the withdrawal of unsecured deposits will have been a drain of collateral assets from commercial banks to central banks.

6. The collateral squeeze and the inflow of funds from abroad

What was happening in financial markets after Lehman Brothers failed? Market makers in financial assets were being required to find additional collateral to secure their financing, while, in the bilateral repo market at least, the required margins of surplus collateral increased and it became impossible to use some assets as collateral for loans.[18] As Section 2 shows, selling assets was a necessary reaction, but an asset sale generates cash at the expense of an asset which might otherwise have been usable as collateral. Likewise secured borrowing involves exchanging an asset for cash. The PDCF and TSLF enabled broker-dealers to exchange assets that were no longer usable as collateral in the market for cash (or Treasury securities that were exchangeable for cash).

In a collateral squeeze, unsecured borrowing (or drawing down of unsecured deposits) is especially valuable, since it generates cash without any immediate loss of collateral. Unsecured borrowing was difficult during the 2008 crisis, except for financial companies which had foreign affiliates which they could induce to place funds with them in the form of new deposits or loans, or to repay existing debts owed to the US operation, as part of intra-group funds transfers.[19] Against this background, the increase of $575 billion in commercial banks' 'net debt to foreign offices' between 3 September and 31 December 2008 shown in Table 2.2 is understandable. Foreign bank affiliates (branches and agencies of foreign banks) in the United States were under greater pressure than US-domiciled banks. They had lost much of the funding they had previously received from money market mutual funds.[20]

---

[18] See Gorton and Metrick (2009), International Monetary Fund (2010b).
[19] See Cetorelli and Goldberg (2009).
[20] The run on money market mutual funds and its effect on foreign banks in the US are documented by Baba *et al.* (2009). Fender and Gyntelberg (2008), p. 9, estimate that investors withdrew $184 billion from money market mutual funds between 10 and 24 September 2008. Another indication of the scale of the run is that drawings on the facility set up by the Fed to finance purchases

Foreign bank branches (the most common type of foreign banking institution operating in the United States) were not allowed to take deposits of less than $100,000 from US citizens and residents, and were thus disqualified from receiving some of the funds that were fleeing from money market mutual funds. Moreover, deposits in foreign bank branches established after 19 December 1991 were not covered by US deposit insurance. Foreign bank affiliates' deposits fell by $258 billion between 3 September and 31 December 2008. Their 'borrowings from others' – presumably mainly from the Fed – increased by $73 billion,[21] and they raised $410 billion from their foreign offices, compared with the $165 billion that US-chartered banks raised from their foreign offices during the same period (see Table 2.2).

Most of the post-Lehman external inflow to the United States took place in October and November. Commercial banks' net debt to foreign offices increased by just $74 billion between 3 September and 1 October, but it had increased by a further $457 billion by 3 December. The inflow was facilitated by the swap lines that the Fed provided to foreign central banks, which enabled the foreign offices of commercial banks located in the United States to remit dollar funds to the United States (see Figure 8.1 below).[22] It seems therefore that the inflow of funds from abroad played a large role in easing the collateral squeeze in US financial markets during October and November, and in financing the large repayments of borrowings from the PDCF.

of commercial paper from MMMFs, which began operations on 22 September 2008, reached $150.7 billion on 2 October.

[21] Why did foreign banks not borrow more from the Fed? Perhaps they were concerned about being stigmatised as weak banks if the fact of their large borrowing became public; perhaps in some cases they did not have the right kind of collateral; perhaps raising funds from foreign affiliates was perceived as less costly than borrowing from the Fed, though the last seems unlikely in the light of the disruption that the withdrawal of dollar funds caused in foreign money markets.

[22] See Committee on the Global Financial System (2010a) on cross-border funding pressures and proposed measures to address them, and Committee on the Global Financial System (2010b).

3 | International liquidity crises outside the USA

1. International flows of funds during the crisis of 2008

Chapter 2 described the liquidity crisis in the USA that followed the failure of Lehman Brothers on 15 September 2008 and explained how it drew in dollar funds to the United States from other countries. This chapter lists all the large international flows of funds in that period, and describes their consequences. International flows of funds through commercial banks in the second half of 2008 are summarised in Table 3.1.

Several features stand out. First, there were very large domestic currency-denominated flows to the United States (discussed in Chapter 2) and Japan (discussed in Section 3 below). Second, in most cases, flows were towards the country of origin of the currency in which they were denominated (most of the entries in the 'domestic currency' column of Table 3.1 are positive). Third, there were large foreign currency-denominated outflows from the euro area, Australia, Denmark, Sweden and Korea. Finally, as Figure 8.1 shows, the inflow of funds to the United States was concentrated in the period after Lehman Brothers failed.

The large flows of dollars to the United States caused severe liquidity problems for commercial banks located outside the United States. Many of them had been financing longer-term US dollar-denominated assets with shorter-term wholesale funding.[1] They needed periodically to renew their funding from commercial sources, and when the flow of dollars to the United States caused sources of wholesale dollar funding elsewhere to dry up, there were severe stresses in financial markets. The withdrawal of external funding from commercial banks outside the United States caused their domestic lending to contract, as Aiyar (2011) shows in the case of the United Kingdom. The shortage

---

[1] See McGuire and von Peter (2008), graph 4.

Table 3.1 *Exchange rate-adjusted changes in commercial banks' net external liabilities in the second half of 2008 (US dollar billions)*

	Total	Domestic currency	Foreign currency
USA	256.8	269.7	–12.9
Japan	134.8	129.8	5.1
Euro area	–311.4	88.2	–399.6
Switzerland	73.5	28.3	45.2
UK	9.9	–47.5	57.4
Australia	–82.1	12.6	–94.6
Denmark	–29.7	–10.1	–19.7
Sweden	–35.7	14.9	–50.5
Korea	–37.8	0.0	–37.8

Note: Countries are included in this table if the total net external liabilities of banks located in that country changed by more than $30 billion in 2008Q4.
Source: BIS international banking statistics, table 2.

of dollars was largely relieved by swap lines provided by the Fed but some of the financial market stresses persisted (see Chapter 4). The provision of dollar funds by the Fed to foreign central banks was closely correlated with the inflow of funds to the United States through banks located in the United States, as Chapter 8 shows.

2. Currency-specific liquidity shortages

The shortage of dollars naturally caused banks to look for ways of converting other currencies into dollars. Moreover, there were shortages of other currencies as well as dollars during the crisis, as will be explained later in this chapter. In normal market conditions, commercial banks can readily convert liquidity from one currency into another using foreign exchange swap markets. Thus a bank which is in need of foreign currency liquidity but can get only domestic currency liquidity can swap the domestic currency into foreign currency using the commercial swap market, selling the domestic currency spot and buying it forward. A shortage of any particular currency can very easily be relieved. However, during the crisis commercial swap markets were seriously impaired, partly by concerns about settlement risk,[2] and currency-specific liquidity shortages developed in many countries.

The Continuous Linked Settlement Bank (CLSB), established in 2002, greatly reduces settlement risk in foreign exchange. The CLSB acts as a central counterparty, which takes one side of all market trades between its members. It is described by Sawyer (2004). The effects of the credit crisis would have been very much worse in its absence. One reason why covered interest differentials and cross-currency basis swap spreads involving the Hungarian forint and the Polish złoty have remained very wide (see Figure 4.2 and Figure 4.5) may be that transactions in neither currency could be settled through the CLSB.

Currency-specific liquidity shortages occurred when commercial banks needed to replace foreign currency deposits (including deposits taken in wholesale markets) which had been withdrawn, but were not able to do so, even if they were able to borrow in other currencies. In order to understand how the liquidity crisis was propagated, it is necessary to consider the characteristics of the currencies in which liquidity shortages were experienced, and the characteristics of the countries in which the shortages were located.

a. Which currencies were in short supply?

It follows from the analysis of the origin of the liquidity shortages that the currencies in which the shortages were experienced had two characteristics:

  i. They were currencies in which were denominated large volumes of assets which could not be liquidated quickly and which were held by banks outside the currency's home territory; and
 ii. Some of the banks concerned were experiencing problems in raising new deposits in the currency in question, or were experiencing the withdrawal of funding previously provided by their offices in other countries.

It is not possible to identify from any available banking statistics precisely which currencies displayed these two characteristics in late 2008. However, the BIS locational international banking statistics contain some suggestive information, summarised in Table 3.2.

---

[2] Settlement risk is the risk that a bank's counterparty in a foreign exchange transaction will not complete the transaction (e.g. because of bankruptcy) and that the bank will suffer a loss as a result.

Table 3.2 *Reporting banks' local assets in foreign currency,*
end-December 2008 (amounts outstanding in US dollar billions)

Currency	vis-à-vis all sectors	vis-à-vis non-banks
All	4,067.2	2,084.5
US dollar	1,927.5	1,015.1
Euro	1,093.7	603.4
Yen	156.5	99.3
Pound sterling	123.3	60.3
Swiss franc	251.5	166.0
Other	216.5	129.0
Unallocated	298.2	11.3

Source: BIS locational international banking statistics (Annex Table 5D).

These data show that the US dollar was the currency most widely used to denominate local foreign currency assets held by banks outside their own territory, followed by the euro and the Swiss franc in that order. Therefore it would not have been surprising if those had been the three currencies in shortest supply during the credit crisis.

In the event, the shortages of US dollars, euros, Swiss francs and yen were all serious enough to warrant the provision of swap facilities by their home central banks. It seems plausible that shortages of US dollars, Swiss francs and yen were related to the earlier use of those currencies as borrowing vehicles for so-called 'carry trades', on account of their relatively low interest rates in the years preceding the credit crunch. The Swiss franc was used for mortgage borrowing by households in some other European countries, owing to its lower interest rates compared with domestic interest rates (see Section 3 below).

The BIS statistics show both local foreign currency assets and liabilities of banks located in individual countries, and their cross-border assets and liabilities denominated in all currencies. Figure 3.1 shows that local foreign currency assets fell in 2008Q2, and fell steadily from 2008Q4 onwards. In 2008Q4, the largest decreases were in assets denominated in US dollars and yen (see Figure 3.1). In 2009Q1, the largest decreases were in assets denominated in euros and US dollars, in that order. Local foreign currency loans in the pound sterling were little changed in either quarter.

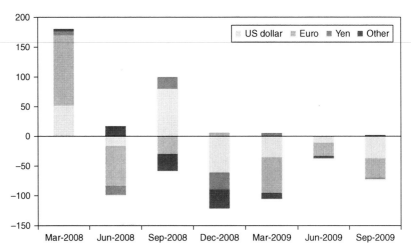

Figure 3.1 BIS reporting banks' local claims in foreign currencies vis-à-vis all sectors (estimated exchange rate-adjusted changes, in US dollar billions).

BIS reporting banks' cross-border foreign currency assets[3] also fell in 2008Q2 and from 2008Q4 onwards. The largest falls were in assets denominated in US dollars, but assets denominated in euros, yen and Swiss francs also fell. This reflected the banks' deleveraging in those currencies, and corroborates the view that they were in short supply (see Figure 3.2). Cross-border foreign currency assets denominated in the pound sterling increased slightly in 2008Q4 and 2009Q1, suggesting no significant deleveraging or shortages in sterling.

b. Which countries experienced foreign currency shortages?

Many countries experienced currency-specific shortages as the financial crisis intensified.[4] In principle, the size of the currency-specific liquidity shortage in any country is equal to the following:

---

[3] We consider BIS reporting banks' cross-border assets in foreign currency, rather than domestic currency, for comparability between currencies of individual countries and of several countries in a monetary union. For the euro, BIS reporting banks' cross-border assets in domestic currency would include cross-border euro positions between countries belonging to the euro area.

[4] US dollar shortages have been analysed in McGuire and von Peter (2009a, 2009b).

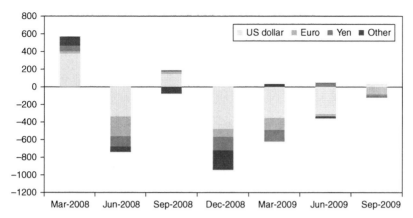

Figure 3.2 BIS reporting banks' cross-border claims in foreign currencies vis-à-vis all sectors (estimated exchange rate-adjusted changes, in US dollar billions).

  i. Banks' total liabilities in the currency in question *minus*
 ii. Banks' total illiquid liabilities in that currency *minus*
iii. The total funds in that currency that banks can raise from depositors, from their affiliates or from other providers, including central banks, or by means of asset sales.

Item (i) minus item (ii) equals the amount of the banks' liabilities that need to be refinanced, and item (iii) is the funding that can be raised for this refinancing. The difference between the two, [(i)-(ii)]-(iii), is therefore the currency-specific liquidity shortage. In practice, none of these components is reported in published statistics. The sizes of currency-specific liquidity shortages have to be estimated using such data as are available.

As a proxy measure of dollar-specific shortages, Figure 3.3 shows the net outstanding dollar cross-border claims on BIS reporting banks by the economies shown, defined as cross-border total liabilities minus claims of all BIS reporting banks vis-à-vis banks and non-banks located in the countries shown.[5] The corresponding proxy measure of euro-specific liquidity shortages is shown in Figure 3.4, and the

---

[5] This measure of currency shortages includes BIS reporting banks' liabilities vis-à-vis monetary authorities in the country concerned.

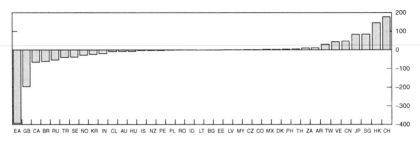

Figure 3.3 Net outstanding US dollar cross-border claims on BIS reporting banks by economies shown[a] (estimated exchange rate-adjusted changes, in US dollar billions, December 2008).

Note: [a] AR = Argentina, AU = Australia, BR = Brazil, BG = Bulgaria, CA = Canada, CL = Chile, CN = China, TW = Chinese Taipei, CO = Colombia, CZ = Czech Republic, EE = Estonia, EA = Euro area, DK = Denmark, HK = Hong Kong SAR, HU = Hungary, IS = Iceland, IN = India, ID = Indonesia, JP = Japan, LV = Latvia, LT = Lithuania, MY = Malaysia, MX = Mexico, PE = Peru, NZ = New Zealand, NO = Norway, PH = Philippines, PL = Poland, RO = Romania, RU = Russia, SG = Singapore, ZA = South Africa, KR = South Korea, SE = Sweden, CH = Switzerland, TH = Thailand, TR = Turkey, GB = United Kingdom, US = United States, VE = Venezuela.

Sources: BIS locational international banking statistics, author's calculations.

corresponding measures for the yen, the pound sterling and the Swiss franc are shown in Figure 3.5–Figure 3.7.[6] The proxy measure of currency-specific liquidity shortages is discussed further in the data appendix.

On this measure, the largest currency-specific liquidity shortage was of dollars in the euro area (around $400 billion). There were shortages of yen in the United Kingdom ($90 billion equivalent), of euros in the United States (about $70 billion equivalent), and of Swiss francs in the euro area (about $30 billion equivalent). There were only small shortages of sterling (with the largest being around $6 billion equivalent for Norway).

Figure 3.8 shows the total cross-border liabilities minus claims of BIS reporting banks vis-à-vis banks and non-banks located in

---

[6] The data underlying Figure 3.3–Figure 3.7 are not published, and the graphs are reproduced here by kind permission of the BIS.

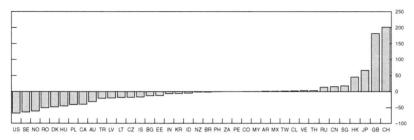

Figure 3.4 Net outstanding euro cross-border claims on BIS reporting banks by economies shown[a] (in US dollar billions, December 2008).
Note: [a] See Figure 3.3 for a list of abbreviations of economies.
Sources: BIS locational international banking statistics, author's calculations.

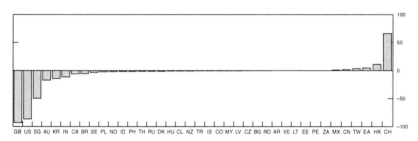

Figure 3.5 Net outstanding Japanese yen cross-border claims on BIS reporting banks by economies shown[a] (in US dollar billions, December 2008).
Note: [a] See Figure 3.3 for a list of abbreviations of economies.
Sources: BIS locational international banking statistics, author's calculations.

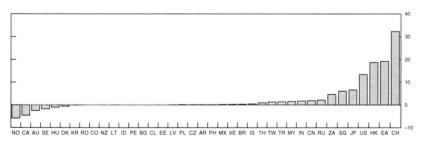

Figure 3.6 Net outstanding pound sterling cross-border claims on BIS reporting banks by economies shown[a] (in US dollar billions, December 2008).
Note: [a] See Figure 3.3 for a list of abbreviations of economies.
Sources: BIS locational international banking statistics, author's calculations.

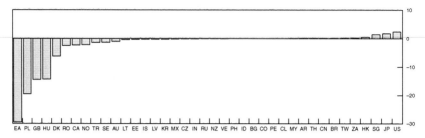

Figure 3.7 Net outstanding Swiss franc cross-border claims on BIS reporting banks by economies shown[a] (in US dollar billions, December 2008).
Note: [a] See Figure 3.3 for a list of abbreviations of economies.
Sources: BIS locational international banking statistics, author's calculations.

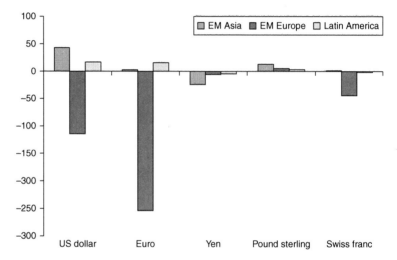

Figure 3.8 Net outstanding cross-border claims on BIS reporting banks by groups of emerging economies shown.

emerging economies as at the end of December 2008. Emerging European economies had by far the largest shortages of foreign currencies on this measure, in euros, dollars and Swiss francs. Other regional groups of emerging countries had surpluses, or small shortages. None of the three groups of emerging economies had shortages in sterling.

3. The unwinding of carry trades

a. Yen carry trades

Section 2 provided evidence of specific shortages of yen, and the market developments which will be described in Chapter 4 corroborate it. The shortages arose from the unwinding of so-called 'carry trades'. Carry trades are operations which involve borrowing in a currency in which interest rates are relatively low in order to finance the purchase of assets denominated in a currency in which interest rates are higher. The carry trader earns the difference between the interest (or other) returns on the purchased asset and the interest due on the borrowing. Foreign exchange risk is inherent in carry trading and the carry trader will gain if the currency of borrowing depreciates relative to the currency of investment, and lose if the opposite is the case. The risk can be mitigated by hedging – e.g. purchasing out of the money options to buy the currency of borrowing in exchange for the currency of investment – but the cost of hedging normally reduces the profitability of the trade.

The long period after 1997 when interest rates were kept very low in Japan provided ample opportunity for carry traders to borrow yen very cheaply and invest in high-yielding currencies. The total amount of yen carry trades has been estimated at around $1 trillion.[7] The attractiveness of yen carry trades diminished with the onset of the financial crisis. The Bank of Japan commented that 'as volatility in the FX markets rose rapidly in summer 2007 and investors' risk-averse behavior became evident, they rushed to unwind their yen-carry positions and higher-yielding currencies consequently depreciated rapidly'.[8] Moreover, the large reductions in short-term interest rates outside Japan in the second half of 2008 will have reduced the expected return from yen carry trades.

Carry-trade outflows from Japan, in the form of increases in Japanese banks' net external yen-denominated assets, continued in the second half of 2007 and the first half of 2008; but there was a large flow of yen-denominated funds into Japanese banks in the second half of 2008 (see Table 3.3), which is most naturally interpreted as a reversal

[7] See Cecchetti, Fender and McGuire (2010).
[8] See Bank of Japan (2009), p. 65.

Table 3.3 *Selected assets and liabilities of banks located in Japan –*
changes from end-July 2008 to end-December 2009 (yen billions)

	Domestically licensed banks	Foreign banks	All banks
Total assets	+21,262 (+2.7%)	–16,642 (–33.7%)	+4,620 (+0.6%)
Net external yen-denominated assets			–18,918

Source: Bank of Japan.

of yen carry trades. This reversal was reflected mainly in a fall in the assets and liabilities of foreign banks located in Japan; domestically owned banks were barely affected. The contraction of foreign banks in Japan was consistent with the general post-crisis tendency for banks to concentrate their activities on their domestic markets and to make disproportionately large cuts in their international activities; conceivably, the fall in the assets of foreign banks in Japan was partly supply-driven. The dollar equivalent of the fall in the banks' net external assets between September 2008 and the end of 2009 was about $185 billion, which suggests that only a moderate proportion of the total of outstanding carry trades was reversed in this way.

b. Swiss franc carry trades

Section 2 also provided evidence of currency-specific shortages of Swiss francs, notably in the euro area, the UK, Poland and Hungary. These were the result of carry trades undertaken over several years. In Austria, Poland and Hungary, it had become very fashionable for households to take mortgage loans denominated in foreign currencies, and particularly in Swiss francs, because Swiss franc interest rates were very low (especially when compared with interest rates in złoty and forints). Auer and Kraenzlin (2011) report that in early 2009, the Swiss franc-denominated debts of households and non-financial firms were CHF 120 billion in central and Eastern Europe, and CHF 80 billion in Austria. The external Swiss franc-denominated assets of banks located in Switzerland reached a peak (in dollar equivalent value) of $169 billion at the end of June 2008, and fell by $43 billion in the second half of the year.[9]

The fall in the external Swiss franc-denominated assets of banks located in Switzerland in the second half of 2008 is most naturally interpreted as having been initiated by the Swiss banks (rather than by the borrowers), in response to the pressure on them, as a result of reported losses, to deleverage and increase their liquidity.

4. The scale of the global crisis

The preceding sections of this chapter have measured the impact of the crisis by currency and by country. This section presents estimates of its global scale. There is no single measure of the magnitude of a financial crisis. Indeed, even in concept, it is difficult to think of a satisfactory measure. For example, a crisis which might have had massively adverse effects if inadequately managed may nevertheless have only small effects if it is well managed. In other words, there is an inescapable inverse relationship between the observed scale of a crisis and the skill with which it is handled. All that can be done is to compare observable indicators of the scale of the crisis, recognising that the effects of the original shock and of the efforts made to contain those effects cannot be separately identified. Two metrics are used in this section, namely the fall in international short-term indebtedness, and the fall in global bank deposits.

The first metric, the total fall in international short-term indebtedness, is taken to mean the total of international bank deposits and international debt securities outstanding with maturity up to one year (see Table 3.4). The fall in total international short-term indebtedness from the peak at the end of 2008Q1 to the end of 2009Q4 was $4,847 billion, or about 15 per cent of the peak level of indebtedness.[10]

---

[9] Figures derived from tables 2a and 2c of the BIS international locational banking statistics.

[10] International debt securities with maturity up to one year include both money market instruments and longer-term debt securities with a residual maturity of less than a year (e.g. Eurobonds). Arguably, for the purpose of the present paper, the fall in international short-term indebtedness should be calculated so as to exclude longer-term debt securities with a residual maturity of less than a year. In fact, it does not make much difference. On the alternative calculation, the fall in international short-term indebtedness from the end of 2008Q1 to the end of 2009Q4 was $4,925 billion, or 16.1 per cent of the peak level.

Table 3.4 *International short-term indebtedness, 2008–09 (US dollar billions)*

	International bank deposits		International debt securities with maturity up to one year		Total international short-term indebtedness	
	At end quarter	Change during quarter (adjusted for exchange rate changes)	At end quarter	Change during quarter (partly adjusted for exchange rate changes)	At end quarter	Change during quarter (partly adjusted for exchange rate changes)
2007Q4	27,131		3,744		29,378	
2008Q1	29,322	+1,113	4,247	+454	32,229	+1,566
2008Q2	28,088	–1,157	4,391	+148	31,074	–1,008
2008Q3	26,838	+10	4,149	–159	29,696	–149
2008Q4	24,342	–1,692	3,944	–157	27,155	–1,849
2009Q1	23,068	–777	3,735	–179	25,771	–956
2009Q2	23,396	–487	3,934	+145	26,311	–343
2009Q3	23,478	–281	4,128	+175	26,528	–106
2009Q4	23,100	–231	3,917	–205	26,085	–436
2010Q1	22,881	+397	3,821	–60	25,756	+337

Sources: BIS locational international banking statistics table 3A, BIS international securities statistics tables 14A and 17B. See data appendix for further informaion.

As to the second metric, it is not a simple matter to calculate changes in bank deposits, and we have made no attempt to compute a global total. Table 3.6 shows percentage changes in the domestic currency value of deposits with commercial banks by country of location in the years September 2007–August 2008, September 2008–August 2009 and September 2009–August 2010 (i.e. in the years just before and after Lehman Brothers failed).[11] The change in the domestic currency value of total deposits between two dates reflects not only the flow of deposits, but also the change in value of foreign currency deposits as at the start date that is accounted for by changes in exchange rates. In countries where foreign currency deposits are significant, these valuation effects can be important. Where possible, we have adjusted the data so as to exclude them. In cases where it has not been possible, owing to absence of data, but where we think that valuation effects are likely to be significant, we have italicised the data in Table 3.6.

It is clear that there was no generalised fall in bank deposits. There were significant falls, defined as a fall which either persists for at least three consecutive months or whose cumulative magnitude exceeds 5 per cent, only in the UK, Russia, Switzerland, Hong Kong and Singapore[12] among the major economies. Significant falls are listed in Table 3.5, which shows changes in bank deposits from the pre-crisis local peak to the date of maximum outflow; some of these falls do not show up in the yearly changes recorded in Table 3.6. In some countries, such as the United States, deposit growth was stronger in the year after the Lehman failure than in the year before. Nevertheless, some banks in such countries did experience liquidity problems. Denmark and Russia were particularly vulnerable to deposit flight because their central banks were committed to maintain their exchange rates within particular limits (in the case of Denmark, against the euro, and in the case of Russia, against a basket of dollars and euros). Danish banks however did not experience any aggregate outflow of deposits. In Russia there was an outflow of deposits amounting to 5.4 per cent

---

[11] Details of the methods used in compiling Table 3.6, and of the data sources, are to be found in the data appendix.

[12] The data for Singapore do not distinguish between deposits and other bank liabilities, so it is not possible to be sure that there was an outflow of deposits there.

Table 3.5 *Significant falls in bank deposits, 2007–10 (percentage changes measured in national currencies)*

Country	Date of peak deposits (end month)	Date of max- imum outflow (end month)	Cumulative outflow as % of peak deposit level
UK	Mar 2008	Jul 2010	–11.5
Switzerland	May 2007	Sep 2010	–15.7[a][b]
Russia	Aug 2008	Nov 2008	–5.4
Hong Kong	Oct 2007	Aug 2008	–7.8
Singapore	Jul 2008	Feb 2009	–11.8[c]

Notes: [a] Liabilities to customers. [b] The cumulative outflow had already reached –15.3 per cent at the end of December 2009. [c] Non-bank deposits with DBUs and ACUs, and inter-bank funds raised by ACUs from outside Singapore.

over three months. The country whose banks fared worst was Iceland, where foreign deposits were immobilised in October 2008. However, total deposits in Icelandic banks were relatively small – just $47 billion at the end of 2007 (and $42 billion at the end of September 2008). There was no sign of the crisis having any effect on deposits in Chinese banks.

The absence of a general flight from the banking system is a remarkable result, bearing in mind the seriousness of the crisis and Fed Chairman Bernanke's assessment that in September–October 2008, 'So out of maybe the 13 – 13 of the most important financial institutions in the United States – 12 were at risk of failure within a period of a week or two.'[13] The resilience of bank deposits in the face of this pressure is likely to have been partly owing to the existence of deposit insurance schemes, which were strengthened in a number of countries to help prevent bank runs. However, deposit insurance typically does not protect large wholesale deposits, and those must have been held in place by the belief, which turned out to be accurate, that governments would not allow systemically important banks to fail, even if a systemically important non-bank like Lehman Brothers had been let go.

[13] See Financial Crisis Inquiry Commission (2011b), p. 24.

Table 3.6 *Changes in bank deposits in and around the 2008–09 finan-cial crisis (percentage changes measured in national currencies)*

Country	Total deposits at end-2007 (US$ billion)	Percentage change in bank deposits		
		Sep 2007– Aug 2008	Sep 2008– Aug 2009	Sep 2009– Aug 2010
USA	6,714[a]	+9.4[b]	+8.9[c]	+3.5[d]
Canada	1,733	+9.6	–1.8	+7.0
Euro area	13,223	+10.1	+6.6	+2.5
UK	11,063	+3.2	-6.5	0.0
Switzerland	1,155	–9.7	–1.1	–2.5
Denmark	221	+6.9	–0.2	+1.3
Iceland	47	+30.8	N/A	N/A
Russia	429	+32.8	+14.5	+21.2
China	5,251	+15.8	+29.0	+19.4
Hong Kong	752	+6.8	+10.8	+3.3
Japan	4,957	+1.8	+1.4	+1.5
Korea	680	+14.7[e]	+14.0[e]	+8.4[e]
Singapore	931[f]	+10.3	-6.4	+5.4
India	760[g]	+22.0[h]	+20.5[i]	+15.0[j]
Australia	1,381	+19.6	+6.5	+5.8
Brazil[k]	429	+33.9	+17.4	+7.3
Mexico	201	+12.0	+12.1	+11.9

Notes: [a] As at 26 December 2007. [b] 29 August 2007–3 September 2008. [c] 4 September 2008–2 September 2009. [d] 3 September 2009–1 September 2010. [e] Year from end-September. [f] Non-bank deposits with DBUs and ACUs, and non-resident inter-bank deposits with ACUs. [g] As at 4 January 2008. [h] 1 September 2007–29 August 2008. [i] 30 August 2008–28 August 2009. [j] 29 August 2009–27 August 2010. [k] The data relate to 'deposit money banks'.
Sources: National data; see data appendix for details.

This section has shown that international short-term indebtedness fell by around 15 per cent during the crisis, and that there was no gen-eralised fall in bank deposits. This does not however imply that banks were not subject to severe liquidity pressure during the crisis. The pres-sures on banks in the United States, and particularly foreign banks, were analysed in Chapter 2. They included off-balance sheet com-mitments to provide liquidity, for example to shadow banks, which crystallised just when liquidity was most difficult to obtain. Section 2 of this chapter explained the pressures on some banks outside the United States, which arose from a drying-up of inter-bank sources of funds rather than non-bank deposits. The fact that there was no general flight from the banks does not imply that the crisis was of only moderate seriousness; more likely it reflects the effectiveness of crisis management, including the existence of credible deposit insurance.

4 | *Effects on financial markets outside the USA*

Chapters 2 and 3 described the effects of the crisis on financial flows in the United States and the rest of the world. The crisis also caused sudden and disruptive changes in financial market conditions outside the United States, and these are described in this chapter.

1. Money and swap markets

This section describes in more detail how the crisis affected financial markets outside the United States and, in doing so, derives market-based indicators of financial stress, which provide another country-by-country and currency-by-currency measure of the severity of the crisis. As Chapter 3 explained, when the credit crisis struck, it became much more difficult, or in some cases impossible, for many banks to attract foreign currency deposits in the wholesale markets. Even in domestic currency markets, the available range of maturities became much shorter. Many banks were therefore forced to use the lending facilities of their home central banks to finance themselves. Such facilities were in normal times typically confined to their domestic currency and to short maturities. Therefore, banks had to replace relatively long-maturity foreign currency financing of foreign currency assets with relatively short-maturity domestic currency financing.

This enforced change in behaviour had several consequences for financial market prices, including the following:

a. Because many banks no longer had access to markets for foreign currency loans and deposits, particularly at longer maturities, quoted prices in those markets became irrelevant for them.

b. There was increased demand to borrow at longer maturities in domestic currency deposit markets, but with domestic depositors also becoming uneasy about bank creditworthiness, and banks hoarding liquidity, interest rates tended to rise.[1]

c. As foreign currency financing of foreign currency assets was replaced by domestic currency financing, banks sold the domestic currency received from the new lender spot for foreign currency, in order to repay the original depositor, and bought it forward so that the currency composition of its assets and liabilities would be matched.[2] Thus the forward price of the domestic currency tended to rise relative to the spot price, particularly at the short maturities at which commercial banks were borrowing from their central banks. In addition, in many countries, foreign investors had purchased domestic currency government securities on a currency hedged basis. In other words, they had bought the domestic currency spot, to pay for the government securities, and sold it forward in order to hedge the foreign exchange risk. When the credit crunch struck, many of them unwound the investment, either because they needed funds themselves or because they became anxious about government credit. When they unwound the investment, they naturally unwound the currency hedge as well, and therefore sold the domestic currency spot and bought it forward. This then was an additional influence driving up the forward price of the domestic currency relative to its spot price.

d. In the stressed market conditions that prevailed during the credit crisis, the cost of raising dollar funding by means of swaps went up as the dollar deposit market became inaccessible to all but a few banks and the demand for swap-related funding rose. In normal conditions, before the crisis, covered interest rate differentials were close to zero (interest parity). During the crisis, they increased sharply as measured by reported market prices, reflecting both upward pressure on interest rates in the currencies in which banks were able to raise deposits, and increasing forward premia on those currencies as banks bought them forward to cover their foreign exchange exposures. At the same time, liquidity in the

---

[1] See for example European Central Bank (2009b), pp. 12–13; Ejerskov (2009), pp. 45–47.

[2] See Mak and Pales (2009), pp. 31–32; Narodowy Bank Polski (2009b), pp. 23–24.

commercial swap market was impaired, probably mainly because of anxiety about counterparty credit risk. Some banks that had previously been able to use swap markets to obtain dollar funding were unable to do so any longer, while others were able to use swap markets only at a restricted range of short maturities. This aggravated the measured changes in covered interest differentials.[3] Covered interest differentials are thus a good market stress indicator.

e. Likewise, as foreign currency financing of foreign currency assets had to be replaced by domestic currency financing, banks adjusted their hedging by means of cross-currency basis swaps, in which banks agreed to pay floating-rate interest in foreign currency and receive it in domestic currency over the life of the swap. Accordingly, the cost of undertaking such swaps increased. In normal conditions, the cost of swapping floating-rate interest at LIBOR into floating-rate interest at LIBOR in any other currency is very small, i.e. a few basis points, but in several currency pairs the spreads became very wide during the crisis.[4] Cross-currency basis swap spreads are therefore the second market stress indicator used here.

f. In some cases, borrowers who had foreign currency debts to repay, and were unable to refinance them, simply bought the needed foreign currency outright, spot or forward. Banks were inhibited from doing so by regulatory limits on their open foreign exchange positions, but non-bank borrowers were generally not thus inhibited, and some of them will in any case have been short of the currency in question. Outright purchases of foreign currencies by those who had borrowed them created pressure for the currencies which had been most widely used as borrowing vehicles to appreciate. The third market stress indicator is therefore spot exchange rates. Of course liquidity pressures were not the only influence on spot exchange rates at the time, but in some cases their behaviour suggests that liquidity pressures were a very important influence on them for a period.

---

[3] See Baba, Packer and Nagano (2008), Baba and Packer (2009), Bank of Korea (2009c), p. 43.

[4] See Baba *et al.* (2008).

To summarise, the three market stress indicators are covered interest differentials, cross-currency basis swap spreads and spot exchange rates.

In some countries, the central bank was willing to lend foreign currency to domestic commercial banks which had lost foreign currency deposit financing of foreign currency assets. In countries where the central bank provided foreign currency in this way, the pressure for the forward price of the home currency to appreciate relative to the spot price was weaker or absent altogether. The central bank's ability to lend foreign currency obviously depended on its own access to foreign currency resources, and the main function of the swap lines set up during the crisis was to augment central banks' foreign currency resources.

Not all central banks lent foreign currency to domestic commercial banks. For example, in some countries where the banks' foreign currency liquidity needs were only moderate, or where most of the banks had foreign parent companies which were able to supply the needed liquidity, the central bank could accept whatever pressure spot purchases of foreign currency might put on the exchange rate, and preferred not to relieve the pressure on the foreign parents of the commercial banks to provide them with liquidity.

2. Incidence of currency-specific liquidity shortages – evidence from market indicators

This section describes the behaviour of the stress indicators identified in Section 1.

a. Covered interest differentials

For the reasons described in Section 1 above, in the stressed conditions that prevailed during the credit crisis, covered interest rate differentials diverged substantially from their normal low levels under pressure from the strong demand from banks which could get access only to domestic currency funding and needed to swap it into the foreign currencies in which the assets that they needed to finance were denominated.

Figure 4.1 provides evidence of stressed foreign exchange swap market conditions. It shows covered interest differentials against US

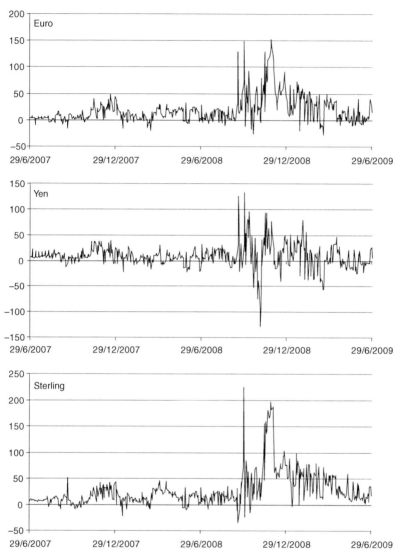

Figure 4.1 Covered interest rate differentials against the US dollar, three-month maturity (basis points).

dollars at the three-month maturity for five currencies – the euro, the yen, the pound sterling, the Swiss franc and the Australian dollar. In late September 2008, in the wake of the Lehman failure, the differentials became much more volatile and much larger in absolute value.

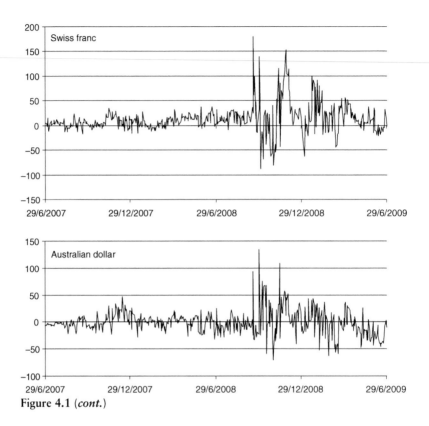

Figure 4.1 (*cont.*)

At times, the cost of borrowing dollars by swapping borrowed Swiss francs and yen was lower than the cost of borrowing dollars directly, but the cost of borrowing dollars by swapping euros and pounds increased sharply in relation to the cost of borrowing dollars directly. Table 4.1 shows average covered interest differentials over the period after the Lehman failure.

The evidence is consistent with the hypothesis that commercial banks needed to get access to dollars, and, at longer maturities, to yen and Swiss francs, presumably to repay debts, and that banks that were unable to borrow those currencies directly for reasons of perceived creditworthiness had to borrow other currencies such as euros and pounds, and swap them into the needed currency, thus putting pressure on covered interest differentials.

Table 4.1 *Average covered interest rate differentials versus US dollar,*
16/09/2008–02/01/2009 (basis points)

Maturity	EUR	GBP	JPY	CHF	AUD
1 month	69	58	46	40	3
3 months	54	64	17	25	4
6 months	38	50	−5	11	6
12 months	20	33	−30	−3	−21

Sources: Bloomberg, BIS calculations.

Curiously, the three-month covered interest differentials of the currencies of Denmark, Norway and Sweden against the euro initially became negative – i.e. it was cheaper to borrow euros indirectly, by borrowing the domestic currency of any of the three domestic currencies and swapping them into euros, than to borrow euros directly (Figure 4.2). In fact the Swedish krona's covered interest differential against the euro remained persistently negative.

In Asia, covered interest rate differentials of the Korean won against the yen turned positive, as Korean banks which were unable to get foreign currency funding turned to the swap market to convert won borrowing into foreign currencies (see Figure 4.3). The profile of Korean covered interest rate differentials against the dollar was very similar.

b. Cross-currency basis swap spreads

As described in Section 2 above, the crisis led to market stresses which drove cross-currency basis swap spreads away from their normal very low levels. Figure 4.4 below shows cross-currency basis swap spreads of the euro, the Swiss franc, the pound sterling, the yen and the Australian dollar against the US dollar. They show stresses developing in summer 2007, increasing in spring 2008 and becoming much more acute after the Lehman failure. This is consistent with the indications from covered interest differentials.

Cross-currency basis swap spreads against the euro of the currencies of some European economies outside the euro area widened in late 2008, in particular in Hungary (HUF) and Poland (PLN), but also in Denmark (DKK), suggesting a shortage of euros in those economies (see Figure 4.5). Cross-currency basis swap spreads against the euro of

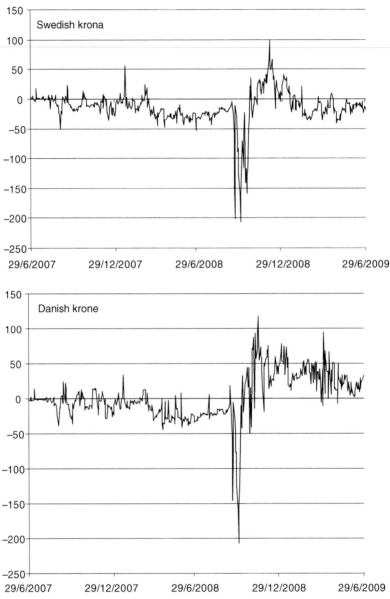

Figure 4.2 Covered interest rate differentials against the euro, three-month maturity (basis points).

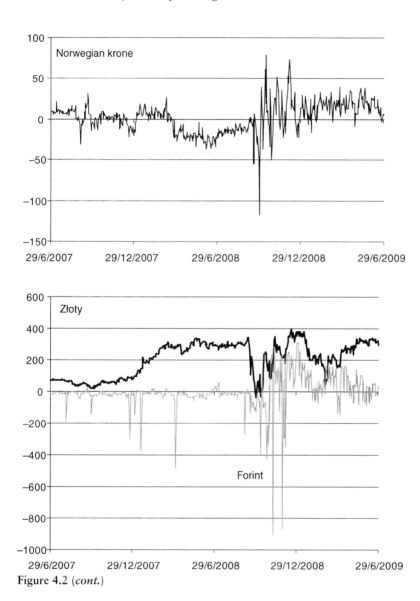

Figure 4.2 (*cont.*)

the Czech koruna, the Swedish krona (SEK) and the Norwegian krone (NOK) also increased in late 2008, but by much less.

Cross-currency basis swap spreads of some Asian currencies against the US dollar increased in late 2008 (see Figure 4.6), in particular the

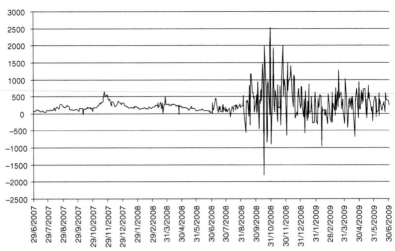

Figure 4.3 Covered interest rate differential of the won against the yen, three-month maturity (basis points).

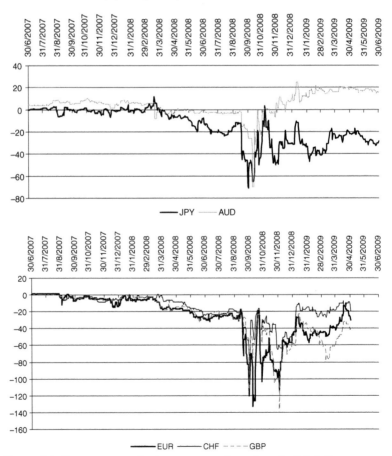

Figure 4.4 Cross-currency basis swap spreads against the US dollar, one-year maturity (basis points).

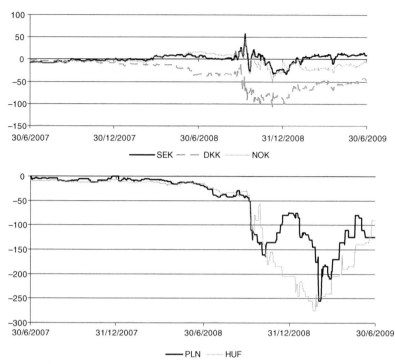

Figure 4.5 Cross-currency basis swap spreads against the euro, one-year maturity (basis points).

Korean won (KRW), consistent with Korea having the largest US dollar shortage among Asian countries on the measure shown in Figure 3.3. By contrast, cross-currency basis swap spreads of the Hong Kong dollar (HKD) and the Singapore dollar (SGD) against the US dollar were little changed, consistent with those two countries having US dollar surpluses on the measure shown in Figure 4.6.

c. Spot exchange rates

As described in Section 2 above, one of the symptoms of market stress in the period immediately after Lehman Brothers collapsed was sharp exchange rate movements as some market participants were forced to buy foreign currencies in order to repay debts. As Figure 4.7 shows, the dollar appreciated against the euro and the pound sterling after the Lehman failure. It was little changed against the Swiss franc, but the

Figure 4.6 Cross-currency basis swap spreads against the US dollar, one-year maturity (basis points).

yen appreciated very sharply against even the dollar, suggesting that deleveraging pressures were particularly intense in yen.

Within Europe, the Hungarian forint and the Polish złoty depreciated sharply against the euro after the Lehman bankruptcy (see Figure 4.8). The Norwegian krone, the Swedish krona and the Czech koruna (CZK) depreciated, too, though more modestly. The Swiss franc appreciated moderately against the euro, and sharply against the forint and the złoty (see Figure 4.9).

In East Asia, the main exchange rate developments were that the Chinese yuan remained effectively pegged against the dollar as from late July 2008, the earlier gradual appreciation which had been in progress since July 2005 having been brought to an end; and that the yen

Figure 4.7 Exchange rates against the US dollar.

appreciated very sharply indeed against a wide range of currencies, including the Indian rupee (INR), the won and the Indonesian rupiah (IDR) (Figure 4.10).

3. Effects of the unwinding of carry trades in destination countries

a. New Zealand

Section 3 of Chapter 3 discussed how the unwinding of carry trades affected the countries whose currencies were used in those trades, and Section 2 of this chapter described how it affected their exchange

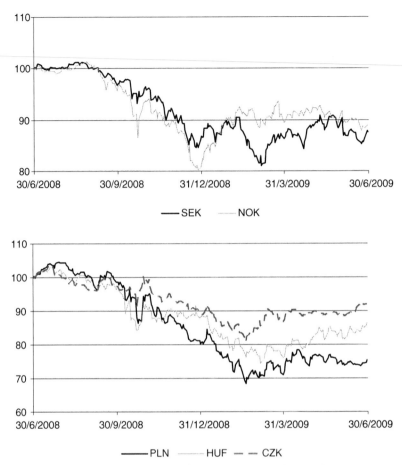

Figure 4.8 Exchange rates against the euro (30 June 2008 = 100).
Note: An increase represents an appreciation against the euro.

rates. The unwinding of carry trades also affected the countries in which the proceeds were invested. New Zealand is a case in point, having received very heavy capital inflows from Japanese purchases of 'uridashi' bonds denominated in New Zealand dollars. The purchasers were attracted by the fact that much higher yields were available in New Zealand dollars than in yen, Japanese bond yields having been depressed by the prospect that short-term yen interest rates would remain very low for a long time. The New Zealand dollar, having appreciated with the support of capital inflows since

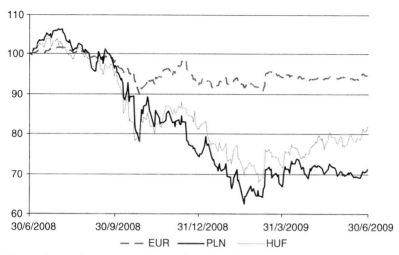

Figure 4.9 Exchange rates against the Swiss franc (30 June 2008 = 100).
Note: An increase represents an appreciation against the Swiss franc.

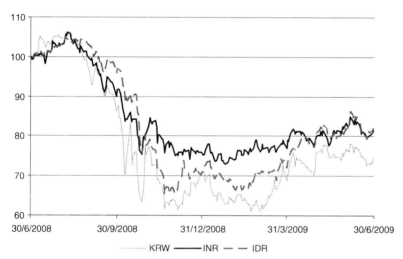

Figure 4.10 Exchange rates against the yen (30 June 2008 = 100).
Note: An increase represents an appreciation against the yen.

2000, depreciated suddenly and heavily after Lehman Brothers failed (Figure 4.11). Meanwhile ten-year New Zealand dollar bond yields had been held down by the capital inflows, despite rising short-term interest rates in the period 2003–08 (Figure 4.12). After the Lehman

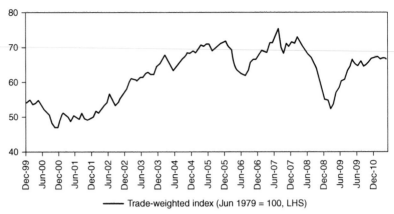

Figure 4.11 New Zealand dollar trade-weighted index.
Source: Reserve Bank of New Zealand.

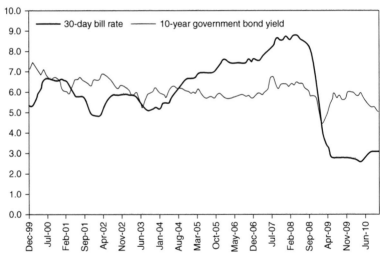

Figure 4.12 New Zealand short-term interest rates and bond yields (%).
Source: Reserve Bank of New Zealand.

bankruptcy, short-term interest rates were cut very heavily: the overnight cash rate fell from around 8% in mid-2008 to around 2.5% a
year later. However, ten-year bond yields remained little changed, after
a brief dip, reflecting the sudden and large fall in demand. Foreign
holdings of New Zealand debt securities fell by NZ$ 14.3 billion,

or 17.6%, in the second half of 2008, and New Zealand's current account balance of payments deficit narrowed sharply, from 8.7% of GDP in 2008 to 2.9% in 2009.

b. Swiss franc mortgages

Carry trades were also undertaken on a large scale in Swiss francs, notably in Hungary, Poland and Austria, where Swiss franc-denominated mortgages became very popular. In Hungary, in the middle of 2008, Hungarian households had outstanding mortgages denominated in 'other foreign currencies' (i.e. other than the euro) of $11.1 billion, and euro-denominated mortgages were just $0.2 billion. Foreign currency mortgages accounted for 51.3% of the total. The Magyar Nemzeti Bank reported (see 2009, p. 39) that most foreign currency household loans were denominated in Swiss francs. In Poland, at the same time, $37.5 billion (58.1%) of housing loans were denominated in foreign currencies, and the Narodowy Bank Polski (2009b, p. 47) reported that 96% of foreign currency mortgages were denominated in Swiss francs.

After October 2008, the Swiss franc value of non-euro foreign currency mortgages began to fall in Hungary (Figure 4.13), while in Poland, its growth rate slowed abruptly (Figure 4.14). The banks that made these mortgage loans had financed them mainly with short-term wholesale market borrowing and when they were unable to roll over the borrowings they were forced to swap their domestic currencies, or sell them outright, for Swiss francs. The pressures thus created led to the drying-up of foreign exchange swap markets and the Hungarian and Polish currencies depreciated sharply in the spot foreign exchange market. The pressures were to some extent relieved when the Swiss National Bank provided facilities for the central banks of Hungary and Poland to swap euros from their reserves for Swiss francs.[5]

c. Banking propagation and bond market propagation

Chapter 3 identified the countries that were likely to experience currency-specific liquidity shortages, by reference to the BIS banking statistics showing outstanding cross-border assets and liabilities. This chapter has identified and applied market price-based stress indicators

---

[5] See Chapter 9.

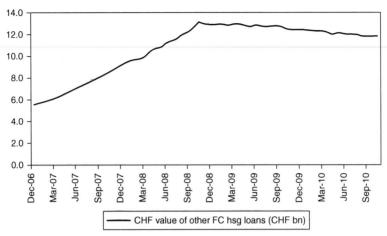

Figure 4.13 Swiss franc value of 'other foreign currency' housing loans to individuals in Hungary (billions).
Sources: Magyar Nemzeti Bank, author's calculations.

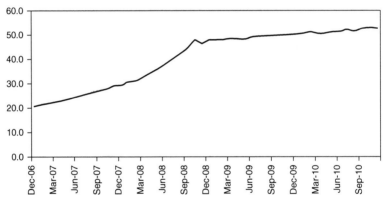

Figure 4.14 Swiss franc value of foreign currency housing loans to individuals provided by Polish MFIs (billions).
Sources: National Bank of Poland, author's calculations.

to ascertain where the banking crisis was particularly severe, and which currencies were likely to have been in particularly short supply. The two methods produce broadly the same results, which suggests that the proxy measure of currency-specific liquidity shortages developed in Chapter 3 has some value.

Yet the banking system was not the only channel through which the economic effects of the crisis were propagated around the world, as is shown by the experience of New Zealand and other countries which received inflows from Japanese bond investors, such as Australia and South Africa. The New Zealand economy was certainly seriously destabilised by the pre-crisis capital inflows and their sudden reversal in 2008, but there was no banking crisis, and although New Zealand received a dollar swap line from the Fed it did not draw on it. The fundamental difference between the experiences of New Zealand and, say, Korea was that New Zealand's external borrowing was in its own currency and for a relatively long term, so that the crisis was reflected in market prices of the New Zealand dollar and New Zealand dollar bonds, whereas Korea's external borrowing was in foreign currencies and relatively short term, so that it had to provide emergency liquidity support to its banks. New Zealand conducted its borrowing in a classically prudent manner; nevertheless it experienced serious economic disruption as a result of the crisis.

5 | The theory of central banking before the crisis and the practice of central banking during the crisis

1. Pre-crisis central bank behaviour

a. The theory and practice of central banking before the crisis

In the years leading up to the crisis, the theory of central banking increasingly regarded an inflation target as the only proper objective of monetary policy. Exchange rate commitments short of full monetary union had been universal in the Bretton Woods era, and widespread in the years that followed its demise, but they gradually went out of fashion, even though they did not disappear completely. From the late 1980s onwards, many countries shifted their monetary policy strategies towards one or other of two polar positions: (a) monetary union (e.g. as in the euro area), and (b) inflation targeting with a floating exchange rate. Both positions appeared sustainable, unlike the Bretton Woods position of 'fixed but adjustable' exchange rates, which, in the light of experience, appeared unstable as capital became more mobile. Thus Economic and Monetary Union has been created in Europe, with seventeen member countries at the time of writing; while inflation targeting with a floating exchange rate, which was invented as a monetary policy technique in New Zealand in the late 1980s, has now been adopted by thirty countries.[1]

Supervision of commercial banks was in many countries conducted by agencies other than the central bank, but central banks were typically assigned responsibility for 'financial stability'. Although there was no widely agreed definition of financial stability, it was clear that it had something to do with preventing financial crises, and, if crises nevertheless occurred, managing them.[2]

---

[1] See International Monetary Fund (2010c), appendix table II.9.
[2] See Allen and Wood (2006) for a discussion of the problems of defining financial stability.

Some central banks treated financial stability as an objective quite separate from monetary policy. This, with the benefit of hindsight, was a mistake. It overlooked the possibility that monetary policy actions might have financial stability consequences, and the possibility that policy actions taken in the interests of financial stability might have consequences for macroeconomic conditions and thus for monetary policy. Moreover the facts that financial stability was ill-defined, and that the macroeconomic models in use for monetary policy analysis were based on assumptions that meant they had nothing to say about financial stability, made it impossible for financial stability analysis to be conducted with the superficial rigour that had become customary in the analysis of monetary policy. Financial stability became a backwater in some central banks. In the Bank of England, for example, the percentage of the budget devoted to financial stability fell steadily from 45 per cent in the financial year 2003–04 to 38 per cent in 2007–08.[3]

All this was reflected in central banking theory. A book written by former Fed Vice-Chairman Alan Blinder in 1999 called *Central Banking in Theory and Practice* was devoted exclusively to monetary policy, narrowly interpreted.[4] It was believed that the only policy weapon that central banks needed was the short-term interest rate on 'risk-free assets'; and domestic currency-denominated government securities were thought to be the only risk-free assets.[5] Central banks' financial operations should be directed at managing risk-free short-term interest rates; that would naturally involve taking no credit risk, it being left to the market to manage credit risk. In retrospect, the life of that model began some time in the late 1980s or early 1990s and ended suddenly in 2007.

While central banks did not all assign a high priority to financial stability issues in the years immediately preceding the crisis, there nevertheless remained an apparently settled crisis management

---

[3] Source: successive Bank of England Annual Reports, author's calculations. Two policy functions were identified in the budgets: financial stability and monetary policy; as financial stability lost, monetary policy gained.

[4] Blinder (1999). The book was based on lectures delivered in 1996.

[5] This begged a few questions that were not addressed, such as what a central bank should do if its government had little outstanding debt (as for example in Australia). It also neglected the possibility that the government could default on its domestic currency debts, as the Russian government did in 1998.

doctrine.[6] In the United Kingdom, this had been expressed by the then newly appointed Governor of the Bank of England Eddie George in a speech in 1993 (George 1993). It recognised the importance of avoiding both the severe economic disruption that could be caused by the failures of financial companies, and the moral hazard that would be caused by guaranteeing financial companies against failure. It thus left open the possibility that a bank would be allowed to fail if its failure were judged likely to have consequences less severe than those of the moral hazard that a rescue would create. The doctrine was put into effect in 1995 when there was no official rescue of the then-distressed Barings Bank. It may be thought of as a late twentieth-century version of Bagehot's prescription for managing a financial crisis.

The doctrine distinguished between problems of liquidity and solvency. During the crisis, liquidity problems were often indicators of concern about solvency – banks were reluctant to lend to one another because of concerns about the valuations of their assets, for example – but before the crisis, liquidity problems had arisen from time to time for more mundane reasons, such as computer failure. In those circumstances, it was clear that the proper policy for central banks was to lend to the temporarily illiquid company until the problem could be resolved.[7]

During the crisis of 2008–09, as described in Sections 2 and 3 below, central banks provided truly massive amounts of liquidity to commercial banks. It was clear that, in many cases, the banks' need for liquidity was indeed a symptom of market anxiety about their solvency. Should central banks and governments have been more cautious in their response to the crisis, out of fear of moral hazard?

In the United Kingdom, the drying-up of liquidity in the market for mortgage-backed securities in the summer of 2007 caused concern about the liquidity of Northern Rock, whose business model depended on its ability to securitise its mortgages. Despite the assessment of the

---

[6] The Bank for International Settlements, however, warned repeatedly in successive Annual Reports during the early-middle years of the first decade of the twenty-first century of an impending financial crisis.

[7] Such lending had taken place on a massive scale in 1985 when the Bank of New York, which acts as a depository for United States government securities, experienced an acute liquidity shortage as a result of computer problems. See Volcker (1985).

Financial Services Authority that Northern Rock's assets were of high quality, the Bank of England was unwilling, on moral hazard grounds, to provide emergency liquidity to the banking system.[8] There was a run on Northern Rock, in which long queues of depositors wishing to withdraw money formed outside Northern Rock branches, as a result of which the Bank of England provided emergency liquidity to Northern Rock alone; when that failed to stop the run, the British government felt impelled to guarantee deposits in Northern Rock. In addition, the failure to support Northern Rock promptly weakened other banks which in turn required support.

The underlying truth is that, in the political environment of the early twenty-first century, no government wanting to retain political support could fail to bail out depositors in any significant bank. Nor could it contemplate the macroeconomic consequences of the failure of any significant bank or group of banks. Bank failures had been allowed to happen in the 1930s, when the banking industry was much smaller, and the consequences had been catastrophic.

Faced with a generalised banking crisis, then, the only realistic policy for governments and central banks was to cast aside concerns about moral hazard and provide whatever support the banks needed. In providing such support, caution could be positively harmful, since it might give rise to doubts about the resolution with which the policy was being implemented. The casting aside of moral hazard concerns could be only temporary. Clearly there had been substantial moral hazard before the crisis. Banks had been able to raise liabilities in amounts and on terms which did not fully reflect the risks of their assets, and it is reasonable to suppose that they had been able to do so because their liabilities were perceived to have a public guarantee.

In the event, shareholders in banks which needed equity support were greatly diluted and suffered heavy losses. It remains a reproach to corporate governance that shareholders were willing to tolerate the risk-taking that cost them so dearly; possible reasons were discussed in Chapter 1. Subordinated debt holders, however, were generally protected, because they could have been forced to absorb losses only in a liquidation, and governments were not prepared to allow significant banks to be liquidated. And depositors lost nothing. Thus the management of the crisis left substantial moral hazard intact. As a result,

---

[8] See Bank of England (2007), King (2007), Darling (2011), pp. 21–26.

it was essential to change the rules of the game after the crisis, and
the post-crisis review of bank regulation has set about reducing or
offsetting moral hazard, as is evident in the Basel 3 regime for bank
supervision, the Dodd-Frank Act in the United States, and the recom-
mendations of the Independent Commission on Banking in the United
Kingdom.

b. Cooperation among central banks

Central banks cooperate naturally when they are committed to maintaining exchange rate relationships among their currencies, as was the
case for example under Bretton Woods and in the European Exchange
Rate Mechanism (which is still in operation for some countries).[9] This
is because maintaining an exchange rate relationship requires domestic monetary policy objectives to be subordinated in some degree, so
that some coordination of monetary policy is unavoidable. Monetary
union – one of the two polar positions to which monetary policy con-
verged after the late 1980s – requires not only cooperation among the
participating central banks, but also common subordination to central
management (such as is provided in the euro area by the European
Central Bank). Until recently, it seemed that the other polar position,
inflation targeting, required no more than exchange of information
among central banks, if that. If one country made a policy error, the
consequences would be largely confined to that country.[10] Accordingly,
cooperation on monetary policy seemed, at least until recently, to have
become less intense. That process has been described succinctly by
Borio and Toniolo (2006):

In the post-Bretton Woods years, the aims of central bank cooperation pro-
gressively shifted from monetary to financial stability, and new tools were
introduced. The experience of the Great Inflation of the 1970s convinced
central banks that domestic monetary stability, their overriding responsibility, could be pursued primarily by domestic policy. After some disappointing
attempts in the 1970s, cooperation on exchange rates became largely subordinated to the pursuit of that objective. ... At the global level, cooperation
on monetary issues became less feasible once the more inflation-conscious

[9] See for example Toniolo (2005).
[10] This has been characterised as the 'house in order doctrine' by Padoa-Schioppa
(2006).

countries or currency areas saw it as not entirely consistent with domestic price stability.[11]

Central banks cooperate more actively on financial stability issues. Financial supervisors from different countries have a natural reason to cooperate, in that many of the private financial companies that they supervise operate in many different countries; and many central banks, though not all, have financial supervision among their functions. However, cooperation went (and still goes) beyond cooperative supervision of individual financial companies to setting of minimum safety standards for banks and other financial companies. This is mainly organised under the auspices of the Bank for International Settlements in Basel, Switzerland, in the Basel Committee on Banking Supervision and the Committee on Payment and Settlement Systems. In addition, the Committee on the Global Financial System, as its name implies, discusses global financial issues.

There are, however, limits to central bank cooperation. It does not extend to the management of foreign exchange reserves, as Section 3b will show. Nor did it extend to contingency planning for the emergency provision of liquidity to international financial markets in a crisis.[12] Goodhart, in his history of the Basel Committee on Banking Supervision from 1974 to 1997 (2011, pp. 379–381) reports that the committee discussed the subject in 1975 and 1976. He comments that 'national procedures of crisis management were too different and idiosyncratic, and the subject matter too delicate to be taken by the Committee'. The committee nevertheless sent a paper on it to the Group of Ten Governors' Committee and other supervisory authorities,[13] but 'In truth, the paper was anodyne and the Governors were presumably not stimulated to ask for more work on this topic. So there was no follow-up on the subject of cross-border crisis management up until the end of 1997.'[14] Thus no contingency plan was produced before 1997, and it seems unlikely that one was produced between then and 2008.

[11] See Borio and Toniolo (2006), p. 25.
[12] There was, however, cooperative contingency planning for the possibility of computer problems in the financial industry connected with the date change from 31 December 1999 to 1 January 2000.
[13] The paper is reproduced in Goodhart (2011), ch. 11, Annex C.
[14] See Goodhart (2011), pp. 380–381.

2. The nature of central banks' reactions to the crisis

The advent of the credit crunch in August 2007, and its subsequent intensification, eroded the hitherto apparently sharp distinction between monetary and financial stability, and led to a revival of central bank cooperation. Crisis prevention having evidently failed, central banks were required to undertake crisis management without much preparation.

a. Interest rate policy

Prior to the financial crisis, the main risk perceived by many central banks was higher inflation, mainly owing to the sharp rise in commodity prices which had continued until mid-2008. For example, oil prices had risen by 470% between the start of 2000 and mid-2008. Higher commodity prices contributed to higher inflation, which doubled from about 2% on average in 2003–05 to 4% in mid-2008 in mature economies, and from about 4% to 8% in emerging economies.[15]

The onset and development of the crisis changed the balance of risks. The objective of monetary policy was unchanged. However, commodity prices fell precipitously and the severe damage done to financial markets by the crisis meant that the economic outlook deteriorated suddenly and massively (see Chapter 1) and the downside risks to inflation became much greater. The threat of deflation was a real one. In these circumstances, interest rates in many countries were reduced to historically very low levels, but interest rate management on its own was inadequate. In some countries it was supplemented by so-called unconventional monetary policy measures, including 'credit easing' and 'quantitative easing', in which central banks bought assets in order to support liquidity in financial markets and increase the 'monetary base'. Such monetary policy measures contributed to an enormous expansion of the balance sheets of major central banks (see Figure 2.1).[16]

They also caused a blurring of what had appeared to be clear demarcation lines between monetary policy and fiscal policy, and between monetary policy and public debt management. Credit easing

---

[15] See Cecchetti and Moessner (2008).
[16] See also Bank for International Settlements (2009), ch. VI, graph VI.4.

blurred the monetary/fiscal demarcation, because the pre-crisis view had conceived of monetary policy operations as involving only 'risk-free' assets, despite the problems of identifying government securities as risk-free assets and despite the fact that historically, and for good reasons, central bank operations had not always been confined to government securities. Official purchases of non-government securities certainly involves some credit risk and confers some benefit on the seller; even if the credit risk and the benefit to the seller are extremely small, on a purist view they can be construed as having a fiscal policy content. Moreover, some of the assets bought by central banks carried more than a little credit risk. And quantitative easing operations, in which central banks bought government securities, blurred the demarcation between monetary policy and debt management, because their net effect was to replace government securities which might have a maturity of several years with deposits in the central bank which were repayable on demand. They were very similar to a purchase of long-term government debt accompanied by an equivalent sale of short-term debt, organised by the official debt management agency.[17]

b. *Official support for banks*

i. Capital support and guarantees

In order to keep the banking system functioning and to prevent bank failures, governments (and some central banks) recapitalised banks that would otherwise have failed or been forced to shrink their balance sheets massively. Governments also provided, in exchange for a fee, asset guarantees which reduced banks' risk exposures. A review and assessment of financial sector rescue programmes is provided in Panetta *et al.* (2009).

ii. Domestic liquidity support

After the onset of the credit crunch, central bank balance sheets expanded enormously, and the range of assets that central banks accepted as collateral for loans was in some cases greatly widened.[18] These changes were the result of national decisions, though the

---

[17] Turner (2011) argues convincingly that the financial crisis has greatly increased the significance of public debt management in macroeconomic policy.
[18] See Bank for International Settlements (2009), ch. VI, graphs VI.4 and VI.5.

decisions were driven by a common cause. For a discussion of the issues surrounding expanded liquidity support by central banks, see Turner (2010).

There were coordinated announcements by major central banks of special measures for enhanced liquidity provision in the central bank's own domestic currencies during the crisis, including in the provision of term funding.[19] There is likely to have been some discussion among central banks about what kind of collateral they would take for loans after August 2007 (e.g. mortgage-backed securities), and perhaps also about the amount of liquidity they would provide to their banking systems. The decisions were purely national although the central banks were no doubt influenced by each other's behaviour. In the words of Fed Vice Chairman Don Kohn (2009), 'Beginning in late 2007, central banks generally reacted to funding problems and incipient runs with similar expansion of their liquidity facilities. They lengthened lending maturities, in many cases broadened acceptable collateral ... Central banks were in constant contact throughout this period, although they arrived at many of these actions separately.' Other instances of coordination include a joint assessment by central banks of measures taken in response to the financial turmoil up to April 2008 (see CGFS 2008), and a coordinated attempt to inform market participants about how central banks operate in a period of uncertainty by publishing a compendium on central bank operating frameworks (see Bank for International Settlements Markets Committee 2008).

iii. Swap networks
The central banks' response to the widespread shortages of foreign currency liquidity was to set up swap facilities so that the home central bank of the currencies in short supply could provide those currencies to the commercial banks outside the home country that needed them. They did so indirectly, using as intermediaries the central banks of the commercial banks that were short of liquidity.

Central bank swaps have been used frequently in the past to help address a wide variety of problems. The mechanics of an

---

[19] For example on 12 December 2007, see www.bankofengland.co.uk/publications/news/2007/158.htm.

inter-central bank swap are very simple. Central bank A credits the account of central bank B in its own books with A's currency; in return, central bank B credits the account of central bank A in its books with an equivalent amount of B's currency. Thus A lends its currency to B and B lends its currency to A; each loan is collateral for the other. There may be a provision for the amounts of the loans to be adjusted as exchange rates change. In principle, both A and B may use the foreign currency which the swap has put at their disposal, but in practice, only one party normally uses the swap proceeds; the other party simply holds them on deposit as collateral for the loan.

Swap facilities make the provision of liquidity by central bank A more effective by extending its geographical scope. Typically, lending to domestic commercial banks by central bank B is denominated in domestic currency; but if the commercial banks need foreign currency liquidity, then something more is required. Swap facilities enable central bank B to provide liquidity to domestic banks in foreign currency.

In effect, the central banks of currencies in short supply – above all the Fed – used foreign central banks to extend the geographical scope of their liquidity-providing operations. Alternatively or in addition, some central banks (such as in Brazil and Korea) used some of their own foreign exchange reserves to provide foreign currency liquidity, converting them into the required currency if necessary by means of market transactions.

3. Scale of central banks' reactions

a. *Short-term interest rates and liquidity provision*

Floating exchange rates prevailed in 2008–09, so that monetary policies did not need to be internationally coordinated and interest rates could be determined by reference to domestic economic objectives. Thus there were large reductions in official interest rates in nearly all the countries shown in Table 5.1 in the last four months of 2008. In Russia, however, the main policy concern in the last few months of 2008 was to maintain the rouble's exchange rate and interest rates were increased (they fell in 2009, however). And in Hungary, the failure of Lehman Brothers, together with market concerns about the

Table 5.1 *Central bank official interest rates, 2008 (in per cent)*

	End of August	End of December
USA	2.00	0.00–0.25
Euro area	4.25	2.50
UK	5.00	2.00
Switzerland	2.25–3.25	0.00–1.00
Canada	3.00	1.50
Japan	0.50	0.10
Russia	11.00	13.00
Australia	7.25	4.25
Denmark	4.60[a]	3.75[a]
Norway	5.75	3.00
Sweden	4.50	2.00
Hungary	8.50	10.00
Poland	6.00	5.00
Korea	5.03[b]	3.02[b]

Notes: [a] CD rate. [b] Call rate.
Sources: National central bank internet sites.

sustainability of domestic policies, had led to such a heavy depreciation of the currency[20] that interest rates had to be raised there, too.

During the crisis central banks provided liquidity on a large scale, both domestically and internationally. The range of assets that they were willing to accept as collateral for loans was in some cases greatly widened.[21] And the range of financial institutions that received support was also widened in some countries, notably in the United States, where the Fed provided liquidity to non-bank broker-dealers and money market mutual funds. These changes were the result of national decisions, though the decisions were driven by a common cause.

Central bank assets increased suddenly and massively after the failure of Lehman Brothers on 15 September 2008 and the subsequent freezing-up of financial markets (see Figure 2.1). More detail is provided in Table 5.2, which shows the expansion in central bank assets,

[20] For an explanation of how the failure of Lehman Brothers caused some currencies to depreciate, see Chapter 4.
[21] See Bank for International Settlements (2009), ch. VI, graph VI.5.

Table 5.2 *Changes in central bank assets, 2008–09*

| Country | Change in central bank assets in year beginning end-August 2008 | | |
	As % of central bank assets as at end-August 2008	As % of commercial bank deposits at end-2007	As % of GDP in 2008
Canada	37.8	1.3	1.3
USA	125.1	17.5	8.1
China	9.7	5.0	6.1
Japan	6.6	1.3	1.4
Korea	22.3	11.1	6.9
India	0.8	0.4	0.2
Singapore	5.2	0.8	4.9
Australia	2.8	0.2	0.2
Russia	4.8	6.9	1.8
Euro area	25.7	4.1	4.1
UK	136.2	2.0	8.8
Switzerland	67.8	6.0	16.5
Denmark	23.0	9.1	5.9
Iceland	58.1	14.7	31.0
Brazil	22.7	22.0	5.7
Mexico	34.9	19.2	3.5
Hong Kong	36.7	8.8	30.8
Weighted average	28.5	5.5	5.4

Note: Countries are included in this table if they publish data on central bank assets and if they meet any of the following criteria: (i) Their 2008 GDP calculated at PPP exchange rates was among the eleven largest in the world. Those eleven countries accounted for 73.9 per cent of global GDP calculated at PPP exchange rates, according to the IMF.[22] (ii) They have a large international financial industry (including Switzerland, Hong Kong, Singapore, Australia). (iii) They had an exchange rate commitment which represented a contingent claim on their foreign exchange reserves (Russia, Denmark). (iv) They were forced to impose exchange controls because the banks could not meet deposit outflows (Iceland).
Source: National data.

[22] See IMF World Economic Outlook database, April 2010, available at www.imf.org/external/pubs/ft/weo/2010/01

country by country, measured in three different ways. The first column shows the increase in central bank assets in the year September 2008–August 2009, expressed as a percentage of the level of such assets at the end of August 2008. The percentage depends significantly on the initial size of the central bank's balance sheet; for example, the Bank of Russia, which has the nation's large foreign exchange reserves on its balance sheet, has much larger assets relative to total bank deposits or GDP than, for example, the Bank of England. The latter has only a moderate amount of foreign exchange reserves on its balance sheet, the majority of the UK's foreign exchange reserves being on the Treasury's balance sheet. The second column shows the increase in central bank assets expressed as a percentage of commercial bank deposits at the end of 2007. This measure depends on the size of the country's commercial banking system. And the third column measures the increase in central bank assets relative to the country's GDP.

Some salient features of Table 5.2 are:

- Countries which are relatively large financial centres tended to provide large amounts of liquidity relative to their GDP (e.g. the USA, the UK, Switzerland, Hong Kong).
- Of the countries in the table, only Iceland was driven to impose exchange controls to protect its banks from unfinanceable deposit withdrawals.

The most heavily used swap network was established by the Federal Reserve. In addition, euro, Swiss franc and Asian and Latin American swap networks were established by other central banks (see Chapter 6). At its peak, on 4 December 2008, the Federal Reserve swap network provided \$586.1 billion in US dollars to other central banks. Swap lines could be set up quickly without the need for extensive negotiation, and could draw on experience with the use of swap lines in the past.

In addition to the additional liquidity provided by central banks, which may have amounted in total to around \$2.7 trillion,[23] governments in many countries facilitated banks' acquisition of liquid assets by providing (in exchange for a fee) guarantees of bonds issued by

---

[23] This is calculated as 28.5 per cent (see Table 5.2) of the total dollar value of the assets of the central banks of the countries listed in Table 5.2 as at the end of August 2008, which was \$9.7 trillion.

banks. The total of such bond issues between October 2008 and May 2009 was about EUR 700 billion, or roughly $1 trillion (see Panetta *et al.*, 2009, p. 49 and graph 3.1).

b. Reserve management

In their capacity as managers of foreign exchange reserves, central banks hold foreign currency deposits in commercial banks. As noted in Chapter 2, central bank reserve management policies have been pro-cyclical in recent years, and they added to foreign currency liquidity shortages in 2008–09.[24]

The bank deposits held by central bank reserve managers fell by more than half between August 2007 and April 2009, and the peak rate of withdrawals coincided with the peak of the crisis in the last four months of 2008. The biggest withdrawals by far were made by the Bank of Russia, which began its move out of bank deposits in summer 2007, though it was accumulating reserves at the time, and continued to move out from September to December 2008, when it was losing reserves. And former US Treasury Secretary Hank Paulson reports that he learned in August 2008 that 'Russian officials had made a top-level approach to the Chinese suggesting that together they might sell large chunks of their GSE [Government-Sponsored Enterprise] holdings to force the US to use its emergency authorities to prop up these companies'.[25] While the Russian withdrawals of bank deposits can be adequately explained by financial considerations, it is also possible that their motivation was partly political. Diplomatic relations between Russia and the United States and several countries in western Europe were coincidentally severely strained at the time of the financial crisis, because of the secession of Kosovo from Serbia and its recognition as an independent state by the United States and several other countries in February 2008, because of the conflicts in Abkhazia and South Ossetia in August 2008, and Russia's subsequent recognition of the two territories as states independent of Georgia, and because of British suspicions that Russia was obstructing police investigations

---

[24] See Pihlmann and van der Hoorn (2010). McCauley and Rigaudy (2011) provide a broader analysis of central bank reserve management during and after the crisis.

[25] See Paulson (2010), p. 161.

into a murder in London that occurred in 2006. McCauley and Rigaudy (2011, p. 27) estimate that central bank deposit withdrawals were predominantly from European banks; they also show that central banks also retreated from US federal agency debentures and securities lending, and describe how they redeployed the funds withdrawn from commercial banks, e.g. in government debt. Whatever the motive for Russia's deposit withdrawals, it remains the case that political events can have serious consequences for international financial relations, as they did in 1931 (see Chapter 11).

The unsecured deposits withdrawn from commercial banks by central bank reserve managers will have largely been replaced by secured loans provided by the home central banks of the commercial banks concerned. The net effect will have been to drain collateral from the commercial banking system and aggravate the collateral squeeze. Thus the withdrawal of deposits from commercial banks by central bank reserve managers might have accounted for about 17 per cent of the $2.7 trillion of additional liquidity that central banks supplied to the commercial banking system in their crisis management capacity.

It was not surprising that central bank reserve managers wanted to reduce their holdings of bank deposits after August 2007, even though each central bank's action added to the liquidity provision task of other central banks. Reserve management was beyond the scope of central bank cooperation, and there was no coordination of the reserve managers' actions.

6 | *Swap lines*

1. History

Central bank currency swaps had been used for a variety of purposes long before the financial crisis of 2008–09. Starting in the 1920s, currency swaps between central banks, in which one central bank was ready to provide its own – or sometimes a third – currency to another central bank, and vice versa, had occasionally been undertaken ad hoc (Toniolo 2005). Such swap lines were usually for a limited duration, e.g. of three months, in order to contain the risks of the transaction (see Chapter 7 for a discussion of the risks) and limit the time during which reserves were immobilised; at the end of its duration, a swap line could be cancelled or put on standby for later reactivation (Toniolo 2005). There had also been a swap arrangement between the Federal Reserve Bank of New York and the Bank of England of $200 million of US gold against sterling in 1925, when sterling returned to the gold standard (Coombs 1976; Sayers 1976).

In October 1955 the Bank for International Settlements offered to accept dollars from the Swiss National Bank in exchange for gold under a swap transaction with a maturity of three or six months, demonstrating that 'knowledge of such swap transactions had been preserved at the BIS during the years of bilateralism' (Bernholz 2007). And at the end of 1959, the Swiss National Bank conducted gold/dollar swaps with the BIS and the Bank of England for $50 million and $20 million, respectively. These gold/dollar swaps helped fund window-dressing dollar/Swiss franc swaps over the year-end by the Swiss National Bank with Swiss commercial banks, so that Swiss commercial banks' balance sheets could show larger amounts of liquid Swiss franc assets; and they contributed to higher reported gold holdings in Switzerland to meet the prescribed cover for note issue (Bernholz 2007).

In February 1961, Max Iklé from the Swiss National Bank proposed gold/dollar swaps to Charles Coombs of the Federal Reserve Bank of

New York at a monthly BIS meeting of central bankers, as well as in a follow-up letter (Bernholz 2007). Iklé had been worried that the decrease in US gold reserves during 1960 could threaten the gold convertibility of the US dollar (Bernholz 2007). Following the revaluation of the Deutsche Mark on 3 March 1961, which put heavy downward pressure on sterling, the Swiss National Bank entered into gold/sterling swaps with the Bank of England (Bernholz 2007). And after the revaluation of the Deutsche Mark led to speculation against the US dollar, the Bundesbank proposed a dollar/Deutsche Mark swap to the Federal Reserve Bank of New York, which was implemented in 1961 (Bernholz 2007).

In the course of 1961 a series of bilateral support measures were set up between the Bank of England and other central banks as well as the BIS under the 'Basel Agreement' in order to counter speculative attacks on the pound sterling. Total support under the Basel Agreement peaked at $904 million at the end of June 1961, with the BIS contributing $154 million in gold swaps in June 1961 (Toniolo 2005).

Starting in 1962, the Federal Reserve developed the use of central bank swap lines further by establishing a network of swap lines involving Western central banks as well as the Bank for International Settlements (Toniolo 2005). The swap arrangements were usually for three months, and could be renewed or maintained on standby if both parties agreed (Coombs 1976).[1] The central bank swap network established by the Federal Reserve grew rapidly from around $2 billion at the end of 1963 (involving eleven foreign central banks and the BIS at the end of November 1963), to $10 billion and $30 billion at the end of 1969 and 1978, respectively, and it was not dismantled with the breakdown of the Bretton Woods system. These swap lines were maintained until the late 1990s, when the Federal Reserve allowed all its swap lines except those with the central banks of Canada and Mexico to lapse, in the light of the introduction of the euro and their disuse for the preceding fifteen years.[2]

---

[1] In 1963 the Federal Open Market Committee approved a one-year limit for the repayment of credits extended under the Federal Reserve swap network. If this one-year limit could not be met, the US Treasury could issue certificates or bonds in the foreign central bank's currency to provide medium-term financing (see Coombs 1976).

[2] See FOMC (1998). The swap lines with Canada and Mexico were retained because they were associated with the North American Framework Agreement, in which the Federal Reserve participated.

The swap network had four main purposes. The first was to support the US dollar exchange rate against temporary fluctuations or 'to help safeguard the value of the dollar in the international exchange markets' (as stated in the Federal Open Market Committee's authorisation of 13 February 1962; see FOMC 1962). The swap network was seen as 'the perimeter defence line shielding the dollar against speculation and other exchange market pressures' (Coombs 1976), and according to a BIS paper its purpose was 'to counter speculative attacks on the dollar or cushion market disturbances that threaten to become disorderly' (BIS G10 1964).

The second purpose of the swap network was to avoid the large drains on the gold holdings of the United States that would occur if central banks converted temporarily-large dollar balances into gold: 'To offset or compensate, when appropriate, the effects on US gold reserves or dollar liabilities of those fluctuations in the international flow of payments to or from the United States that are deemed to reflect temporary disequilibriating forces or transitional market unsettlement' (FOMC 1962); 'to avoid a bunching of gold losses resulting from rapid accumulation of excess dollar balances by foreign central banks – especially if these accumulations were likely to be reversed within a foreseeable period; swap arrangements were not, however, designed to avoid gold losses resulting from a persistent payments deficit' (BIS G10 1964). The swap network was described as a 'temporary alternative to international gold settlements in the form of central bank credit facilities' (Coombs 1976).

The third purpose of the swap network was to enhance international monetary cooperation between central banks and international institutions and avoid adverse effects on foreign exchange reserves positions: to 'further monetary cooperation with central banks of other countries maintaining convertible currencies, with the International Monetary Fund, and with other international payments institutions' (FOMC 1962), to 'supplement international exchange arrangements such as those made through the International Monetary Fund' (FOMC 1962), 'Together with these banks and institutions, to help moderate temporary imbalances in international payments that may adversely affect monetary reserve positions' (FOMC 1962).

The fourth purpose of the swap network was to aid in the provision of international liquidity in the longer term: 'In the long run, to provide a means whereby reciprocal holdings of foreign currencies may contribute to meeting needs for international liquidity as required in terms of an expanding world economy' (FOMC 1962); 'in the longer run, when the US balance of payments had returned to equilibrium, to provide a means whereby reciprocal holdings of foreign currencies might contribute to meeting needs for international liquidity' (BIS G10 1964). The fourth purpose of contributing to meeting the needs for international liquidity was essentially the same as the one served by the swap network established in the financial crisis of 2007–08.

Other central banks also used this central bank swap network to support their currencies, for example the Bank of Italy in support of the Italian lira in March 1964; they also used them to manage seasonal pressures arising in foreign exchange markets, for example due to operations of commercial banks at year-end (Toniolo 2005). The Federal Reserve also entered into some swap lines with the BIS enabling the Fed to convert one foreign currency into another without affecting foreign exchange markets by large transactions (BIS G10 1964).

Following the terrorist attacks on the United States on 11 September 2001, the Federal Reserve established temporary central bank swap lines for a duration of 30 days with the European Central Bank and the Bank of England, and temporarily increased its existing swap line with the Bank of Canada.[3] Their purpose was to provide emergency US dollar liquidity in response to the disruption of the financial infrastructure. For example, the press statement accompanying the swap line for $30 billion established between the Federal Reserve and the Bank of England on 14 September 2001 specified that 'The US dollar proceeds, would, if necessary, be made available to banks in the United Kingdom to facilitate the settlement of their US dollar transactions.'

2. Which swap networks were set up during the crisis?

In total, four overlapping swap networks were established:

a. The Fed network, set up to supply dollars (the Fed also set up swap facilities with certain foreign central banks under which it could obtain foreign currencies from them).

---

[3] See press releases by the Federal Reserve, www.federalreserve.gov/boarddocs/ press/general/2001/20010913/default.htm, www.federalreserve.gov/boarddocs/ press/general/2001/20010914/default.htm and www.federalreserve.gov/ boarddocs/press/general/2001/200109144/default.htm.

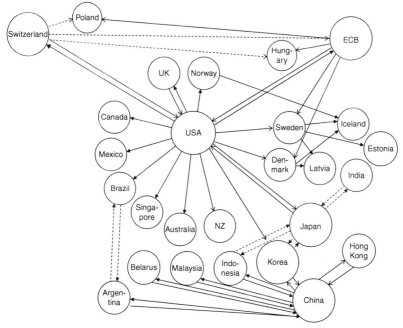

Figure 6.1 Swap networks created in 2007–09.

b. The euro network, under which the ECB supplied euros. There were also what might be regarded as extensions to the euro network under which Danmarks Nationalbank, the Norges Bank and the Sveriges Riksbank provided euros to other central banks.
c. The Swiss franc network.
d. The Asian and Latin American network.

The entire network of swap facilities is illustrated in Figure 6.1, and the swap lines that were set up are listed in the appendix at the end of this chapter.

a. The Fed network

The Federal Reserve was the first in the field. It set up its first crisis-related swap lines in December 2007, and the number and size of its swap lines increased steadily in the following months. In reporting the initial phase of the extension of swap facilities in December 2007, the Federal Reserve Bank of New York commented as follows:

From mid-November to year-end, trading liquidity in the foreign exchange swaps market was severely impaired. The re-emergence of funding pressures in term dollar, euro, and pound sterling money markets caused by balance sheet constraints and typical year-end funding pressures made it difficult to identify the appropriate interest rates at which to price forward transactions. These factors were exacerbated by increased demand for dollar funding by offshore banks that are typically structurally short US dollars and that use the foreign exchange swaps market to obtain such funding. As a result, trading volumes in the foreign exchange swaps market diminished considerably, trade sizes contracted, and bid-ask spreads on transactions became much wider than normal. Additionally, concerns about counterparty credit risk prompted some market makers to temporarily withdraw from the market. Credit tiering also became evident, with counterparties viewed as less creditworthy finding it more difficult and costly to enter into transactions than counterparties perceived to be more creditworthy. Despite the impairment to the swaps market, spot foreign exchange market liquidity for major currencies was generally healthy during the quarter.[4]

The swap network was part of a broader programme of facilities that the Fed established to provide liquidity to financial markets. Access to other Federal Reserve liquidity facilities is confined to banks and primary securities dealers in the United States,[5] so that banks outside the United States which did not have affiliates in the United States, and which needed to raise dollars, did not have access to them. The swap lines established by the Federal Reserve also had the aim of reducing US dollar funding market pressure in the United States, as the following statements make clear:

However, we did explicitly coordinate to address problems in dollar funding markets. The Federal Reserve entered into foreign exchange swaps with a number of other central banks to make dollar funding available to foreign

---

[4] See Federal Reserve Bank of New York (2008).
[5] For information about access to the discount window, see Board of Governors of the Federal Reserve System (2005). For information about access to the Term Auction Facility and the Primary Dealer Credit Facility, see www.federalreserve. gov/newsevents/press/monetary/20071212a.htm and www.federalreserve.gov/ newsevents/press/monetary/20080316a.htm, respectively.

banks in their own countries. By doing so, we reduced the pressure on dollar funding markets here at home. (Kohn 2009)

During this period, foreign commercial banks were a source of heavy demand for US dollar funding, thereby putting additional strain on global bank funding markets, including US markets, and further squeezing credit availability in the United States. To address this problem, the Federal Reserve expanded the temporary swap lines that had been established earlier with the European Central Bank (ECB) and the Swiss National Bank, and established new temporary swap lines with seven other central banks in September and five more in late October, including four in emerging market economies. (Bernanke 2009a)

Chapter 2 explained how the collateral squeeze in the United States pulled in dollar funds from other countries. The Fed swap lines enabled banks outside the United States to repay deposits provided by banks in the United States, and thereby both prevented widespread failures among banks outside the United States and relieved the domestic collateral squeeze.

The minutes of the conference call held by the Federal Open Market Committee on 6 December 2007, at which it was decided to establish the first of the swap lines, records that the swap proposal was 'aimed at improving market functioning'. The extension of swap lines by the Federal Reserve took place in four main phases, as market liquidity deteriorated. The first swap lines were set up in December 2007, and they were extended, both in size and in geographical spread, in March 2008, May 2008 and September/October 2008. The last phase of extensions was by far the largest. It followed the failure of Lehman Brothers on 15 September. In response to the ensuing deterioration in market conditions, it was announced that foreign central banks (the ECB and the central banks of Japan, Switzerland and the UK) would auction term and forward dollar funding, in parallel with the Fed's domestic Term Auction Facility. To facilitate these auctions, the upper limits on the amounts of the Fed's swap lines with these central banks were removed entirely.

The four economies with the largest US dollar shortages according to the measure shown in Figure 3.3, namely the euro area, the United Kingdom, Canada and Brazil, all received swap lines from the Fed. Among the fifteen economies with the largest US dollar shortages, all received US dollar swap lines from the Fed except for Russia, Turkey,

India, Chile, Hungary and Iceland (see Figure 6.1). Of these countries, Russia had substantial foreign currency reserves (see Table 13.1),
India received a US dollar swap line from the Bank of Japan, and
Hungary and Iceland received IMF standby arrangements. In addition,
Switzerland, Japan, Singapore, Mexico and Denmark received US dollar swap lines from the Fed, despite having US dollar surpluses on the
measure shown in Figure 3.3.

In April 2009, the Fed announced that, as a precautionary measure, it had established swap lines to enable it to borrow foreign currencies from the ECB and the central banks of Switzerland, the UK
and Japan, so that it would have the means to relieve shortages of
foreign currencies in the United States should they arise.[6] These swap
lines were not used. All of the Fed swap lines expired on 1 February
2010.[7]

On 9 May 2010, amid the market stresses related to the crisis in
Greek public finances, the Fed re-established temporary swap lines
with the Bank of Canada, the Bank of England, the ECB and the Swiss
National Bank. Owing to liquidity pressures in international financial
markets and their possible impact on liquidity in the yen money market, the Fed swap line with the Bank of Japan was re-established on 10
May 2010.[8] These swap lines, and other consequences of the sovereign
debt crisis in the euro area, are, however, not part of the story told in
this book.

---

[6] In each case, it already had in place a swap line under which it could supply
dollars to the foreign central bank in question.
[7] See FOMC press release of 27 January 2010, www.federalreserve.gov/
newsevents/press/monetary/20100127a.htm.
[8] The swap lines with the Bank of England, the Bank of Japan, the ECB and
the Swiss National Bank allow tenders of US dollars at fixed rate for full
allotment, while the swap line with the Bank of Canada allows drawings up
to $30 billion, as had been the case previously. See FOMC press releases of 9
May 2010 and of 10 May 2010, www.federalreserve.gov/newsevents/press/
monetary/20100509a.htm and www.federalreserve.gov/newsevents/press/
monetary/20100510a.htm, and Bank of Japan press release of 10 May 2010,
www.boj.or.jp/en/type/release/adhoc10/mok1005a.pdf. The Fed explained the
reopening of the swap lines with the Bank of Canada, the Bank of England, the
ECB and the Swiss National Bank as being 'in response to the re-emergence of
strains in US dollar funding markets in Europe'. The Bank of Japan explained
that its swap line had been reopened 'in view of recent liquidity pressures in the
international financial markets and the possible impact of those on liquidity in
the Yen money market'.

b. The euro network

As Chapter 3 noted, the euro is less widely used than the US dollar to denominate foreign currency bank loans outside its home territory. Moreover, its external use in trade in goods is concentrated in those parts of Europe outside the euro area (see Bertuch-Samuels and Ramlogan 2007).[9] At the end of June 2008, euro-denominated reserves comprised 30% of total world holdings of official foreign exchange reserves for which the currency composition is known, while dollar-denominated reserves comprised 63%.[10] In 2004, the euro surpassed the dollar as the most important currency of issue for international bonds and notes.[11] In international banking, 23% of all assets and 20% of all liabilities were denominated in euros at the end of June 2008, compared with 55% and 56%, respectively, that were denominated in dollars.[12] In foreign exchange markets, the euro was the second most widely traded currency after the dollar in April 2007 (see Bank for International Settlements 2007).

There is good evidence that financial trading in euros is largely concentrated in time zones close to those of the euro area, so that there is much less risk of stresses emerging in euro money markets at a time of day when normal central bank liquidity facilities are not available than there is in the case of the dollar.[13] Nevertheless, euro-specific liquidity shortages developed in 2008 in several European countries outside the euro area; the market symptoms were noted in Chapter 4 above. The ECB set up facilities with the Danish, Hungarian, Polish and Swedish central banks to assist commercial banks in those countries in getting access to euro liquidity and thereby relieving localised shortages. In Hungary and Poland, commercial banks had made extensive domestic mortgage loans in foreign currencies, financing themselves in wholesale markets which became much less liquid as the credit crisis intensified.[14]

---

[9] Evidence on the external role of the euro is provided in European Central Bank (2008) and Bertuch-Samuels and Ramlogan (2007). See also Galati and Wooldridge (2006) on the role of the euro as a reserve currency, and McGuire and Tarashev (2007) on its role in international banking.

[10] Source: IMF, Composition of Foreign Exchange Reserves; see www.imf.org/external/np/sta/cofer/eng/index.htm.

[11] Source: BIS international securities statistics, table 13B.

[12] Source: BIS international banking statistics, table 5A.

[13] See European Central Bank (2008), ch. 2.

[14] See for example the 2007 IMF Article 4 reports on Hungary and Poland (www.imf.org/external/pubs/ft/scr/2007/cr07250.pdf and www.imf.org/

Among the seven economies with the largest euro shortages according to the measure shown in Figure 3.4, all received euro swap lines from the ECB except for Norway and Romania (see Figure 6.1).[15] Norway had substantial foreign exchange reserves (see the discussion in Chapter 9 below), but it nevertheless received a swap line from the Fed. Romania received an IMF standby arrangement. In addition to the swap lines provided by the ECB, further swap lines were provided indirectly to Iceland, Estonia and Latvia in an extended euro swap network by the central banks of Denmark, Norway and Sweden (see Figure 6.1). The Czech Republic, Lithuania, Bulgaria and Turkey also had euro shortages on the measure shown in Figure 3.4, but did not receive euro swap lines.

c. The Swiss franc network

The euro area, Poland and Hungary were three of the four economies with the largest Swiss franc shortages according to the measure shown in Figure 3.7, and they all received Swiss franc swap lines from the Swiss National Bank (see Figure 6.1). The United Kingdom also had a large Swiss franc shortage (see Figure 3.7), but did not receive a Swiss franc swap line. Under the SNB's swap lines with Hungary and Poland, Swiss francs were provided against euro collateral, not against the national currency of the counterparty central bank.

The SNB's purpose in providing these swap facilities was to enable foreign central banks to provide their commercial banks with Swiss franc liquidity and thereby satisfy the strong demand for Swiss franc funding.[16] The SNB implements its monetary policy by fixing a target range for the three-month Swiss franc LIBOR rate. The SNB reduced the upper bound of its target range from above 3 per cent to 0.75 per cent in the course of the financial crisis, and sought to bring down the LIBOR rate within this target range. However, the efforts of foreign banks to obtain the Swiss franc funding that they needed put upward pressure on the LIBOR rate. Easing the Swiss franc funding problems

---

external/pubs/ft/scr/2008/cr08130.pdf). See also Narodowy Bank Polski (2008). The loans were predominantly in Swiss francs.

[15] The swap facility under which the ECB could supply dollars to the Fed was however set up only in April 2009.

[16] See Roth (2009).

of foreign banks by providing swap lines was therefore expected to help bring down the SNB's policy rate within the target range, thereby aiding in achieving the SNB's monetary policy objectives. Explaining the extension of the EUR/CHF foreign exchange swaps with the ECB, Narodowy Bank Polski and Magyar Nemzeti Bank on 25 June 2009, the SNB stated in its Monetary Policy Report that 'The aim of this measure is to further ease the situation on the short-term Swiss franc money market.'[17]

In addition to providing these swap facilities, the Swiss National Bank also supplied Swiss franc liquidity directly to foreign commercial banks through its regular repo operations. Auer and Kraenzlin (2011, p. 6) comment that: 'The original intention of allowing foreign banks to access the Swiss REPO system was to reduce the dependence on the few large Swiss financial institutions, to improve the general liquidity, and to thereby facilitate the steering of a longer term money market rate, namely the three-month Swiss franc LIBOR.'

The provision of the swap facilities probably also partly reflected the SNB's concern about the appreciation of the Swiss franc, as well as its concern about conditions in credit markets. Indeed, on 12 March 2009, the SNB announced that it would act 'to prevent a further appreciation of the Swiss franc against the euro', including by purchasing foreign currency on the foreign exchange markets.[18] It therefore seems likely that the provision of Swiss franc swap facilities to the ECB and to the central banks of Hungary and Poland was partly motivated by the same concern.

d. The Asian and Latin American network

Before the credit crisis began, there was already an extensive network of inter-central bank swap lines in East Asia, created since 2000 under the Chiang Mai initiative.[19] These facilities were set up after the Asian financial crisis of 1997–98 in order to enable East Asian central banks to provide mutual financial support in the event of a future crisis, and they are part of a larger programme of economic integration in East Asia, as Kawai (2007) describes. The provisions of the swap facilities

---

[17] See Swiss National Bank (2009), p. 26.
[18] See www.snb.ch/en/mmr/reference/pre_20090312/source.
[19] See Kawai (2007).

are fairly conservative, in that only the first 20 per cent of the committed amount is available in the absence of IMF conditionality. The remainder is provided in association with an IMF programme. To the author's knowledge, no drawings were made under this network during 2007–09. The Chiang Mai network needed to be supplemented to address the pressures created by the credit crisis.[20]

During the crisis, the Bank of Japan established yen swap lines with the Federal Reserve and the Bank of Korea (see Figure 6.1); the United States and Korea were among the six economies with the largest yen shortages according to the measure shown in Figure 3.5. No drawings were made on either of them. In addition, in June 2008, the Bank of Japan, acting as agent for the Ministry of Finance, established a US dollar swap line with India.

The People's Bank of China was active in establishing new swap lines during the crisis. It appears to have had two separate objectives: first, to help in dealing with financial stress, and second, to promote bilateral trade and investment in the partner countries' own currencies, with a view to establishing these currencies as international trading and investment vehicles in the longer term. It is reasonable to believe that the PBOC's pursuit of both these objectives was motivated by the financial crisis. The need for liquidity was obvious. And the desire to promote non-dollar currencies as trading and investment vehicles is consistent with the views on international monetary reform expressed by the Governor of the PBOC in a speech on 23 March 2009.[21]

These objectives were set out in the English language versions of the PBOC's announcements of the establishment of the various swap lines, as Table 6.1 shows.

The PBOC's second objective, of promoting bilateral trade in the trading partner countries' own currencies, with a view to establishing their own currencies as international trading vehicles, is by its nature a longer-term project, and this is reflected in the fact that the PBOC's swaps all had three-year terms, much longer than the terms of the swaps set up by other central banks purely to address market liquidity strains.

---

[20] In late 2009, the Chiang Mai network of bilateral facilities was multilateralised. Each member country was assigned a 'contribution amount' and a 'purchasing multiplier', and is able to draw US dollars up to the product of its contribution amount and purchasing multiplier. See for example www.pbc.gov.cn/english/detail.asp?col=6400&id=1451.

[21] See Zhou (2009).

Table 6.1 *Language of swap announcements by the People's Bank of China*

Date	Counterparty	Short-term liquidity?	Bilateral trade?
12 December 2008	Bank of Korea	Yes	Yes
20 January 2009	Hong Kong Monetary Authority	Yes	Yes[a]
8 February 2009	Bank Negara Malaysia	No	Yes[b]
11 March 2009	National Bank of Belarus	No	Yes[b]
23 March 2009	Bank Indonesia	Yes	Yes[c]
2 April 2009	Central Bank of Argentina	No	No

Notes: [a] 'This will bolster investor confidence in Hong Kong's financial stability, promote regional financial stability and the development of yuan-denominated trade settlement between Hong Kong and the mainland'. [b] Announcement refers to 'bilateral trade and investment'. [c] Announcement refers to 'bilateral trade and direct investment'.
Sources: English language versions on PBOC internet site.

Hong Kong had substantial surpluses in the US dollar, euro, yen and pound sterling on the measure shown in Figure 3.3–Figure 3.7, and so had no obvious need for swap lines for providing liquidity in these foreign currencies; of the other countries which received swap lines from China, Malaysia had small surpluses, and Indonesia small shortages. Korea is discussed in Chapter 9.

Only a few economies had shortages in the pound sterling according to the measure shown in Figure 3.6, while many economies were close to balance in the pound sterling or had surpluses. This is consistent with the absence of any swap lines in the pound sterling.[22]

[22] With the exception of the undrawn swap line provided to the Fed, listed in Section 2 of the Appendix to this chapter.

Appendix: list of swap lines

List of swap lines extended between December 2007 and April 2009

Date	Counterparty central bank	Amount (bn)	Expiry date
1. Swap lines extended by the Fed to provide dollars			
12 December 2007	European Central Bank	20	Jun 2008
	Swiss National Bank	4	Jun 2008
11 March 2008	European Central Bank*	30	Sept 2008
	Swiss National Bank*	6	Sept 2008
2 May 2008	European Central Bank*	50	Jan 2009
	Swiss National Bank*	12	Jan 2009
30 July 2008	European Central Bank*	55	Jan 2009
18 September 2008	European Central Bank*	110	Jan 2009
	Swiss National Bank*	27	Jan 2009
	Bank of Japan	60	Jan 2009
	Bank of England	40	Jan 2009
	Bank of Canada	10	Jan 2009
24 September 2008	Reserve Bank of Australia	10	Jan 2009
	Sveriges Riksbank	10	Jan 2009
	Danmarks Nationalbank	5	Jan 2009
	Norges Bank	5	Jan 2009
26 September 2008	European Central Bank*	120	Jan 2009
	Swiss National Bank*	30	Jan 2009
29 September 2008	Bank of Canada*	30	Apr 2009+
	Bank of England*	80	Apr 2009
	Bank of Japan*	120	Apr 2009
	Danmarks Nationalbank	15	Apr 2009
	European Central Bank*	240	Apr 2009
	Norges Bank*	15	Apr 2009+
	Reserve Bank of Australia	30	Apr 2009+
	Sveriges Riksbank*	30	Apr 2009+
	Swiss National Bank*	60	Apr 2009+
13 October 2008	Bank of England*	Unlimited	Apr 2009+
	European Central Bank*	Unlimited	Apr 2009+
	Swiss National Bank*	Unlimited	Apr 2009+
14 October 2008	Bank of Japan*	Unlimited	Apr 2009+
28 October 2008	Reserve Bank of New Zealand	15	Apr 2009+

29 October 2008	Banco Central do Brasil	30	Apr 2009+
	Banco de Mexico	30	Apr 2009+
	Bank of Korea	30	Apr 2009+
	Monetary Authority of Singapore	30	Apr 2009+

* Denotes an extension or enlargement of an existing facility.
\+ The expiry date of these swap lines was extended first to October 2009 and later to February 2010.

2. Swap lines under which the Fed could receive foreign currencies

6 April 2009 2009**	Bank of England	GBP 30	Oct
	European Central Bank	EUR 80	Oct 2009**
	Bank of Japan	JPY 10,000	Oct 2009**
	Swiss National Bank	CHF 40	Oct 2009**

** The expiry date of these swap lines was later extended to February 2010.

3. Swap lines extended by the European Central Bank to provide euros

20 December 2007	Sveriges Riksbank	10	
16 October 2008	Magyar Nemzeti Bank	5	Not specified
27 October 2008	Danmarks Nationalbank	12	'As long as needed'
21 November 2008	Narodowy Bank Polski	10	Not specified

4. Other swap lines in the extended euro network

a. Danmarks Nationalbank supplying euros

16 May 2008	Central Bank of Iceland	0.5	Extended in Nov 2008 until end-2009

b. Norges Bank supplying euros

16 December 2008	Bank of Latvia	0.125	
16 May 2008	Central Bank of Iceland	0.5	Extended in Nov 2008 until end-2009

c. Sveriges Riksbank

16 May 2008	Central Bank of Iceland	EUR 0.5	Extended in Nov 2008 until end-2009

| 16 December 2008 | Bank of Latvia | EUR 0.375 | |
| 27 February 2009 | Bank of Estonia | SEK 10 | |

5. Swap lines extended by the Swiss National Bank to provide Swiss francs

15 October 2008	European Central Bank	Not specified	Jan 2009*+
7 November 2008	Narodowy Bank Polski	Not specified	Jan 2009*+
28 January 2009	Magyar Nemzeti Bank	Not specified	Apr 2009+*

*+ The expiry dates of these swap lines were later extended to April, then
to October 2009 and again until January 2010. Swap operations were
discontinued after 25 January 2010.
+* The expiry date was later extended to October 2009, then to January
2010. Swap operations were discontinued after 25 January 2010.

6. Asian swap lines
a. People's Bank of China

12 December 2008	Bank of Korea	CNY 180 KRW 38,000	3 years
20 January 2009	Hong Kong Monetary Authority	CNY 200 HKD 227	3 years
8 February 2009	Bank Negara Malaysia	CNY 80 MYR 40	3 years
11 March 2009	National Bank of Belarus	CNY 20 BYR 8,000	3 years
23 March 2009	Bank Indonesia	CNY 100 IDR 175,000	3 years
2 April 2009	Banco Central de la Republica Argentina	CNY 70 ARS 38	3 years

b. Bank of Japan

30 June 2008	Reserve Bank of India	USD 3	
12 December 2008	Bank of Korea	USD 20	Jan 2009***
6 April 2009	Bank Indonesia	USD 12	

*** The expiry date was later extended first to October 2009, and later to
February 2010.
Sources: Central banks.

7 | *Which countries received swap lines?*

A swap network needs membership rules; in other words, criteria to determine which countries are to be offered swap facilities. In the circumstances of late 2008, decisions had to be taken very quickly and there was not much time for analysis and reflection. This chapter first discusses the risks in providing swap facilities from the standpoint of the country providing them, and then discusses the issues for the prospective recipients. It then examines what actually happened in 2008, by looking at the relationship between currency-specific liquidity shortages and the distribution of swap lines.

1. Risks to liquidity providers

As Chapter 5 explained, swap arrangements were used during 2007–09 as a means of providing currency-specific liquidity to banks outside the home territory of the currency concerned, thus, in effect, widening the geographical reach of national open-market operations. The central banks which provided liquidity through swaps avoided the credit risk involved in lending to commercial banks by lending to the central banks in which they were located;[1] the latter central banks took the credit risk of lending to commercial banks in their territories. The central banks which provided liquidity in effect took sovereign credit risk by lending to other central banks.

The risk was mitigated by the fact that they took deposits, normally in the counterparty central bank's currency, as collateral, but it was not entirely eliminated. For example, the counterparty central bank might not be able to return the currency that it had drawn when the swap arrangement expired. In that case, the central bank that provided the currency would have to try to liquidate its collateral, which is normally in the form of the borrowing country's currency. However, the

---

[1] See Bernanke (2009b).

currency might have depreciated in the foreign exchange market,[2] and, even if the amount of collateral had been adjusted to take account of any exchange rate depreciation, it might be very difficult to sell a large amount of the currency in a short time in a possibly illiquid market.

Central banks must take account of this risk in deciding whether to extend swap facilities. One way of dealing with the risk is to extend a swap line, but against another major currency rather than the domestic currency of the recipient country. For example, when the Swiss National Bank lent Swiss francs to the central banks of Hungary and Poland, the swaps were against euros, rather than forints and złotys. Another way is to take high-quality assets denominated in the currency of the liquidity provider as collateral. Thus the ECB's facilities for Hungary and Poland simply enabled the central banks of those two countries to repo high-quality euro-denominated assets in their reserves in exchange for euro cash (so that the facilities were not swap lines, strictly speaking).

In some cases, the unavailability of foreign currency liquidity was not confined to particular banks but extended to the country as a whole, including its government. This might reflect market doubts about the sustainability of the country's macroeconomic policies. In those cases, swaps could in principle be used to provide foreign currency liquidity to governments that were no longer able to obtain it in financial markets. If such market doubts were warranted, then it would normally be thought undesirable to provide swap lines, since their probable effect would be to delay necessary macroeconomic adjustment. Moreover, the risks to central banks providing swap lines might be judged unacceptable. In such cases, swap lines would normally be extended only after the country concerned had reached a financing agreement with the IMF involving macroeconomic policy adjustments, or at least when it was clear that such an agreement would be reached.

Iceland is a case in point. It had serious problems in its banking system, which was extremely large in relation to the Icelandic economy. Icelandic commercial banks had severe liquidity difficulties and, in order to try to help resolve them, the Central Bank of Iceland tried to arrange swap facilities with a number of other central banks. It was able to agree (on 16 May 2008) swap facilities with the central

---

[2] The Fed avoids this risk by denominating the loan repayment and interest in dollars. See Bernanke (2009b).

banks of Denmark, Norway and Sweden totalling EUR 1,500 million.[3] However, as it relates in a remarkable statement, it had no further success.[4] The statement makes it clear that the potential counterparty central banks were concerned about the risk they would be taking in entering a swap agreement with Iceland, and specifically about the large size of the Icelandic banking system. Later, Iceland obtained emergency financing from the IMF, and, having done so, it was able to extend the swap facilities it had received earlier.

As another example, the Bank of Latvia concluded on 16 December 2008 an agreement with the central banks of Sweden and Denmark under which it could draw up to EUR 500 million in total, as bridging loans to an expected IMF programme.[5]

Bridging loans to IMF programmes carry the risk that the IMF programme may not be agreed and the supporting funds may not be disbursed as had been expected at the time when the loan was made. In that case, the bridge could be a 'bridge to nowhere'. However, the countries which extend the loan presumably have good information about the progress of the loan negotiations, partly because they are themselves members of the IMF. Moreover they can feel confident that the IMF will make an adequate amount of money available on *some* terms, and can assess the likelihood that the government of the distressed country will reach an agreement with the IMF.

A separate risk for central banks providing liquidity in their own currency to foreign central banks is governance. The Federal Open Market Committee discussed this and the other risks involved at its meeting on 28–29 October 2008 when considering the proposal to set up swap arrangements with Mexico, Brazil, Korea and Singapore. The minutes report that:

In their remarks, participants focused on the outlook for complementarity between these swaps and the new short-term liquidity facility that the

---

[3] See www.sedlabanki.is/?PageID=287&NewsID=1766.
[4] See www.sedlabanki.is/?PageID=287&NewsID=1890.
[5] See www.bank.lv/eng/main/press/sapinfo/lbpdip/1612/. The President of the ECB, Jean-Claude Trichet, however, made a statement in support of Latvia when he said 'I have full confidence the government of Latvia will take the appropriate decisions needed on a domestic basis without any change in the currency' (*Financial Times*, 5 June 2009). Mr Trichet's choice of words makes it clear that he thought that macroeconomic adjustment was needed.

International Monetary Fund was considering; on the governance and structure of the swap lines; and on the particular countries included. Several participants pointed to the international reserves held by the countries and the importance of ensuring that these temporary swap lines, like the others that had been established during the period, be used only for the purposes intended. On balance, the Committee concluded that in current circumstances the swap arrangements with these four large and systemically important economies were appropriate ...[6]

This discussion suggests that, in view of the risks, the Fed preferred to provide swap lines only in cases where other sources of financing were not available or not thought to be adequate, and to countries that are large and systemically important. One member of the FOMC (William Poole) dissented from the decision to establish the initial swap lines (and later decisions to extend the network) on the grounds that he viewed the swap agreement as unnecessary in the light of the size of the dollar-denominated foreign exchange reserves of the recipient central bank.[7]

It should not be imagined that countries which did not get a swap line from the Fed were *ipso facto* deemed to be too risky, too small or systemically unimportant. The minutes of the FOMC meeting held on 16 September 2008 record that:

The Committee considered a proposal intended to provide the flexibility necessary to respond promptly to requests from foreign central banks to engage in temporary reciprocal currency ('swap') arrangements to be used in supporting dollar liquidity in their jurisdictions.[8]

This makes it clear that the Fed made decisions about which countries should receive swap lines by responding to requests. It is reasonable to think that there were countries to which the Fed would have been quite willing to provide a swap line, but which did not ask for one.

Central banks need to be concerned about political as well as economic risks. Measures such as swap facilities, which appear on the surface to benefit only foreigners, are vulnerable to criticism from politicians, especially in hard economic times. The Fed has legal authority

---

[6] See Federal Open Market Committee (2008b).
[7] See Federal Open Market Committee (2007).
[8] See Federal Open Market Committee (2008a).

under the Federal Reserve Act to enter into swap agreements with foreign central banks. Nevertheless Chairman Bernanke was questioned aggressively in the US House of Representatives by Congressman Alan Grayson of Florida in July 2009 about why the Fed had provided the large amounts of money it had lent through swap lines to foreigners and not to Americans.[9]

2. Objectives of liquidity takers

The countries which accepted swap lines providing foreign currency were concerned above all to maintain the stability of their banking systems, and in particular to ensure that commercial banks had the means to repay foreign currency liabilities as they fell due.

It is possible that some countries could have achieved this objective without the use of swap lines. For example, they could have provided the necessary liquidity to commercial banks in their domestic currency. However, the commercial banks would have been required to swap massive amounts of domestic currency into foreign currency to repay depositors who did not wish to roll over foreign currency deposits, and already-stressed swap markets in many currencies would have been unable to handle the necessary volume of transactions. And, in conditions of ample domestic currency liquidity, sales of the domestic currency might have led to large depreciations and loss of welfare to the citizens of the country concerned.

Alternatively, they could have used their own foreign exchange reserves to provide the needed foreign currency liquidity. However, in many countries the reserves were simply not large enough to meet the need. And even in countries where they were large enough, they might not have been held in the particular currencies that were needed, and selling other currencies (or swapping them) to raise the needed currencies would have aggravated foreign exchange market stresses, and might have drained scarce foreign currency liquidity from the domestic banking system. In some cases, the reserves might have been invested in temporarily illiquid assets, even if the assets were denominated in the needed currency. Moreover, in countries whose reserves were only modest in size relative to the liquidity need, and in the febrile

---

[9] Figure 8.1, which shows that the funds lent through swap lines all found their way back into the US banking system, is an effective answer to such questions.

atmosphere that prevailed at the time, the use of a large percentage of the reserves to provide liquidity support to commercial banks could have undermined confidence in the currency and led to a disproportionate depreciation of the exchange rate. In countries which used a pegged exchange rate as their monetary policy anchor, a large percentage fall in the reserves occurring in this way could have seriously undermined the credibility of monetary policy. Finally, in some countries, the purposes to which the reserves can be put are constrained by statute, and the permissible purposes might not include providing liquidity support to commercial banks.

Augmenting the reserves by means of official foreign currency borrowing would have been expensive, if not impossible, for many countries in the circumstances of the time. A further alternative, for countries in which the majority of banks are foreign owned, was to do nothing, leaving it to the parent companies of the banks to solve their liquidity problems. This was a successful strategy in some small countries. A variant of doing nothing was to provide limited and expensive foreign currency liquidity facilities intended for use by domestically owned banks only.

Most countries had powerful reasons to accept swap facilities if they were available, both to enable them to provide foreign currency liquidity without using their own reserves, and no doubt because the signal of international support that the swap lines conveyed was extremely valuable amid the prevailing economic and financial uncertainty.

3. Relationship between currency shortages and probability of receiving a swap line

This section examines the relationship between the level of a country's currency-specific liquidity shortages based on the BIS locational international banking statistics by residence of counterparty as shown in Figure 3.3–Figure 3.7, and whether the country received a swap line in that currency. It does so by considering a probit regression model of the dependent variable, y^c_i, which equals 1 if the country received a swap line in the currency, c, under consideration and 0 otherwise, on the level of countries' currency-specific shortages,[10] s^c_i, as well as on a

---

[10] A country's currency-specific shortage is defined as in Figure 3.3–Figure 3.7, but here we take shortages to have positive sign.

constant term. The sample of countries consists of those included in Figure 3.3–Figure 3.7. The vector of explanatory variables is defined as $x^c_i = (1, s^c_i)$. The probit model models the probability that a country i receives a swap line in currency c, i.e. that $y^c_i = 1$, as a function of the explanatory variables, namely a constant term and the currency-specific shortage, s^c_i, according to

$$P(y^c_i = 1 \mid x^c_i) = \Phi(x^c_i{}' \beta) \qquad (7.1)$$

where $\Phi(.)$ is the standard normal cumulative distribution function, the vector of coefficients is $\beta = (\beta_1, \beta_2)$, c denotes the currency considered, i.e. the US dollar, euro, yen or the Swiss franc, and s^c_i is the measure of the shortage in that currency (where a shortage is defined as positive in the regressions), in billions of US dollars or US dollar equivalent.[11] The estimated coefficients in the regression in equation (7.1) are shown in Table 7.1. The estimated probability of a country receiving a swap line in the euro, yen and the Swiss franc depends significantly on the measures of currency-specific shortage in the currency considered. The estimated relationship is significant at the 1 per cent level for the euro and Swiss franc, and at the 5 per cent level for the yen. The estimated coefficient β_2 of the currency-specific shortage is largest for the Swiss franc, followed by the euro and the yen. Consistent with this, the goodness-of-fit of the probit model as measured by the McFadden R^2 measure, is largest for the Swiss franc (at 0.44), followed by the euro (at 0.41) and the yen (at 0.19).

The marginal effect of the currency shortage on the probability of receiving a swap line in that currency is given by[12]

$$\partial \Phi(x^c_i{}' \beta)/\partial s^c_i = \phi(x^c_i{}' \beta)^* \beta_2 \qquad (7.2)$$

where $\phi(.)$ denotes the standard normal density function. This marginal effect depends on the value of the shortage. For the values of the shortages in our sample of countries, it ranges from close to zero to around 0.05 for the Swiss franc, to around 0.02 for the euro, and to around 0.01 for the yen.

---

[11] We do not consider sterling since no swap lines were granted in that currency, with the single exception of the swap line provided by the Bank of England to the Fed in April 2009.
[12] See Verbeek (2004).

Table 7.1 Results for probit and logit models by currency

	US dollar		Euro		Yen		Swiss franc	
	Eq. 7.1	Eq. 7.3	Eq. 7.1	Eq. 7.3	Eq. 7.1	Eq. 7.3	Eq. 7.1	Eq. 7.3
Constant, β_1	-0.25	-0.41	-1.87**	-3.17**	-1.73**	-3.04**	-1.85**	-3.53**
	(0.21)	(0.34)	(0.50)	(0.95)	(0.38)	(0.80)	(0.40)	(0.99)
Currency-specific shortage, β_2	0.004	0.006	0.043**	0.073**	0.021*	0.036*	0.130**	0.252**
	(0.003)	(0.005)	(0.014)	(0.025)	(0.01)	(0.018)	(0.048)	(0.097)
McFadden R^2	0.04	0.04	0.41	0.39	0.19	0.18	0.44	0.46
Number of observations	39		39		39		39	

Note: ** and * denote significance at the 1 per cent and 5 per cent level, respectively; standard errors are given in parentheses.

Next, the probability that a country i receives a swap line in currency c, i.e. that $y^c_i = 1$, is estimated as a function of the explanatory variables, a constant term and the estimated currency-specific shortage, s^c_i, using the logit model which is an alternative binary choice model to the probit model, in which the standard normal probability distribution function is replaced by a logistic probability distribution function

$$P(y^c_i = 1 | x^c_i) = F(x^c_i{}' \beta) \tag{7.3}$$

Here, $F(.)$ is the standard logistic distribution function, $F(w) = \exp(w)/(1+\exp(w))$.

In the logit model the marginal effect of the estimated currency shortage on the probability of receiving a swap line in that currency is given by[13]

$$\partial F(x^c_i{}' \beta)/\partial s^c_i = \exp(x^c_i{}' \beta)/(1+ \exp(x^c_i{}' \beta))^2 {}^* \beta_2 \tag{7.4}$$

This marginal effect again depends on the value of the shortage. For the values of the shortages in the chosen sample of countries, it ranges from close to zero to around 0.06 (per \$1 billion) for the Swiss franc, to around 0.02 for the euro and to around 0.01 for the yen.

The probit and logit models give similar results for the significance of the coefficients (see Table 7.1) and for the magnitudes of the marginal effects of the currency shortages on the probability of receiving a swap line in that currency for the Swiss franc, euro and yen where the effect is significant.

By contrast, in the specifications reported in Table 7.1 the relationship between the currency-specific shortage and the probability of receiving a swap line is not significant for the US dollar. One possible explanation is related to differences in time zones. In countries with time zones remote from the United States, US financial markets are closed during part or all of the trading day, for example the mornings in European countries. When US markets are closed, commercial banks with US dollar shortages in such time zones, for example in Europe, are likely to have tried to obtain US dollar funding in the markets of other large international financial centres outside the USA, such as Japan and Singapore. Thus US dollar shortages were likely to have been passed from one time zone to another. An international

---

[13] See Verbeek (2004).

Table 7.2 *Probit model for probability of receiving US dollar swap line*

	From any country	From the Federal Reserve (equation 7.5)
Constant, β_1	−0.73**	−0.96**
	(0.27)	(0.30)
US dollar shortage, β_2	0.026*	0.026*
	(0.010)	(0.011)
Dummy for large int. financial centre, β_3	4.94**	5.24**
	(1.87)	(1.93)
McFadden R²	0.31	0.35
Number of observations	39	39

Note: ** and * denote significance at the 1 per cent and 5 per cent level, respectively; standard errors are given in parentheses.

financial centre which initially had a dollar surplus might experience large inter-bank outflows which had the effect of turning the surplus into a shortage. Furthermore, many commercial banks in locations remote from US time zones may not have affiliates in the United States from which they could obtain US dollar liquidity, and would therefore be likely to look for US dollar funding outside the USA. Consequently, given the international role of the US dollar, it is reasonable to hypothesise that the Federal Reserve supplied US dollar funding via swap lines to the central banks of large international financial centres in remote time zones, so that the latter could distribute US dollar liquidity on to commercial banks while US markets were closed.

To test this hypothesis, a dummy variable, d_i^{lfc}, is added to the probit regression for the probability of the country receiving a US dollar swap line from any country, which equals one if an economy is a large international financial centre (i.e. Australia, the euro area, Hong Kong, Japan, Singapore, Switzerland and the United Kingdom) and zero otherwise. The vector of explanatory variables in the probit regression of equation (7.1) is now defined as $x_i^c = x\$_i = (1, s\$_i, d_i^{lfc})$, and the vector of coefficients is $\beta = (\beta_1, \beta_2, \beta_3)$. The results are shown in the middle column of Table 7.2. The coefficient on the dummy variable for an economy which is a large international financial centre is statistically significant at the 1 per cent level, consistent with the hypothesis. Moreover, when controlling for whether a country is a large international financial centre, the proxy measure of the US dollar shortage becomes statistically significant at the 5 per cent level in the probit regression. For the values of the US dollar shortages in the sample of countries, the marginal effect of the estimated US dollar shortage on the probability of receiving a US dollar swap line ranges from close to zero to around 0.01 (per \$1 billion), similar to what was found for the yen above. These results suggest that economies with larger US dollar shortages, and economies that are large international financial centres, had a higher probability of receiving a US dollar swap line.

Next, this exercise is repeated in the probit regression for the probability of the country receiving a US dollar swap line from the Federal Reserve, rather than from any country.[14] The dependent variable in the probit regression is now the probability that a country i receives a US dollar swap line from the Federal Reserve, $y^{Fed}_i = 1$, and the explanatory variables are again $x\$_i = (1, s\$_i, d_i^{lfc})$, with the vector of coefficients being $\beta = (\beta_1, \beta_2, \beta_3)$,

$$P(y^{Fed}_i = 1 | x\$_i) = \Phi(x\$_i' \beta) \tag{7.5}$$

The results are reported in Table 7.2 (right-hand column).

For swap lines provided by the Fed, the estimated coefficients on both the US dollar shortage and the dummy for a large international financial centre are statistically significant. These results suggest that countries with larger US dollar shortages, and countries that are large international financial centres, were more likely to receive a US dollar swap line from the Federal Reserve.

Finally, a variable is added for the difference in time zones between each country and New York, tz_i (in hours), in the probit regressions for the probability of the country receiving a US dollar swap line from any country. The vector of explanatory variables in the probit regression of equation (7.1) is now defined as $x^c_i = x\$_i = (1, s\$_i, d_i^{lfc}, tz_i)$, and the vector of coefficients is $\beta = (\beta_1, \beta_2, \beta_3, \beta_4)$. The results are reported in Table 7.3 (middle column). The estimated coefficient on the difference in time zones is not statistically significant in the

---

[14] India and Indonesia received a swap line from the Bank of Japan, but not from the Fed. All the other countries receiving US dollar swap lines did so from the Fed.

Table 7.3 *Probit model for probability of receiving US dollar swap line,*
taking into account time zone difference

	From any country	From the Federal Reserve
Constant, β_1	−0.61	−0.40
	(0.50)	(0.51)
US dollar shortage, β_2	0.026*	0.027*
	(0.011)	(0.011)
Dummy for large int. financial	4.99**	5.74**
centre, β_3	(1.89)	(2.09)
Time zone difference to New	−0.02	−0.10
York, β_4	(0.07)	(0.08)
McFadden R^2	0.31	0.39
Number of observations	39	39

Note: ** and * denote significance at the 1 per cent and 5 per cent level,
respectively; standard errors are given in parentheses.

regression. Next, the analogous regression for the probability of a
country receiving a US dollar swap line from the Fed is run. The vector of explanatory variables in the probit regression of equation (7.5)
is now defined as $x\$_i = (1, s\$_i, d_i^{lfc}, tz_i)$, and the vector of coefficients is
$\beta = (\beta_1, \beta_2, \beta_3, \beta_4)$. A similar result holds in this case (see Table 7.3, right-
hand column). This regression is also consistent with the view that
the Federal Reserve was more likely to extend swap lines to countries
which had large US dollar shortages or were large international financial centres.[15,16]

Next, we examine the actual amounts drawn on swap lines provided by the Federal Reserve at the end of 2008. The hypothesis is
that the amounts drawn at end-2008, $draw\$_i$ (in US dollar billions),
depend significantly on the country's US dollar shortage, $s\$_i$ (in US

[15] In studying the provision of swap lines by the Federal Reserve to emerging
economies, Aizenman and Pasricha (2009) find that the exposure of US
banks to emerging economies is significant in explaining the probability of an
emerging economy receiving a Fed swap line.

[16] Yehoue (2009) finds that 'countries with bigger economies and depreciating
currencies are more likely to seek cross-country FX swap facilities'. These
conclusions are not inconsistent with our analysis, since bigger economies are,
other things being equal, more likely to have larger currency-specific liquidity
shortages than smaller ones; and depreciating currencies are one of the
indicators of market stress that we identified in Section 2.

Table 7.4 *Drawings on US dollar swap lines from the Federal Reserve at end-2008*

	Equation (7.6)	Equation (7.7)	Equation (7.8)
Constant, β_1	−2.53	−16.7	−2.20
	(6.96)	(15.8)	(8.63)
US dollar shortage, β_2	0.36+	0.39*	0.42*
	(0.17)	(0.17)	(0.18)
Dummy for large international financial centre, β_3	69.6*	59.0	—
	(31.5)	(34.9)	
Time zone difference to New York, β_4	—	2.85	—
		(3.12)	
Dummy for large int. financial centre × time zone difference, β_5	—	—	7.73+
			(3.55)
Adjusted R^2	0.56	0.53	0.55
Number of observations	14	14	14

Note: **, * and + denote significance at the 1 per cent, 5 per cent and 10 per cent levels, respectively; White heteroscedasticity-consistent standard errors are given in parentheses.

dollar billions), for the sample of countries which received a swap line from the Federal Reserve. Data on drawings on Fed swap lines at the end of 2008 are shown in Table 8.1.

The following regression is estimated by OLS (with White heteroscedasticity-consistent standard errors),

$$\text{draw}^\$_i = \beta_1 + \beta_2{}^*s^\$_i + \beta_3{}^*d_i^{lfc} + e_i \tag{7.6}$$

as well as the regression also including a variable for the difference in time zones, tz_i,

$$\text{draw}^\$_i = \beta_1 + \beta_2{}^*s^\$_i + \beta_3{}^*d_i^{lfc} + \beta_4{}^*tz_i + e_i \tag{7.7}$$

and a specification including the dummy variable for large international financial centres interacted with the difference in time zones,

$$\text{draw}^\$_i = \beta_1 + \beta_2{}^*s^\$_i + \beta_5{}^*d_i^{lfc}{}^*tz_i + e_i \tag{7.8}$$

Estimation results are shown in Table 7.4.

The estimated coefficient of the US dollar shortage is significant at the 5 per cent level in two of the specifications, and at the 10 per cent level in the remaining one. The dummy variable for large international financial centres is significant at the 5 per cent level in the first specification, and the dummy variable for large international financial centres multiplied by the variable for the difference in time zones is significant at the 10 per cent level in the third specification. Goodness of fit of these regressions, as measured by the adjusted R^2, is around 0.55. These results suggest that actual US dollar funding obtained by drawing on the Fed's swap lines at the end of 2008 was larger for countries with higher US dollar shortages on the proxy measure, and for economies which are large international financial centres.

8 | *Did the swap providers achieve their objectives?*

This chapter discusses the extent to which the providers of swap lines achieved their objectives, and compares their experiences.

1. Experiences of swap providers

a. The United States

The Fed's objectives in setting up swap lines were to make dollar funding available to banks outside the United States, and thereby to ease funding pressures inside the United States (see Chapter 6). The Fed has published copious information about the use of the swap network, including data showing the amounts drawn by individual foreign central banks day by day. The total amount drawn rose during 2008 as the crisis intensified, especially after Lehmans' failure, and, at the end of the year, total drawings were \$553.7 billion[1] (see Table 8.1). This was more than half of the total of BIS reporting banks' local claims on non-banks denominated in US dollars (see Table 3.2 above), which is a striking measure of the severity of the crisis.

The establishment of swap lines with the Fed might have been expected to ease pressures in foreign exchange swap markets involving the dollar. Some evidence is shown in Table 8.2.

The establishment of swap lines in December 2007 had no perceptible effect on covered interest differentials. As regards the progressive extension of swap lines in the second half of September 2008 – immediately after the failure of Lehmans on 15 September – the evidence suggests that the swap lines did not have a clear-cut constructive effect, and that any effect they may have had was overwhelmed by other pressures. Broadly speaking, the Fed repeatedly increased the

---

[1] The peak was \$586.1 billion, not including interest, on 4 December.

Table 8.1 *Drawings of US dollars on Fed swap lines (US dollar millions, end-quarters)*

End of	2007Q4	2008Q1	2008Q2	2008Q3	2008Q4	2009Q1	2009Q2	2009Q3	2009Q4
Canada	0	0	0	0	0	0	0	0	0
ECB	20,000	15,000	50,000	174,742	291,352	165,717	59,899	43,662	6,506
Switzerland	4,000	6,000	12,000	28,900	25,175	7,318	369	0	0
Japan	0	0	0	29,622	122,716	61,025	17,923	1,530	545
UK	0	0	0	39,999	33,080	14,963	2,503	13	0
Denmark	0	0	0	5,000	15,000	5,270	3,930	580	0
Australia	0	0	0	10,000	22,830	9,575	240	0	0
Sweden	0	0	0	0	25,000	23,000	11,500	2,700	0
Norway	0	0	0	0	8,225	7,050	5,000	1,000	0
New Zealand	0	0	0	0	0	0	0	0	0
Korea	0	0	0	0	10,350	16,000	10,000	4,050	0
Brazil	0	0	0	0	0	0	0	0	0
Mexico	0	0	0	0	0	0	3,221	3,221	3,221
Singapore	0	0	0	0	0	0	0	0	0
TOTAL	24,000	21,000	62,000	288,263	553,728	309,918	114,585	56,576	10,272

Source: Federal Reserve Bank of New York, 'Treasury and Federal Reserve Foreign Exchange Operations', various releases.

size of its swap lines, reacting very quickly as the crisis intensified. For example, on 18 September 2008, in the week Lehman Brothers failed, it increased the total amount available on swap lines from $67 billion to $247 billion. The following week it added another $43 billion (in two stages on 24 and 26 September), taking the total to $290 billion. Then on 29 September, the total was more than doubled to $620 billion. On 13 and 14 October, the Fed removed the quantity limits from the swap lines with the ECB and the central banks of the UK, Switzerland and Japan. And this removal of limits did finally appear to lead to a substantial narrowing in the covered interest differentials of some major currencies against the dollar (see Table 8.2).[2] As to other indicators of market stress, the appreciation of the dollar began to reverse from early March 2009.

Much of the sudden demand for dollar funding in international markets immediately after Lehmans' failure resulted from the drawing of dollar funds by commercial banks in the USA from their related foreign offices. Figure 8.1 shows a close correspondence in the weekly data between US commercial banks' net debt to related foreign offices and the total amount outstanding on Fed swaps to foreign central banks, which shows that the funds lent by the Fed through swap lines found their way back to the United States through the foreign offices of banks located in the United States.[3] The main counterpart to the increase in US commercial banks' net debt to related foreign offices was a massive increase in cash assets.[4] In fact, most of the drawing-in of funds was done by foreign-related institutions in the USA, rather than domestically chartered banks. Foreign-related institutions' ratio of cash assets to total assets increased from 4.2 per cent on 3 September 2008 to 19.1 per cent on 31 December. This was a much bigger increase than for domestically chartered banks, or for foreign banks in other jurisdictions such as Switzerland. The

---

[2] This conclusion is the same as that reached by Baba and Packer (2009).

[3] The loans made by the Fed represented an outflow in the US balance of payments, and there had to be a corresponding inflow, since the balance of payments must balance. However, the fact that the corresponding inflow was through the net debt of commercial banks located in the United States to their related foreign offices indicates that the Fed swaps were effective in relieving stress in US domestic financial markets.

[4] For further discussion of banking and other US cross-border financial flows during the crisis, see Bertaut and Pounder (2009).

Table 8.2 *Announcements of swap lines and covered interest differentials against US dollar[a]*

Average differential during:	EUR	GBP	JPY	CHF
Using deposit rates:				
5 days after 1/1/2007 (i.e. pre-crisis)	3	1	0	1
5 days before 12/12/2007[b]	17	19	15	7
5 days after 12/12/2007[b]	32	20	23	7
15/9/2008 – 17/9/2008 (i.e. 3 days before 18/9/2008[b])	63	4	58	81
19/9/2008 – 26/9/2008[b]	26	3	3	22
30/9/2008 – 10/10/2008 (i.e. 9 days before 13/10/2008[b])	54	57	63	-7
5 days after 13/10/2008[b]	4	10	6	-5
5 days before 1/10/2009	0	-7	-3	4
Using Libor rates:				
5 days after 1/1/2007 (i.e. pre-crisis)	-1	0	-1	0
5 days before 12/12/2007[b]	12	16	5	10
5 days after 12/12/2007[b]	30	22	22	14
15/9/2008 – 17/9/2008 (i.e. 3 days before 18/9/2008[b])	87	29	80	109
19/9/2008 – 26/9/2008[b]	127	102	102	126
30/9/2008 – 10/10/2008 (i.e. 9 days before 13/10/2008[b])	159	170	131	101
5 days after 13/10/2008[b]	32	35	6	-24
5 days before 1/10/2009	38	19	31	30

Notes: [a] Three-month maturity, in basis points. [b] Date when Fed swap facilities were introduced or extended.
Sources: Bloomberg, author's calculations.

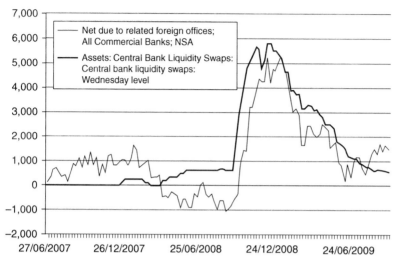

Figure 8.1 US commercial banks' net debt to related foreign offices and Fed swaps outstanding (in US dollar billions).
Source: Federal Reserve tables H4.1 and H8.

reasons for the inflow of funds to the United States were discussed in Chapter 2.

The availability of the swap lines evidently helped to stabilise financial markets and the amount outstanding fell quite quickly during 2009. By the end of 2009, the share of foreign exchange swaps in total assets of the Federal Reserve had fallen back to below 0.5 per cent, from over 25 per cent in late 2008. The Fed's objectives were to ease dollar funding pressures in foreign countries and thereby relieve financial stress in the United States. On the evidence, the swap lines, taken together with the other measures that were implemented, can be said to have achieved these objectives.

b. The euro area

The European Central Bank was economical in explaining its provision of euro liquidity to other countries. It said merely that: 'In October and November 2008 the ECB signed agreements to provide euro liquidity to a number of EU central banks outside the euro area. The ECB's intention in establishing these agreements was to support various measures taken by these central banks, all of which were aimed at improving euro liquidity in their respective domestic financial markets.'[5]

The ECB has published little information about the use of the swap lines. The external use of the euro takes place largely in time zones close to the euro area, and many of the commercial banks involved have affiliates in the euro area and thus have access to euro-denominated liquidity provided by the ECB, so that the need for euro swap facilities was not as great as in the case of the dollar. Nevertheless, there evidently was a need. It may be inferred from the ECB's statement that its objectives in providing swap lines to neighbouring central banks were to help other European Union countries avoid the economic disruption that an unrelieved euro liquidity shortage might have caused. The implied restriction of ECB swap facilities to EU member countries means that even Norway was not considered eligible for a swap line, and is revealing about the ESCB's attitude to the internationalisation of the euro.[6] When the euro was established, the ESCB said that it would 'take a neutral stance towards an international role of the euro. It will neither hinder nor deliberately encourage the development of this role, but will rather leave this to market forces'.[7] Its neutral stance seems to have excluded the provision of swap lines beyond the borders of the EU in 2008–09. In this respect, the ESCB's attitude to the international use of its currency is in sharp contrast to that of the Fed, and its objectives in providing swap lines were narrower in scope. Moreover, even within the EU, the ECB was not as prompt in providing assistance to other countries as the Fed; for example, Denmark received a dollar swap line from the Fed on 24 September 2008, and it was increased in size on 29 September. It did not receive a swap line from the ECB until 27 October (see Chapter 9). Information about the scale of the ECB's operations is provided in Table 8.3.

The assessment of the ECB's success in meeting its objectives is largely the same as the assessment of the success of the recipients of the ECB's swap lines in meeting their objectives, and that assessment is made in Chapter 9.

---

[5] See European Central Bank (2009a), p. 103.
[6] The ESCB is the European System of Central Banks. It consists of the European Central Bank and the national central banks of the member countries of the European Union.
[7] See Duisenberg (1998).

Table 8.3 *Selected items from Eurosystem balance sheet (euro billions)*

Last Friday of	External foreign currency assets	Monthly changes	Domestic foreign currency assets	Monthly changes	External euro liabilities	Monthly changes
Nov-07	142.2		25.2		28.7	
Dec-07	135.2	−7.0	41.9	16.7	45.1	16.3
Jan-08	140.0	4.9	36.4	−5.6	51.0	5.9
Feb-08	137.8	−2.2	24.7	−11.6	34.4	-16.6
Mar-08	141.1	3.3	34.8	10.1	47.9	13.5
Apr-08	138.7	−2.5	40.1	5.3	58.1	10.2
May-08	136.3	−2.4	54.9	14.8	73.4	15.3
Jun-08	135.3	−1.0	56.3	1.3	77.5	4.1
Jul-08	135.5	0.3	54.9	-1.4	78.0	0.5
Aug-08	135.4	−0.2	55.1	0.2	80.1	2.1
Sep-08	134.4	−1.0	103.1	48.0	127.5	47.4
Oct-08	155.1	20.8	205.8	102.7	303.4	175.9
Nov-08	159.7	4.6	208.2	2.4	278.4	−25.0
Dec-08	149.6	−10.0	229.5	21.3	286.0	7.6
Jan-09	159.2	9.5	171.2	−58.3	232.2	−53.8
Feb-09	155.7	−3.5	134.6	−36.6	202.6	−29.6
Mar-09	152.4	−3.3	140.8	6.2	207.2	4.6
Apr-09	157.9	5.6	125.3	−15.5	184.2	−23.0
May-09	158.0	0.1	103.0	−22.3	156.4	−27.7
Jun-09	159.7	1.7	75.1	−27.9	117.9	−38.6
Jul-09	159.6	−0.1	61.2	−13.9	98.3	−19.6
Aug-09	197.2	37.6	59.3	−1.9	93.4	−4.9
Sep-09	196.3	−0.9	58.1	−1.2	85.7	−7.7

Note: The Eurosystem consists of the European Central Bank and the national central banks of the euro-area countries.
Source: ECB.

External euro liabilities include the euros credited to the Fed and the Swiss National Bank as collateral for the dollars and Swiss francs borrowed on the swap facilities received by the ECB, as well as euros lent to central banks to which the ECB provided swap facilities. Domestic foreign currency assets include dollars and Swiss francs lent to euro-area commercial banks. External foreign currency assets include the foreign currency that the ECB received as collateral from the central banks to which it provided swap lines, for example Denmark and Sweden. Such assets increased by roughly EUR 21 billion between the last Fridays of September and October 2008, but the amount is normally quite volatile from week to week and it is not possible to be confident that this figure represents accurately the amount provided by the ECB through swap facilities.

c. Switzerland

The Swiss National Bank provided Swiss francs to foreign central banks by means of foreign exchange swaps against euros, beginning in October 2008. The facilities provided by the SNB included swap lines with the ECB and with the National Banks of Hungary (MNB) and Poland (NBP). The SNB also provided swaps through auctions to its normal commercial repo counterparties. Although the counterparties of these swaps were domestic commercial institutions rather than foreign central banks, it is nevertheless likely that they helped to relieve the shortage of Swiss francs in international markets. The ECB, the MNB and the NBP distributed Swiss francs drawn on their swap lines to commercial banks through auctions which coincided with those organised by the SNB. The SNB's swap programme ended in January 2010.[8] In addition, as noted in Chapter 6, the SNB also provided Swiss francs directly to commercial banks located outside Switzerland through its regular repo operations, to which such banks had access.

The amounts provided through swap facilities are reported in Table 8.4, which reports not only the total amount outstanding (from the SNB's balance sheet reports) but also calculations of the amounts outstanding from auctions conducted by the SNB, the ECB, the MNB and the NBP (from the announcements of the auction results). There is a residue, which in principle reflects amounts drawn by the ECB, the MNB and the NBP on their swap lines but not distributed, less any Swiss francs distributed by those central banks which were not obtained from their swap lines.

The amounts provided to commercial banks outside Switzerland through repo operations have not been published in digital form, but

[8] See the SNB's press release of 18 January 2010, www.snb.ch/en/mmr/reference/pre_20100118/source/pre_20100118.en.pdf.

Table 8.4 *Amounts of Swiss francs provided by Swiss National Bank through swaps (in billions)*

End of	Total		Auctioned by SNB		Auctioned by ECB		Auctioned by MNB		Auctioned by NBP		Residue	
	CHF	EUR	CHF	EUR	CHF	EUR	CHF	EUR	CHF	EUR	CHF	EUR
Oct-08	38.8	26.3	18.6	12.6	18.8	12.8	0.0	0.0	0.0	0.0	1.3	0.9
Nov-08	46.3	30.1	23.2	15.0	21.8	14.2	0.0	0.0	0.2	0.1	1.2	0.8
Dec-08	50.4	33.8	22.4	15.0	26.0	17.4	0.0	0.0	0.5	0.3	1.5	1.0
Jan-09	51.0	34.3	18.1	12.2	30.7	20.7	0.0	0.0	0.6	0.4	1.5	1.0
Feb-09	61.8	41.7	22.6	15.3	36.2	24.5	0.8	0.5	0.3	0.2	1.9	1.3
Mar-09	62.2	41.2	23.0	15.3	36.5	24.1	0.8	0.5	0.8	0.5	1.2	0.8
Apr-09	53.7	35.6	15.2	10.1	35.8	23.7	0.9	0.6	0.3	0.2	1.6	1.0
May-09	60.9	40.3	22.6	15.0	36.1	23.9	0.6	0.4	0.2	0.1	1.4	0.9
Jun-09	48.5	31.8	15.0	9.9	30.5	20.0	0.5	0.4	0.2	0.1	2.2	1.5
Jul-09	32.0	21.0	11.5	7.5	18.9	12.4	0.1	0.1	0.2	0.1	1.4	0.9
Aug-09	29.4	19.4	12.5	8.2	15.5	10.2	0.0	0.0	0.2	0.1	1.2	0.8
Sep-09	12.3	8.1	1.8	1.2	9.9	6.5	0.0	0.0	0.1	0.0	0.6	0.4

Note: The euro amounts are the equivalent of the Swiss franc amounts, converted at the contemporaneous spot exchange rate (Source: Bloomberg).

Sources: Swiss National Bank, ECB, Magyar Nemzeti Bank (MNB), Narodowy Bank Polski (NBP), author's calculations.

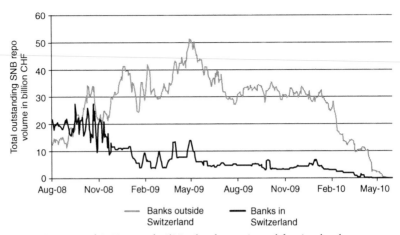

Figure 8.2 Use of SNB repo facilities by domestic and foreign banks.

Figure 8.2, reproduced with kind permission from Auer and Kraenzlin (2011, figure 3) shows that the total provided in this way exceeded CHF 50 billion in May 2009. Thus the total provision of Swiss francs to relieve liquidity shortages outside Switzerland, including funds provided by both swaps and repos, must have easily exceeded CHF 100 billion, or around $90 billion. This was more than half of BIS reporting banks' Swiss franc-denominated local foreign currency assets (see Table 3.2) or about 3 per cent of the total assets of the commercial banks located in Switzerland.

Had the SNB not made Swiss franc liquidity available to commercial banks outside Switzerland, it is likely that many of the short-term deposits that commercial banks in Switzerland had placed with them could not have been repaid on time, and that the banking crisis in Switzerland, and in other parts of Europe, would have been considerably worse than it actually was. Nevertheless, market indicators continued to show signs of stress notwithstanding the SNB's actions. For example, cross-currency basis swap spreads involving the złoty remained very wide well into the summer of 2009, after the SNB's liquidity provision had peaked (see Figure 4.5). And, as Figure 8.3 shows, the Swiss franc appreciated on balance in the last quarter of 2008, followed by a period when it appeared to be on a plateau until the monetary policy change announced on 12 March 2009, when the

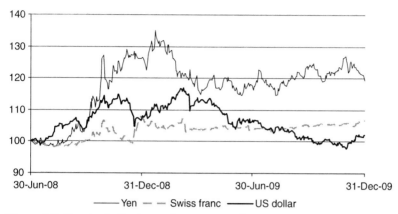

Figure 8.3 Nominal effective exchange rate indices (30 June 2008 = 100).
Source: Bank of England.

central bank declared its intention to buy foreign currencies. It seems reasonable to suppose that the swap lines contributed to containing the appreciation of the Swiss franc in early 2009, but the appreciation was reversed (and then only partly) only when the SNB announced official sales of Swiss francs.

d. Asia and Latin America

The motivations for the establishment of the Asian/Latin American network seem to have been diverse, and largely of a longer-term nature. It is much too soon to attempt any assessment of these longer-term objectives. However, the provision or enlargement of swap lines by China and Japan to Indonesia and Korea was clearly intended also to address immediate market problems. Korea also received a swap line from the Federal Reserve. The success of these operations in alleviating tensions in Korean financial markets is assessed in Chapter 9.

The Bank of Japan's provision of yen through swap lines seems to have been on a much smaller scale than the Fed's provision of dollars, if indeed it provided any yen at all. Table 8.5 compares the item 'foreign currency assets' in the Bank of Japan accounts with the Bank of Japan's drawings of dollars on its account with the Fed

Table 8.5 *Bank of Japan foreign currency assets and drawings on the swap line with the Fed*

	1	2	3	4	5	6	7	8
	Foreign currency assets			Drawings on Fed swap			Other deposits	
	Amount outstanding (JPY 100mn)	Amount outstanding (USD bn)	Change in quarter (USD bn)	Amount outstanding (USD bn)	Change in quarter (USD bn)	Residual change in foreign currency assets (=3–5) (USD bn)	Amount outstanding (JPY 100mn)	Amount outstanding (USD bn)
Jun-08	54,138	51.0		0.0			234	0.2
Sep-08	85,466	80.5	29.6	29.6	29.6	0.0	31,503	29.7
Dec-08	172,870	190.7	110.2	122.7	93.1	17.1	118,224	130.4
Mar-09	108,647	109.0	–81.7	61.0	–61.7	–20.0	57,739	57.9
Jun-09	72,068	74.8	–34.2	17.9	–43.1	8.9	17,645	18.3
Sep-09	50,061	55.8	–19.0	1.5	–16.4	–2.6	1,630	1.8

Sources: Bank of Japan, Federal Reserve Bank of New York, Bloomberg (exchange rates), author's calculations.

(published by the Federal Reserve).[9] It shows an increase in foreign currency assets in the fourth quarter of 2008 amounting to some $17 billion in excess of what is explained by the drawing on the Fed swap line. This 'excess increase' was reversed in the first quarter of 2009, but there was a further 'excess increase' of some $9 billion in the second quarter of 2009 (see column 6). It is tempting to think that the 'excess increase' in the fourth quarter of 2008 partly or wholly reflects drawings on swap lines provided by the Bank of Japan; but in fact the Bank of Korea did not draw on the $20 billion swap line set up on 12 December 2008[10] (the swap line with Indonesia was not set up until April 2009). Any drawings that were made in the second quarter of 2009 could in principle have been made by any country which had a swap line open with the Bank of Japan at the end of June.

Table 8.5 also shows 'other deposits' at the Bank of Japan, which include the yen deposits held by the Fed as collateral for the swap line. 'Other deposits' were very small in June 2008, before the swap line was opened, and they rise and fall closely with the total of swap drawings as reported by the Fed. They were down to $1.8 billion by the end of September 2009, when the amount outstanding on the swap was down to $1.5 billion.

As regards the market stress indicators, the very sharp appreciation of the yen after Lehman Brothers failed (see Figure 4.7) demonstrated the severity of the stresses in yen financial markets. The appreciation of the yen was partly reversed in the spring of 2009 as market stresses eased, but nevertheless by the middle of 2009 the yen had appreciated on balance by very large amounts, particularly against other Asian currencies.

It is not possible to make any assessment yet of the provision of swap lines by China, partly because no information is readily available about their use, and partly because their objectives are clearly mainly longer-term in nature.

---

[9] Drawings by the Bank of Japan would add to 'foreign currency assets' because they would lead either to a rise in the Bank of Japan's balance at the Fed, or to a rise in the Bank of Japan's dollar claims on Japanese banks. Drawings by a foreign central bank on a swap line provided by the Bank of Japan would lead to a rise in the balance on the Bank of Japan's account at the foreign central bank, denominated in that central bank's currency.

[10] Information provided to the author by the Bank of Korea.

2. Comparison of the experiences of swap providers

The central banks which provided their own currencies through swap facilities have made it clear that their main objective was to reduce stresses in financial markets. The Fed largely achieved its objectives (see Section 1a); and the ECB's objective appears to have been to relieve liquidity shortages in EU countries not in the euro area (see Section 1b). The Swiss National Bank was clearly concerned about the strength of market demand for Swiss francs and announced in March 2009 that it would sell Swiss francs for foreign currencies so as to contain the pressure for currency appreciation. More generally, the President of the SNB discussed at length the SNB's changing attitude to the internationalisation of the Swiss franc.[11]

After Lehman Brothers failed, the effective exchange rate index of the yen, as calculated by the BIS, appreciated much more than those of the dollar and the Swiss franc (see Figure 8.3). The relatively modest appreciation of the dollar is probably partly explained by the Fed's willingness to provide very large amounts of dollar liquidity through swaps quickly and flexibly as market tensions mounted. As noted above, the Fed provided $586 billion in dollar liquidity at the peak, which represented more than half of BIS reporting banks' local US dollar assets vis-à-vis non-banks of $1,015.1 billion. The amount provided by the Swiss National Bank was comparable. As noted above, it amounted in total to at least $90 billion at the peak, including amounts provided through swap facilities to commercial counterparties, and through repo transactions with foreign banks, compared with local Swiss franc assets of $166.0 billion.

The fact that the yen appreciated by so much more than the dollar and the Swiss franc may therefore be partly explained by differences in the provision of swap facilities. Another possible explanation is the decision by the Swiss National Bank to sell Swiss francs for foreign currencies; however, that can be only a partial explanation, because the decision was made only in March 2009, by which time the relatively powerful appreciation of the yen was already well established. The Bank of Japan commented that the 'rapid yen appreciation was mainly caused by unwinding of the yen-carry positions, reflecting

---

[11] See Roth (2009).

investors' diminished risk-taking capacity against the background of the stock price declines and increased volatility, as well as tightening of interest rate differentials between Japan and overseas'.[12] It is likely that only a small fraction of the yen carry trades were captured in the BIS international banking statistics quoted in Chapter 3.

[12] See Bank of Japan (2009).

9 | *How did the swap lines affect the recipients?*

This chapter reviews the effects of the swap lines on the countries which drew on them to obtain foreign currency, and considers how the swap lines helped those countries meet their objectives. In total, we review the experiences of twelve countries (or territories), which are summarised in the table below, classified into three groups. Table 9.1 sets out salient facts country by country.

1. Large international financial centres: the euro area, Switzerland, the United Kingdom, Japan and Australia

There were large outflows of funds from the United Kingdom and Switzerland in the second half of 2008, as the first column of Table 9.1 shows. However, the scale of the withdrawals of funds from banks, in relation to the initial level of claims, differed widely. In Switzerland, the reduction in claims on banks began at the beginning of 2008, and over the year as a whole it amounted to $362 billion (26.7 per cent), perhaps partly because of the difficulties of UBS, one of the two very large Swiss banks. In the UK, the reduction over the last three quarters of 2008 was $460 billion (11.1 per cent), again probably aggravated by the problems of one particular bank, namely Royal Bank of Scotland.

In all the five large international financial centres that received and drew on swap lines from the United States, namely Australia, the euro area, Japan, Switzerland and the United Kingdom, covered interest differentials against the dollar widened and became more volatile as commercial banks used domestic currency financing to replace dollar financing which had been withdrawn (Figure 4.1). And cross-currency basis swap spreads turned negative as banks went into the market seeking to pay floating-rate dollar interest and receive floating-rate interest in their domestic currency (Figure

Table 9.1 *Summary statistics: countries which received swap lines (US dollar billions, unless otherwise specified)*

	Change in BIS reporting banks' claims on country in the second half of 2008[a]	Change in commercial banks' net external foreign currency liabilities in the second half of 2008[b]	Peak foreign currency liquidity support provided to domestic banks	Drawings on swap lines (highest reported level)	Foreign exchange reserves at end Aug-08
Large international financial centres					
Australia	+61.6	−94.6	26.7	26.7	28.0
Euro area	N/A	−399.6	293.4 (USD)[c] 35 (CHF)[c]	313.8 (USD) 35 (CHF)	212.4
Japan	+13.7	+5.1	127.6	127.6	971.6
Switzerland	−182.9	+45.2	31.1	31.1	44.5
United Kingdom	−504.1	+51.1	85.5[d]	94.5	46.2[e]
Smaller international financial centres					
Denmark	−12.3	−19.7	20.4	19.8	30.6
Sweden	+42.8	−50.5	30.8	25.0	27.6
Norway	+13.2	−10.0	9.1	9.0	41.7
Countries which are not international financial centres					
Korea	−0.1	−37.8	48.0[f]	16.4	242.7
Mexico	+5.5	−3.8	3.2	3.2	96.1
Hungary	−3.9[g]	−4.5[h]	1.8	0 (see text)	25.2
Poland	+0.2[i]	+0.4[j]	0.7	0 (see text)	78.6

Notes: [a] Source: BIS international banking statistics table 2A, plus author's calculations, unless otherwise stated. [b] Source: BIS international banking statistics table 2C, plus author's calculations, unless otherwise stated. [c] The dollar and Swiss franc amounts shown are the peak amounts made available through auctions conducted by the ECB. The peak dollar and Swiss franc amounts were recorded at different times. See Chapter 8 for further discussion. [d] Maximum quantity of dollars provided through auctions. See text for further discussion. [e] HM Treasury plus Bank of England. [f] As at the end of December 2008. More support was provided later. [g] Increase in MFIs' gross short-term external liabilities in all currencies in 2009 Q2 and Q3. Source: Magyar Nemzeti Bank plus author's calculations. [h] Increase in MFIs' net short-term external liabilities in all currencies in 2009Q2 and Q3. *Source:* Magyar Nemzeti Bank plus author's calculations. [i] Increase in MFIs' gross external liabilities in all currencies in 2009Q2 and Q3. Source: Narodowy Bank Polski. [j] Increase in MFIs' net external liabilities in all currencies in 2009Q2 and Q3. Source: Narodowy Bank Polski.

4.4).[1] With the exception of the yen, all five currencies depreciated against the dollar immediately after Lehmans' collapse (Figure 4.7). All five central banks drew large amounts of dollars from their swap lines.

For the euro area, the United Kingdom, Japan and Switzerland, the evidence presented in Table 8.2 indicates that the dislocations in foreign exchange swap markets of their currencies against the US dollar were alleviated by the US dollar swap lines received by the ECB, the Bank of England, the Bank of Japan and the SNB after the limits on drawings were removed in October 2008 (see also Figure 4.1). Table 8.2 also shows that at the end of September 2009, foreign exchange swap spreads of the euro, yen, Swiss franc and sterling against the US dollar at the three-month maturity, based on deposit rates, had largely normalised at values of up to seven basis points. Note, however, that the foreign exchange swap spreads of the four currencies against the US dollar at the three-month maturity based on LIBOR rates remained more elevated at around 20–40 basis points (see Table 8.2). This might, however, reflect remaining dislocations in the short-term money markets and problems of defining LIBOR rates. At the end of September 2009, cross-currency basis swap spreads of these four currencies against the US dollar at the longer maturity of one year remained wider than before the crisis, at around –20 to –40 basis points, suggesting continuing problems at longer maturities (see Figure 4.4).

Moreover, Figure 9.1 shows that the amounts of US dollars allotted in auctions by the ECB, Bank of England and Swiss National Bank, all or most of which presumably originally came from the Fed swap lines, fell back strongly in mid-2009 from their peaks reached in late 2008, suggesting that the need for drawing on the Fed swap lines had decreased significantly in the case of the ECB, and largely disappeared in the case of the Bank of England and Swiss National Bank.

The European Central Bank provided US dollars to commercial banks by means of loans against collateral eligible at the ECB. The total amount provided by auctions of dollar liquidity peaked at $293 billion in early December 2008, at which time the ECB had drawn $313 billion from the Fed on the swap line. It is not clear what

---

[1] Curiously, the USD/AUD basis swap spread became positive towards the end of 2008.

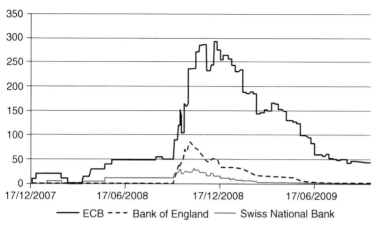

Figure 9.1 US dollar auction allotments (in US dollar billions, cumulative).
Note: Amounts outstanding in US dollar repo operations and US dollar FX swap operations.

happened to the residual $20 billion; possibly it was lent bilaterally by national central banks in the euro area to commercial banks in distress. The ECB's dollar provision to commercial banks fell steadily during the first half of 2009, as did the amount outstanding on the swap line (see Table 9.2). This suggests that market conditions had begun to stabilise and that banks' need for official support had decreased. The amount outstanding on the ECB's swap line from the Fed was still substantial ($43.7 billion) at the end of September 2009, suggesting that there was still some residual need for US dollar liquidity provided by the ECB; it had fallen to $6.5 billion at the end of the year. The ECB was thus relatively slow to repay its swap drawings, and this foreshadowed the banking problems that later emerged in the euro area.

The ECB also provided Swiss francs to commercial banks through swaps, drawing on its swap line with the Swiss National Bank. Details are given in Chapter 8 and in Table 9.2. The amount of foreign currency liquidity that the ECB provided to commercial banks was well in excess of the total foreign exchange reserves of the Eurosystem; however, the Eurosystem also had $292.3 billion of gold reserves. Without the swap lines, the Eurosystem could not have provided as much foreign currency liquidity to its banks as it did, unless it had sold or pledged some of its gold.

Table 9.2 *Foreign currency auction allotments and foreign exchange reserves in the euro area (US dollar billions, or equivalent)*

End of	US dollars provided at auctions reported by the ECB	Swiss francs provided at auctions reported by the ECB	Eurosystem foreign exchange reserves
Sep-08	150.7	0	210.3
Oct-08	271.2	17.4	210.2
Nov-08	244.0	19.2	204.2
Dec-08	265.7	25.8	202.0
Jan-09	187.3	27.8	191.1
Feb-09	144.5	32.5	186.4
Mar-09	165.7	33.1	189.2
Apr-09	130.1	33.0	187.9
May-09	99.7	35.4	191.9
Jun-09	59.9	29.9	192.5
Jul-09	48.3	18.6	197.9
Aug-09	46.1	15.4	197.8
Sep-09	43.7	10.1	195.0

Sources: ECB, BIS calculations, IMF.

Lending of dollars to commercial banks by the Swiss National Bank peaked at $31.1 billion in late October 2008, after the Fed had removed the limit on swap line drawings. This peak amount was nearly three-quarters of Switzerland's total foreign exchange reserves that month (see Table 9.3). The swap line allowed the SNB to provide dollar liquidity without drawing down the foreign exchange reserves. The amounts of US dollars allotted in auctions by the SNB fell to $0.02 billion at the end of July 2009, implying that foreign exchange market conditions had largely stabilised.

The Bank of England's provision of dollar funding to UK banks through auctions peaked at $85.5 billion on 17–19 October 2008 (see Table 9.4). However swap drawings peaked at $95 billion on 15 October, when the amount allotted by auctions was $48.5 billion. Possibly the remaining $46.5 billion drawn on the swap line on 15 October was lent by the Bank of England to the Royal Bank of Scotland or Halifax Bank of Scotland on the bilateral facilities whose

Table 9.3 *US dollar auction allotments and for-eign exchange reserves in Switzerland (US dollar billions)*

End of	US dollar auction allotment by the SNB	Foreign exchange reserves of Switzerland
Sep-08	28.9	44.2
Oct-08	28.5	43.3
Nov-08	20.9	43.1
Dec-08	10.9	44.2
Jan-09	6.1	43.5
Feb-09	2.0	43.3
Mar-09	1.0	49.1
Apr-09	1.0	49.3
May-09	1.0	51.7
Jun-09	0.02	75.3
Jul-09	0.02	75.0
Aug-09	0.01	75.1
Sep-09	0	78.9

Sources: SNB, IMF, BIS calculations.

existence was disclosed on 24 November 2009.[2] The amount out-standing on the swap line fell to $33.1 billion at the end of December 2008 and to $0.01 billion at the end of July 2009, implying that mar-ket conditions had stabilised to the point at which the swap line was no longer needed.

Although the outflows of funds from Japan[3] were very modest in 2008Q3, and were more than offset in 2008Q4 by inflows, commer-cial banks in Japan nevertheless experienced liquidity shortages in dol-lars. The Bank of Japan drew on its swap line with the Fed to finance lending of dollars to commercial banks. The Bank of Japan's foreign currency assets peaked at $191 billion at the end of December 2008 (see Table 8.5). However, in June–August 2008, before the credit crisis intensified, those assets had been around $50 billion, so the increase was about $140 billion. Analysis of the auction results published

[2] See Bank of England (2009).
[3] In currencies other than the Japanese yen.

Table 9.4 *US dollar auction allotments and foreign exchange reserves in the United Kingdom
(US dollar billions)*

End of	US dollar auction allotment by the BoE	Foreign exchange reserves[a]
Sep-08	40.0	43.2
Oct-08	72.4	44.1
Nov-08	54.3	45.4
Dec-08	33.1	45.2
Jan-09	23.5	40.3
Feb-09	16.0	40.3
Mar-09	15.0	43.7
Apr-09	13.5	43.0
May-09	2.5	47.0
Jun-09	2.5	43.2
Jul-09	0.01	44.3
Aug-09	0.01	43.7
Sep-09	0.01	43.1

Note: [a] In the UK, both the Treasury and the Bank of
England hold foreign exchange reserves. The figures
quoted show the sum of the two holdings.
Sources: Bank of England, BIS calculations, IMF.

by the Bank of Japan shows that the amount of dollars it supplied
through auctions peaked at \$127.6 billion in December 2008. As
Table 8.5 shows, the quarterly profiles of the Bank of Japan's foreign
currency assets and its drawings on the Fed swap matched closely,
except that the Bank of Japan acquired some net foreign currency
assets in 2008Q4 that were not matched by drawings from the Fed
(see Chapter 8 for discussion). The swap line had been all but repaid
by the end of September 2009.

In response to the crisis, the Reserve Bank of Australia opened a
swap line with the Fed. Its initial upper limit, set on 24 September
2008, was US\$ 10 billion, but it was trebled in size to US\$ 30 billion on
29 September. In commenting on the decision that it and other central
banks had taken to provide US dollar funding to domestic commercial
banks, the Reserve Bank of Australia said that: 'the decision to provide

Table 9.5 *Reserve Bank of Australia balance sheet – selected items (US dollar billions)*

Wednesdays	Liabilities to overseas	Amount drawn on Fed swap	Gold and foreign exchange assets
27/08/2008	1.6	0	39.1
24/09/2008	1.7	0	37.2
29/10/2008	20.9	17.8	57.7
26/11/2008	23.6	21.6	59.1
31/12/2008	25.5	22.8	62.2
28/01/2009	11.9	10.2	46.4
25/02/2009	11.3	10.2	44.0
25/03/2009	11.4	9.6	45.0
29/04/2009	5.1	3.6	45.0
27/05/2009	3.5	2.2	47.0
24/06/2009	1.1	0.2	46.4
29/07/2009	0.9	0	46.3
26/08/2009	0.8	0	44.2
30/09/2009	0.7	0	45.6

Source: Reserve Bank of Australia, Federal Reserve.

US dollar funding by some of these central banks, including the RBA, does not reflect vulnerabilities in their own banking sectors; rather, it is intended to alleviate global pressures by improving the distribution of US dollar liquidity across different time zones and locales.[4]

The evolution of the key features of the RBA's balance sheet is shown in Table 9.5. 'Gold and foreign exchange assets', which include US dollar loans to Australian commercial banks, increased by about US$ 23 billion between the end of August 2008 and the end of the year.[5] This was more or less exactly matched by drawings on the Fed swap. The liquidity situation seems to have improved after the beginning of 2009, probably helped by the stabilisation of commodity prices, and the swap had been repaid by the end of September.

[4] Reserve Bank of Australia (2008), box B.
[5] Analysis of the auction results indicates that the peak level of US dollar loans was $26.7 billion, reached on 31 October.

In all five cases, central bank dollar loans to commercial banks and
the amounts outstanding on the Fed swap had fallen back substantially
by the middle of 2009. On 24 September the ECB, the Bank of England
and the SNB were able to announce that in light of reduced demand
for funds, they intended to discontinue the current eighty-four-day US
dollar repo operations after a final operation at the start of October,
though the seven-day US dollar repo operations would continue until
January 2010.[6] This strongly suggests that the objective of the swap
lines, to stabilise market conditions, had been largely achieved.

Could it have been achieved without the swap lines? Japan's foreign
exchange reserves were much larger than the amount of dollars that the
Bank of Japan lent to commercial banks (though most of the reserves
are managed by the Ministry of Finance and not the Bank of Japan),
so it could be said that Japan did not need its swap line. The same
could not be said of any of the other financial centres. In Australia and
Switzerland, the attempt to finance dollar liquidity provision out of
foreign exchange reserves would have led to such a heavy percentage
depletion of reserves as to run the risk, in the nervous atmosphere prevailing at the time, of loss of market confidence in the creditworthiness
of the country concerned. The foreign exchange reserves of the euro
area and the United Kingdom would simply have been insufficient to
finance their central banks' peak dollar liquidity provision (see Table
9.1). What might have happened had the swap lines not been provided
is discussed at the end of this chapter.

Among other large international financial centres, Hong Kong did
not experience unusual flows of foreign currency funds during the
crisis. However, there was a strong demand for Hong Kong dollars,
reflecting the closing out of carry trades which had been financed using
Hong Kong dollars. Under the Convertibility Undertaking embodied in
the currency board arrangement, the Hong Kong Monetary Authority
provides Hong Kong dollars in exchange for US dollars at a rate of
HK$ 7.75 = US$ 1. In addition, the Monetary Authority announced
on 30 September 2008 five temporary measures to provide HK dollar liquidity to commercial banks, through loans or swaps, including Hong Kong dollar swaps against US dollars.[7] Between the end of

---

[6] See www.bankofengland.co.uk/publications/news/2009/072.htm, www.ecb.int/
   press/pr/date/2009/html/pr090924_2.en.html., www.snb.ch/en/mmr/reference/
   pre_20090924_1/source/pre_20090924_1.en.pdf.
[7] See Hong Kong Monetary Authority (2008), box 4.

August and the end of December 2008, Hong Kong's official reserve assets increased by US$ 24.5 billion, and they increased by a further US$ 73.3 billion in 2009.[8] It was announced on 26 March 2009 that the swap facility would be made permanent.[9] We know of no indications that Hong Kong used the swap line that it had obtained from the People's Bank of China, and there is no obvious reason why the swap line should have been used.

Singapore did experience outflows of funds, however. BIS reporting banks' assets vis-à-vis Singapore fell by US$ 121.5 billion (14.1 per cent of the initial total) in 2008Q4 and 2009Q1. The Monetary Authority of Singapore received a US$ 30 billion swap line from the Fed but did not draw on it.

2. Smaller international financial centres: Denmark, Sweden and Norway

Denmark, Sweden and Norway were all seriously affected by the credit crisis. Figure 4.2 and Figure 4.5 show how covered interest differentials and basis swap spreads reacted. The Norwegian krone and the Swedish krona both depreciated against the euro (see Figure 4.8).

Denmark faced a war on two fronts. It had two kinds of contingent claims on its reserves – one being its exchange rate commitment and the other being the possible need to provide emergency foreign currency liquidity to distressed banks.[10] Denmark is not a member of the euro area, the electorate having rejected membership in a referendum in 2000. The Danish krone is a member of ERM2 and Danmarks Nationalbank accordingly undertakes to maintain the krone within a fluctuation band ± 2.25 per cent around its central rate against the euro. In fact the krone normally remains within a much narrower margin around the central rate. The krone remained very close to its ERM2 parity against the euro throughout the credit crisis, with the support

[8] Source: SDDS returns. See http://dsbb.imf.org/Pages/SDDS/ReserveTemplates. aspx.
[9] See Hong Kong Monetary Authority (2009), p. 50.
[10] Russia was in the same position, having both an exchange rate target for monetary policy purposes and a need to provide foreign currency liquidity to commercial banks. Russia had very large reserves and no need of a swap line. In the event, Russia abandoned its exchange rate target at the beginning of 2009.

of official outright purchases of kroner, which amounted to DKK 64.6 billion (EUR 8.7 billion) in September and October 2008.[11]

Danish banks, like others, experienced withdrawals of foreign currency deposits, and Danmarks Nationalbank began intervening in the swap market on 18 September, using its own reserves, to help banks meet these withdrawals.[12] It established two swap lines, one with the Fed, opened on 24 September for $5 billion and increased to $15 billion on 29 September, and the other with the ECB for EUR 12 billion opened on 27 October. It used swap drawings to finance auctions of euro and dollar deposits to commercial banks.[13] The amounts involved are shown in Table 9.6, which shows the monthly reserve totals published by the Nationalbank, together with predetermined outflows, which reflect the proceeds of swap drawings. During September–November 2008, the Nationalbank lent the equivalent of DKK 115.6 billion in euros and dollars. Total swap drawings reached DKK 116.3 billion (EUR 15.6 billion) at the end of November. Had Danmarks Nationalbank made the foreign currency loans without the support of the swap lines, its reserves would have fallen to DKK 52.7 billion (EUR 7.1 billion) at the end of October 2008, less than a third of what they had been at the end of August, before the crisis began.

During October, the Danish government issued a guarantee of bank deposits (on 5 October); and the Nationalbank raised interest rates (the lending rate and the CD rate) by 40 basis points on 7 October and by a further 50 basis points on 24 October, while ECB rates were falling. That marked the turning point, and funds began to flow back into Denmark during November, as Table 9.6 shows. The fact that a moderate positive interest differential vis-à-vis the euro area was able to attract funds back to Denmark in these circumstances demonstrates the credibility of Denmark's exchange rate commitment.

Danmarks Nationalbank was then able to begin purchasing foreign exchange, and over the eleven months November 2008–September 2009, it sold DKK 193.3 billion for foreign exchange worth about EUR 25.9 billion – more than three times the amount of reserves it had spent in intervention during September and October 2008. The market

---

[11] See Danmarks Nationalbank (2009a), p. 10. Figures come from balance sheet data published by Danmarks Nationalbank.

[12] See Danmarks Nationalbank (2008 and 2009a), Bernstein (2010) and Table 12.1.

[13] See Danmarks Nationalbank (2009b), pp. 47–50.

Table 9.6 *Denmark: influences on international liquidity*

End of	Gold and foreign exchange reserves DKK bn	Predetermined outflows DKK bn	Intervention during month to purchase foreign exchange (net) DKK bn	Foreign currency lending to banks DKK bn	equivalent in USD (USD bn)	EUR (EUR bn)	Reserves net of predetermined outflows DKK bn
Aug-08	166.7	0.4					167.1
Sep-08	163.8	−25.0	−0.7	25.5	4.8	3.4	138.8
Oct-08	133.7	−81.0	−63.9	85.3	14.6	11.4	52.7
Nov-08	176.4	−116.3	31.6	114.6	19.5	15.4	60.1
Dec-08	223.7	−108.2	24.7	116.0	21.8	15.6	115.5
Jan-09	226.2	−96.6	12.1	93.6	16.1	12.6	129.6
Feb-09	241.8	−71.3	10.1	70.6	12.0	9.5	170.5
Mar-09	267.3	−55.7	18.1	44.3	7.9	5.9	211.6
Apr-09	291.3	−43.6	8.9	44.3	7.9	5.9	247.7
May-09	331.1	−34.4	28.5	34.5	6.6	4.6	296.7
Jun-09	334.4	−36.0	6.7	36.4	6.9	4.9	298.4
Jul-09	340.1	−33.4	6.6	33.6	6.4	4.5	306.7
Aug-09	377.8	−15.1	26.9	15.6	3.0	2.1	362.7
Sep-09	398.0	−6.0	19.1	6.3	1.2	0.8	392.0

Source: Danmarks Nationalbank, Bloomberg (exchange rates).

demand for Danish kroner in and after November 2008 partly reflected the differential between the lending rates of Danmarks Nationalbank and the ECB, which remained wider than usual. It is possible that Danmarks Nationalbank's decision to maintain an unusually wide interest rate margin over the euro area was motivated partly by a desire to build up the reserves out of a concern that the financial crisis had shown that they were not large enough. On the other side of the account, Denmark provided euro swap lines to Iceland and Latvia, but the amounts were relatively small (see the appendix to Chapter 6 for details).

In Sweden, commercial banks experienced shortages of foreign currencies, and their net external foreign currency liabilities fell by $50.5 billion in the second half of 2008 (see Table 9.1). The Riksbank opened a swap line with the Fed on 24 September; initially for $10 billion, it was increased to $30 billion on 29 September. The Riksbank began auctioning dollar loans to Swedish banks as from 1 October. By the end of October, it had lent $23.9 billion and by the end of the year the total was up to $25 billion.[14] There were net repayments in January 2009 but the demand for foreign currency liquidity support then increased again and the amount outstanding reached $30.9 billion at the end of April. Not all of the foreign currency loans to domestic banks were financed by drawings on the Fed swap (see Table 9.7); the Riksbank evidently committed some of its own reserves to foreign currency liquidity support. Nevertheless, having repaid $15 billion of swap drawings in January 2009, the Riksbank increased its drawings as the commercial banks' demand for foreign currency liquidity increased, and drawings on the Fed swap returned to their earlier peak level of $25.0 billion from 9–14 May 2009. On 12 June, the Riksbank and the ECB announced that the Riksbank was borrowing EUR 3 billion from the ECB under a EUR 10 billion swap agreement that had been made on 20 December 2007. The Fed swap was fully repaid on 23 October 2009. Sweden's foreign exchange reserves were $27.6 billion just before the crisis, and the Riksbank therefore

---

[14] Bryant, Henderson and Becker (2012) describe the management of the crisis by the Swedish authorities in detail. They point out that some of the commercial banks' pre-crisis dollar borrowing had been swapped into kronor and used to finance krona-denominated assets.

Table 9.7 Sveriges Riksbank balance sheet – selected items (Swedish krona billions, unless otherwise specified)

End of	External foreign currency claims	(USD bn)	Domestic foreign currency claims	(USD bn)	External kronor liabilities	External foreign currency liabilities	(USD bn)	Domestic foreign currency liabilities	(USD bn)	Drawing on Fed swap (USD bn)
Aug-08	174	26.9	0	0.0	0	16	2.6			0.0
Sep-08	235	34.0	0	0.0	0	65	9.4			0.0
Oct-08	186	23.9	186	23.9	150	51	6.6			20.0
Nov-08	204	25.2	187	23.1	189	35	4.3			25.0
Dec-08	200	25.6	196	25.0	189	9	1.1			25.0
Jan-09	207	24.8	131	15.7	79	60	7.1			10.0
Feb-09	207	23.0	246	27.2	194	58	6.5			23.0
Mar-09	196	23.7	247	30.0	194	58	7.0			23.0
Apr-09	199	24.8	248	30.8	196	59	7.3			23.0
May-09	189	25.0	197	26.1	132	60	7.9			16.5
Jun-09	281	36.5	138	17.9	124	37	4.8	66	8.6	11.5
Jul-09	278	38.6	84	11.7	65	38	5.2	66	9.2	4.2
Aug-09	304	42.8	66	9.3	53	37	5.2	66	9.3	2.7
Sep-09	297	42.7	26	3.7	20	8	1.2	91	13.1	2.7

Source: Sveriges Riksbank.

could not have provided as much foreign currency liquidity as it did to domestic commercial banks without the help of the Fed swap line.

Sweden extended swap lines to Iceland (EUR 500 million), Latvia (EUR 375 million) and Estonia (SEK 10 billion) during the crisis. These swap lines were too small to have any material effect on Sweden's own finances.

In Norway, there was an outflow of foreign currency from the banks in the second half of 2008 as their net external foreign currency liabilities fell modestly (see Table 9.1); Norges Bank reported that 'banks' market funding became both more expensive and less readily available during the autumn'.[15] In response, Norges Bank greatly expanded the scale of its krone liquidity provision. In addition, having obtained a swap line from the Fed for $5 billion on 24 September 2008, increased to $15 billion on 29 September, in October it began providing dollar fixed-rate loans. Moreover, Norges Bank provided krone loans against euros and dollars both domestically and to foreign banks active in the Norwegian money market.[16]

Table 9.8 shows the evolution of relevant parts of Norges Bank's balance sheet. 'Other domestic assets', which include foreign currency lending to Norwegian banks, increased to $9.1 billion at the end of November 2008.[17] Its foreign currency component, which was $8.3 billion at the end of December, fell to $5.1 billion at the end of June 2009 and $1.0 billion at the end of September. Its rise and fall were closely matched by drawings on the Fed swap line.

'Other foreign assets', which include krone loans to foreign banks active in the Norwegian money market, rose very quickly to the equivalent of $8.7 billion at the end of November 2008, and its domestic currency component fell from $8.0 billion at the end of December to $5.3 billion at the end of June 2009 and $1.1 billion at the end of September.

Norway's foreign exchange reserves were $41.7 billion just before the crisis, at the end of August 2008, and this would, in the event, have been amply sufficient to provide Norwegian commercial banks with the foreign currency liquidity that they needed. In addition, Norway

[15] See Norges Bank (2008), p. 21.
[16] See Norges Bank (2008), p. 28.
[17] Analysis of the auction results published by Norges Bank suggests that the foreign currency lending component was $8.9 billion.

Table 9.8 Norges Bank balance sheet – selected items (Norwegian krone billions, US dollar billions in parentheses)

	International reserves	Other foreign assets	of which NOK-denominated	Other domestic assets	of which foreign currency-denominated	Foreign liabilities	of which deposits	Drawings on Fed swap (USD bn)
Aug-08	257.7 (46.6)	0.2 (0.0)		1.0 (0.2)		46.8 (8.6)	0.1 (0.0)	
Sep-08	261.7 (44.6)	8.6 (1.5)		4.9 (0.8)		44.9 (7.7)	0.1 (0.0)	
Oct-08	263.4 (39.2)	50.5 (7.5)		20.3 (3.0)		109.4 (16.3)	33.9 (5.0)	5.5
Nov-08	296.8 (42.3)	61.1 (8.7)		63.9 (9.1)		165.5 (23.6)	61.0 (8.7)	8.9
Dec-08	357.3 (51.4)		55.8 (8.0)		57.6 (8.3)	175.1 (25.2)	55.9 (8.0)	8.2
Jan-09	333.8 (48.3)		47.3 (6.9)		48.6 (7.0)	161.3 (23.3)	47.6 (6.9)	7.1
Feb-09	349.7 (49.7)		47.3 (6.7)		48.4 (6.9)	156.6 (22.2)	47.5 (6.7)	7.1
Mar-09	314.5 (46.7)		47.3 (7.0)		48.0 (7.1)	147.2 (21.8)	47.4 (7.0)	7.1
Apr-09	315.2 (48.1)		34.2 (5.2)		34.0 (5.2)	124.7 (19.0)	34.3 (5.2)	5.0
May-09	307.8 (48.9)		34.2 (5.4)		32.5 (5.2)	114.0 (18.1)	34.2 (5.2)	5.0
Jun-09	308.4 (47.9)		34.2 (5.3)		32.6 (5.1)	112.3 (17.5)	34.2 (5.2)	5.0
Jul-09	301.1 (49.2)		6.5 (1.1)		7.9 (1.3)	59.2 (9.7)	6.5 (1.1)	1.0
Aug-09	270.9 (45.0)		6.5 (1.1)		6.1 (1.0)	59.2 (9.8)	6.5 (1.1)	1.0
Sep-09	282.8 (49.0)		6.5 (1.1)		5.8 (1.0)	61.0 (10.6)	6.5 (1.1)	1.0

Sources: Norges Bank, Federal Reserve, Bloomberg (exchange rates).

had at its disposal the resources of its Government Pension Fund, which were around NOK 2 trillion, or around $370 billion, at the end of 2007. It was perhaps partly in order to forestall the risk of disruptive asset sales by the Government Pension Fund that the Fed extended a swap line to Norway.

In Denmark, Sweden and Norway, the amount of dollar loans to commercial banks and the amounts outstanding on swap lines fell back substantially during 2009, suggesting that the objectives of the swap lines had been achieved. In Denmark, as already noted, the objective was to ensure not only that the banks could repay their deposits on time but also that Denmark's exchange rate commitment, which is the foundation of its monetary policy, could be maintained. In the event, the credibility of the exchange rate commitment proved to be robust, but it might have been threatened if there had been a much larger fall in the reserves. It is doubtful whether Denmark or Sweden could have provided effective support to their banks as they did had they not received swap lines very quickly from the Fed after the Lehman failure, and later from the ECB, since the necessary provision of liquidity would have used up most of their reserves.

3. Countries which are not international financial centres: Korea, Mexico, Hungary and Poland

Korea was hit very hard by the financial crisis, despite having large foreign exchange reserves. Korean banks encountered funding problems, as they had done in the crisis of 1997–98, when there had been a massive depreciation of the won and a very large contraction in domestic demand. The won depreciated very heavily after Lehman Brothers failed; by the end of November 2008 the depreciation had reached 25 per cent against the dollar and 33 per cent against the yen (see Figure 4.10). In addition, covered interest rate differentials against the yen turned positive, as Korean banks which were unable to get foreign currency funding turned to the swap market to convert won borrowing into foreign currencies (see Figure 4.3). The profile of covered interest rate differentials against the dollar was very similar.

There was a big outflow of funds. The net external liabilities of Korean banks fell by $37.8 billion in the second half of 2008 (see Table 9.1), and there were heavy sales of Korean local currency bonds by non-residents (see Figure 9.2), of KRW 18.6 trillion (roughly $18 billion) between June 2008 and May 2009.

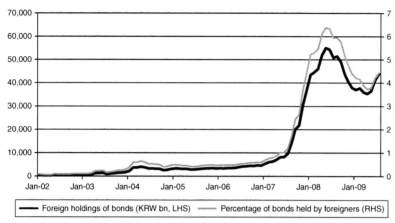

Figure 9.2 Foreign holdings of Korean local-currency bonds.

On 21 October 2008, the Korean Ministry of Strategy and Finance issued a press release on the financial crisis, in which it said that, among other measures, the government and the Bank of Korea would provide additional dollar liquidity, amounting to $30 billion, to the banking sector by utilising foreign exchange reserves.[18]

The Bank of Korea obtained swap lines from three sources, to reinforce the foreign exchange reserves. On 30 October 2008, it obtained a $30 billion swap line from the Fed; and on 12 December it obtained swap lines of CNY 1,800 billion or KRW 38 trillion from the People's Bank of China and of $20 billion equivalent from the Bank of Japan. The Bank of Korea reported that 'the establishment of the currency swaps themselves actually had a positive announcement effect in stabilizing the financial market unrest, as price variables have shown rapid recoveries'.[19] By the end of 2008, it had drawn $10.35 billion on the Fed swap, to finance foreign currency lending to commercial banks. It made no drawings, then or later, on the swap lines with the People's Bank of China or the Bank of Japan.[20] The funds drawn on the Fed swap were lent to commercial banks, and, in addition, the

[18] See Korea Ministry of Strategy and Finance (2008).
[19] See Bank of Korea (2009b).
[20] Information provided to the author by the Bank of Korea. In a document published on 28 January 2009 (see Korea Ministry of Strategy and Finance 2009), the Bank of Korea commented, in relation to the swap agreement with the People's Bank of China, that 'the two sides have agreed to explore the possibility and extent of converting the swap currencies into reserve currencies'.

Bank of Korea supplied $10.27 billion to commercial banks through swap transactions between October and December 2008, financed out of its own reserves.[21]

Korean government funds also provided foreign currency liquidity. The Bank of Korea noted (Bank of Korea 2009b, footnote 8) that

the government (Foreign Exchange Stabilization Fund) also announced its own foreign currency liquidity supply plans for 10.0 billion US dollars by swap trading, 14.0 billion US dollars by competitive auction loans, and 11.0 billion US dollars by support for trade finance, for a total of 35.0 billion US dollars. An additional 27.4 billion US dollars was supplied through the Export-Import Bank of Korea.

By the end of December 2008, government funds had provided $27.4 billion in foreign currency liquidity in addition to the $20.6 billion provided by the Bank of Korea, making a total of $48 billion.[22] Between the end of August and the end of December, Korea's foreign exchange reserves fell by $42.0 billion (however, this will have included changes in the dollar value of non-dollar currencies held in the reserves), and Korea drew $10.35 billion from the Fed. The foreign currency liquidity of the Korean monetary authorities thus fell by an amount of the order of $52 billion. The difference of roughly $4 billion between the fall in the foreign exchange reserves and the amount of foreign exchange liquidity provided to commercial banks through loans or swaps may have represented the amount spent on outright purchases of won for dollars.

The Bank of Korea's provision of foreign currency liquidity continued into 2009, and in January, it lent a further $6.0 billion (net) to commercial banks, financed by drawings on the Fed swap line. Those drawings peaked at $16.35 billion, from 22 January to 18 March 2009. In the first quarter of 2009, Korea's reserves increased by $5.1 billion, but the Bank of Korea drew a further $5.6 billion net from the Fed. Therefore it seems likely that transactions by the Korean monetary authorities in the first quarter of 2009 were such as to generate only a small net outflow of foreign exchange, and possibly an inflow.

[21] See Bank of Korea (2009a). Also, between December 2008 and February 2009, the Bank of Korea supplied $0.15 billion of foreign exchange through the purchase of export bills.
[22] Information provided to the author by the Bank of Korea.

In the second and third quarters of 2009, there was a clear improvement in Korea's international liquidity: the foreign exchange reserves increased by $43.8 billion while $12.0 billion was repaid to the Fed. And the won stabilised somewhat in foreign exchange markets, as Figure 4.10 shows.

Korea's reserves, which were $243.2 billion at the end of August 2008, would have been easily large enough to meet the demand for foreign currency liquidity. The swap facilities were in that sense not essential to the financing of the liquidity provision. However, there is no reason to doubt the Bank of Korea's assertion that their availability had a positive effect on market sentiment; and market sentiment might have deteriorated further if there had been a larger fall in the reserves, particularly after an ill-judged official statement that the reserves would not be allowed to fall below $200 billion. In other words, the demand for foreign currency liquidity might have been greater still in absence of the swap facilities. In spite of the foreign currency liquidity that the Korean authorities provided, financial market stresses clearly remained in the third quarter of 2009: for example, covered interest differentials between the won and the yen (and the dollar) were very wide (see Figure 4.3).[23] The Bank of Korea commented in April 2009 that: 'This seems chiefly attributable to the rise in risk premiums caused by the competition to secure dollars in the international financial market and by concerns about the rising credit risks of domestic financial institutions.'[24]

To the extent that the residual stresses reflected the credit risks of financial institutions, they could not have been alleviated by additional liquidity provision. However, additional liquidity provision might have reduced the competition to secure dollars (or other foreign currencies) in the international financial market.

As the crisis abated, Korea was quick to rebuild its foreign exchange reserves, even though they were still very large. Moreover Korea has been the main proponent of a 'financial safety net' to provide emergency liquidity to countries experiencing sudden capital outflows.

---

[23] The forward exchange market in Korea is heavily influenced by large-scale transactions by shipbuilding companies. However, the fact that covered interest differentials were much wider in the third quarter of 2009 than in the third quarter of 2007 suggests that the financial crisis had a lasting effect.

[24] Bank of Korea (2009c), p. 43.

After two financial crises in little more than a decade, Korea's dominant concern seems to be to secure more liquidity as a protection against future possible financial instability.

In Mexico, the peso depreciated very sharply after Lehman Brothers failed; its effective exchange rate index fell by 23.3 per cent between the end of August 2008 and the end of February 2009. Covered interest differentials curiously turned sharply negative for a period: in other words, it was cheaper to borrow dollars indirectly, by borrowing pesos and swapping them, than directly. The differentials returned to moderate negative levels, of around 100 basis points, in early January 2009. There were net foreign sales of Mexican government securities, amounting to MXN 81.2 billion (about $6 billion) between 15 September 2008 and the low point on 23 April 2009, as Figure 9.3 shows.[25]

The Banco de Mexico responded initially to the crisis by undertaking regular and at times very large official purchases of pesos for dollars,[26] partly in order to help relieve liquidity pressures in the spot foreign exchange market related to corporate losses on derivative positions.[27] Mexico's foreign exchange reserves fell by $13.8 billion during October 2008. The Fed established a swap line for $30 billion with the Banco de Mexico on 29 October 2008, and it seems to have had a positive announcement effect: in the five trading days after the announcement, the peso was 5.8 per cent stronger against the dollar on average than in the five trading days before the announcement. However, the swap line was not drawn on until April 2009, when the Banco de Mexico auctioned dollar deposits to commercial banks, drawing $3.2 billion on the swap for the purpose.[28] Also in April 2009, Mexico obtained a Flexible Credit Line from the IMF for some $47 billion.

Mexico appears to have overcome the crisis using mainly its own foreign exchange reserves (which were $96.1 billion at the end of August 2008). It also received backup support from the IMF. The Fed swap was probably helpful in improving Mexico's market credibility,

---

[25] For fuller discussion of the effects of the credit crisis on Latin America, see Jara, Moreno and Tovar (2009).

[26] See Banco de Mexico (2009), p. 84, and International Monetary Fund (2009), p. 12.

[27] See International Monetary Fund (2009), p. 20.

[28] See Banco de Mexico (2009), p. 48. The swap line, for a maximum of $30 billion, had been opened on 29 October 2008.

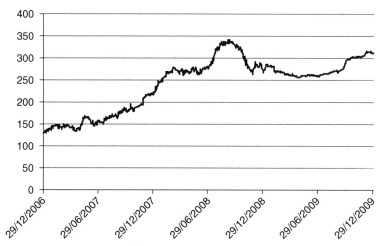

Figure 9.3 Net position of foreign residents in Mexican government securities, 2006–09 (in MXN billions).
Source: Banco de Mexico series SF 65218.

but, although they were used, the funds that it provided seem to have played only a minor role.

Following the failure of Lehman Brothers on 15 September 2008, the currencies of Hungary and Poland depreciated heavily in the foreign exchange market (see Figure 4.8). In both countries, covered interest differentials and cross-currency basis swap spreads against the euro widened substantially and remained very wide by historical standards (Figure 4.2 and Figure 4.5).

In early October, the impairment in foreign currency swap markets triggered problems in Hungary, including in the form of a fall in the share price of OTP Bank (viewed as vulnerable since, although mainly foreign-owned, its ownership was dispersed rather than concentrated) and a sharp reduction in foreign demand for local currency bonds.[29, 30] Foreign holdings of Hungarian forint-denominated government securities fell by HUF 1.2 trillion, or about EUR 4.3 billion, between October 2008 and June 2009 (see Figure 9.4). Many mortgage borrowers were exposed to foreign exchange risk: total foreign

[29] In mid-October, there were no bidders at local currency government bond auctions, leading to an increase in local currency bond spreads.
[30] See Mihaljek (2010).

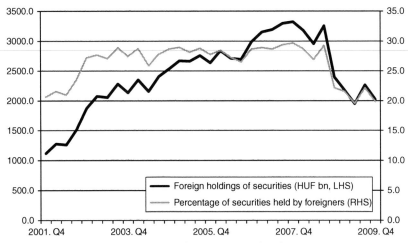

Figure 9.4 Foreign holdings of Hungarian local-currency government securities.
Sources: National data, author's calculations.

currency housing loans, mostly denominated in Swiss francs, were the equivalent of EUR 7.6 billion, or 7.2 per cent of GDP, at the end of August 2008. The forint depreciated sharply, with commercial banks no longer prepared to exchange foreign currencies for forints in swap markets.[31] The events in Hungary had spillover effects in Poland and the Czech Republic, leading to an increase in the yields of national currency-denominated government bonds.[32]

These events led several central banks, including the Magyar Nemzeti Bank (MNB), to take the role of counterparties in swap transactions in which they provided euros and Swiss francs to banks in swaps against their domestic currencies.[33] The MNB obtained euro financing facilities from the ECB against high-quality euro collateral, and Swiss franc financing from the Swiss National Bank, using the latter's CHF/EUR swap arrangements. Neither of these facilities increased the amount of foreign currency available to Hungary; the ECB facility simply enabled the MNB to turn high-quality euro assets into cash, and the SNB facility enabled it to exchange one foreign currency for another. However,

---

[31] For a discussion of the swap market in forints, see Mak and Pales (2009).
[32] For a fuller account, see Austrian National Bank (2008), pp. 17ff.
[33] See Austrian National Bank (2008).

in November 2008, the Hungarian government reached agreement with the IMF and the European Commission on a standby credit facility of up to EUR 20 billion, of which EUR 6.9 billion was drawn in 2008Q4.[34] External borrowing of foreign currency will have reduced depreciation pressure on the forint by helping the central bank finance foreign currency swaps with commercial banks, and thereby reducing the need for commercial banks and others to sell forints in the spot market for foreign currencies at a time when the foreign currency swap market was not functioning. The MNB's swaps with credit institutions, which from March to August 2009 included one-week CHF/EUR, three-month EUR/HUF and six-month EUR/HUF central bank foreign exchange swaps, peaked in April–May 2009 at HUF 362 billion, or the equivalent of EUR 1.3 billion (see Table 9.9). On average in September 2009, the MNB's swaps with credit institutions were down to to HUF 159 billion (EUR 0.6 billion).[35]

The announcement of the ECB facility on 16 October 2008 and the announcement on 25 June 2009 that the SNB swap line would continue until the end of October, appear to have had some immediate positive impact on cross-currency basis swap spreads against the euro. The first announcement of the SNB swap line on 28 January 2009 had no immediate positive impact, though it was followed by a narrowing of spreads (see Table 9.10 and Figure 4.5). However, three-month covered interest differentials and one-year cross-currency basis swap spreads against the euro were still much wider on average over the third quarter of 2009 than before the financial crisis, at around 58 basis points and 88 basis points respectively, but nevertheless much lower than in early 2009 (see Figure 4.2 and Figure 4.5). This suggests that the market stresses engendered by the crisis were persistent.[36]

---

[34] See Magyar Nemzeti Bank (2009), p. 20, box 1–1.

[35] A time series of the MNB's swaps with credit institutions is shown in graph 8 of the MNB's 'Charts to the press release on the statistical balance sheet of the MNB, August 2009', available at http://english.mnb.hu/Engine.aspx?page=mnben_statisztikai_idosorok&ContentID=11489.

[36] It may be argued that the three-month deposit and swap markets, and the one-year basis swap market, are not very liquid in Hungary, so that the data quoted in this paragraph do not constitute strong evidence of persisting market stresses. However, the fact that those markets are not very liquid is in itself a sign of stress. And covered interest differentials against the euro were still substantial even at shorter maturities. The average differentials in 2009Q3 at the one-week and one-month maturities were 37 and 26 basis points, respectively.

Table 9.9 *Hungary: selected data*

	Swaps with credit institutions[a] (monthly averages)		Foreign exchange reserves (end period)	Loan drawings (end period)
	HUF billion	EUR billion	EUR billion	EUR billion
May-08			16.7	0
Jun-08			17.1	0
Jul-08			17.0	0
Aug-08			17.1	0
Sep-08			17.2	0
Oct-08			17.6	0
Nov-08			22.7	
Dec-08			23.9	6.9
Jan-09			24.4	
Feb-09			24.7	
Mar-09	297.1	1.0	27.7	
Apr-09	361.9	1.2	26.7	
May-09	361.9	1.3	26.5	
Jun-09	356.0	1.3	26.8	
Jul-09	252.5	0.9	29.3	
Aug-09	200.9	0.7	29.4	
Sep-09	159.4	0.6	29.4	

Note: [a] This item includes one-week CHF/EUR, three-month EUR/HUF and six-month EUR/HUF central bank FX-swaps.
Sources: MNB, IMF, Bloomberg (exchange rates), author's calculations.

Since the MNB's facilities with the ECB and the SNB could not augment its reserves, it can be said that Hungary financed all of its support for the foreign currency liquidity of its commercial banks from its own reserves, together with external official borrowing undertaken by the government.

The post-Lehman intensification of the financial crisis also affected Poland, even though its macroeconomic fundamentals were strong and it did not need a standby agreement with the IMF (see Figure 4.2, Figure 4.5 and Figure 4.8). As in Hungary, there was a large volume of foreign currency loans to households, which were the equivalent

Table 9.10 *Hungary: cross-currency basis swap spreads against the euro*[a]

Before crisis	5 days from	01.01.2007	−8
ECB Swap line	5 days before	16.10.2008	−108
	5 days from	16.10.2008	−95
SNB Swap line	5 days before	28.01.2009	−227
	5 days from	28.01.2009	−232
SNB Swap line	5 days before	25.06.2009	−118
	5 days from	25.06.2009	−89
Autumn 2009	5 days before	1.10.2009	−95

Note: [a] At the one-year maturity, in basis points; averages over periods shown.
Sources: Bloomberg, author's calculations.

of EUR 29.5 billion (8.1 per cent of GDP) at the end of August 2008. Settlement of currency options (foreign currency calls) written by Polish enterprises added to the demand for foreign currencies (see NBP 2009b). The NBP, like the MNB, obtained euro financing facilities from the ECB against high-quality collateral, and a Swiss franc swap line against euro collateral from the Swiss National Bank. As in the case of Hungary, these facilities did not augment the country's international reserves. By March 2009, the NBP had not drawn on the ECB facility, though it had obtained Swiss francs from the SNB using euros from its reserves as collateral.[37] In addition, Poland established a one-year flexible credit line of $20.6 billion with the IMF in May 2009, on which it did not draw.

There is no evidence that the swap line announcements had an immediate positive impact on cross-currency basis swap spreads (see Table 9.11 and Figure 4.5), or any lasting effect on covered interest differentials (Figure 4.2). As in Hungary, basis swap spreads and covered interest rate differentials both remained unusually wide: the average three-month covered interest differential against the euro over the third quarter of 2009 was 49 basis points and the average one-year basis swap margin was 98 basis points.

The NBP offered foreign exchange swaps in USD/PLN and EUR/PLN to commercial banks from 17 October 2008 at a seven-day maturity, with the first swap being concluded on 21 October 2008 (see NBP

---

[37] See NBP (2009b), p. 13.

Table 9.11 *Poland: cross-currency basis swap spreads against the euro*[a]

Before crisis	5 days from	01.01.2007	−7
SNB Swap line	5 days before	07.11.2008	−152
	5 days from	07.11.2008	−150
ECB Swap line	5 days before	21.11.2008	−135
	5 days from	21.11.2008	−135
SNB Swap line	5 days before	16.01.2009	−80
	5 days from	16.01.2009	−89
SNB Swap line	5 days before	25.06.2009	−125
	5 days from	25.06.2009	−125
Autumn 2009	5 days before	01.10.2009	−92

Note: [a] At the one-year maturity, in basis points; averages over periods shown.
Sources: Bloomberg, author's calculations.

2009a). On 17 November 2008 the NBP began conducting foreign exchange swap transactions in CHF/PLN, also at a seven-day maturity. On three occasions in 2008 the NBP also conducted CHF/PLN swaps with an eighty-four-day maturity. The NBP deliberately made the terms that it offered for these swaps expensive, so as to encourage banks to look for funding elsewhere, and in particular, in the case of foreign-owned banks, to seek funding from their parent banks. By the end of 2008, the balance of foreign exchange swaps had risen to about PLN 2 billion equivalent, or about EUR 0.5 billion,[38] and at the end of April 2009 it was PLN 1.8 billion (about EUR 0.4 billion). As in the case of Hungary, this must have been financed entirely from Poland's own reserves, because neither of the NBP's central bank facilities, with the ECB and the SNB, increased the amount of foreign currency available to Poland. The NBP reported in June 2009 that it had not drawn on the ECB facility,[39] but it did use the swap line with the SNB to obtain Swiss francs in exchange for euros (see Table 8.4). At the end of March 2009, the NBP announced that it would liberalise access to central bank credit as from the end of May, including lengthening the maximum maturity of normal foreign exchange swap operations to a month. Table 9.12 shows that Poland's reserves net of predetermined

[38] See NBP (2009a), fig. 9.
[39] See NBP (2009b), p. 13.

Table 9.12 Poland: foreign exchange reserves net of predetermined outflows (euro billions)

	Foreign exchange reserves	Predetermined outflows		Reserves net of predetermined outflows	
		Foreign currency loans, securities, and deposits	Other	Level	Change in month
May-08	48.9	-5.4	-11.9	31.6	-0.2
Jun-08	50.0	-5.7	-10.9	33.4	+1.8
Jul-08	52.3	-5.7	-12.2	34.4	+1.0
Aug-08	53.3	-3.7	-11.7	37.8	+3.5
Sep-08	49.4	-4.5	-8.0	36.9	-1.0
Oct-08	48.0	-4.7	-4.8	38.5	+1.6
Nov-08	46.9	-4.6	-3.6	38.7	+0.2
Dec-08	41.8	-4.6	-1.3	36.0	-2.7
Jan-09	43.5	-3.2	-1.8	38.5	+2.6
Feb-09	46.1	-3.2	-1.8	41.2	+2.6
Mar-09	43.5	-2.8	-1.3	39.4	-1.7
Apr-09	45.5	-2.8	-2.6	40.2	+0.6
May-09	45.9	-3.0	-2.5	40.4	+0.2
Jun-09	45.2	-2.6	-2.1	40.4	0.0
Jul-09	48.2	-3.0	-2.6	42.7	+2.3
Aug-09	49.4	-3.0	-2.1	44.3	+1.6
Sep-09	49.4	-3.0	-2.0	44.4	+0.1

Sources: NBP, author's calculations.

outflows fell by just EUR 1.9 billion between the end of August and the end of December 2008 (including valuation effects). Thus liquidity provision by the NBP made only a modest contribution to relieving the shortage of foreign currency.

In both Hungary and Poland, all the market indicators suggest that the effects of the credit crisis were very substantial, and that they persisted after the crisis appeared to be over elsewhere. As noted in Chapter 3, the fact that transactions in the forint and the złoty cannot be settled through the Continuous Linked Settlement Bank may help to explain why covered interest differentials involving these currencies are so wide. It cannot be said that the central bank swap technique failed to deal with the problems, because the facilities provided could not augment either country's reserves. The swap technique strictly speaking was not really tried. It does seem likely, however, that the facility under which the central banks of Hungary and Poland could obtain Swiss francs from the Swiss National Bank through swaps against euros was useful in replacing market sources of Swiss franc funding for domestic banks.

By contrast to the experiences of Hungary and Poland, in the Czech Republic cross-currency basis swap spreads increased only mildly, and returned to the very low value of 6 basis points at the end of September 2009, close to pre-crisis levels, suggesting that stresses in cross-currency swap markets were much less severe there, and that the Czech Republic had no need to obtain swap lines (see Figure 4.5).

4. Summary

Not all the countries which received swap lines from the Fed used them, but many of the countries which did use them drew very heavily on them. As Table 9.1 shows, several countries drew amounts on the swap lines that were larger than their own foreign exchange reserves. Had the Fed not made swap lines available to foreign central banks, it is likely that more money would have been drawn from the Fed through its domestic liquidity-providing facilities to relieve the collateral squeeze in the United States, but it is also likely that more commercial banks outside the United States, unable to repay dollar deposits, could not have been supported by their home central banks and would have failed. Likewise, some banks in Hungary and Poland might have failed had it not been for the Swiss National Bank's provision of Swiss franc liquidity. Without the swap lines, it is likely that the financial crisis would have done much more damage to the world economy than it actually did.

10 | Propagation and scale of the 1931 crisis

This chapter and the next are about the banking crisis of 1931, and Chapter 12 will compare the recent crisis with that of 1931. This chapter describes the 1931 crisis and presents estimates of its scale.

1. International flows of funds in 1931

During the spring and summer of 1931, there was an epidemic of severe banking or exchange rate crises in Europe, and some European countries suffered heavy outflows of gold from their reserves while trying vainly to support their banking systems and remain faithful to the gold standard simultaneously. It is now conventional wisdom that the disastrous events of 1931 were crucial in turning the recession following the stock market crash of 1929 into the Great Depression of the 1930s.[1]

The banking crisis began in May 1931 with the disclosure of massive losses at Creditanstalt in Vienna.[2] The ensuing crisis in Austria was followed immediately by a crisis in Hungary and shortly afterwards by one in Germany. The central banks of the affected countries provided liquidity support to their commercial banks, and imposed controls on outflows of funds so as to contain the loss of gold and foreign exchange reserves. Pressures on sterling, which had been chronic ever since the UK had returned to the gold standard in 1925, became acute during the summer of 1931 and the UK left the gold standard in September.

It is not obvious why the crisis was propagated from Austria to Germany. James (1992) comments that 'in the most famous case, the

[1] See e.g. Friedman and Schwartz (1963), Bernanke and James (1991), Ahamed (2009), Ritschl (2009) and James (2009), ch. 2.
[2] Williams (1963) denotes the period that began in May 1931 as the 'final phase' of the crisis and describes how the crisis developed until then. For an account of the Austrian crisis, see Cottrell (1995).

Austrian crisis around the Creditanstalt in May 1931 is supposed to have provoked the German bank collapse of June–July, although the extent of German financial involvement in Austria was very limited, and it would be impossible to argue that the Austrian developments directly weakened German institutions'.[3] James suggests that the key issue in the early 1930s was market anxiety about budget deficits, which were thought to threaten a likely departure from gold. Eichengreen (1992) thinks that 'lacking timely information on the state of German finances, investors took the Austrian crisis as a warning'.[4]

The banking crises in central Europe added decisively to the pressure on sterling in 1931. For one thing, London was the world's main international financial centre, and people and companies needing liquidity on account of the crises in central Europe would naturally have drawn it from London. In particular, London merchant banks (accepting houses) had provided extensive acceptance credits to central European borrowers, especially in Germany.[5] After the crises, the borrowers could not pay the bills on time, and the acceptors were therefore liable to the holders of the bills. Standstill agreements were reached under which the creditors agreed not to call in the debts, and the existing credits were frozen on their original terms but interest payments were guaranteed.[6] The German agreement provided that there was to be no discrimination among the creditors, but that the German authorities would discriminate in authorising foreign payments in favour of remittances due under the agreement.[7] German debtors were required to provide bills for acceptance. As Roberts (1995, p. 164) aptly remarks, 'Under this agreement German bills remained in the [London] market and were repeatedly renewed on expiry, the sort of practice which had hitherto caused apoplexy in the Discount Office [of the Bank of England].'

The central European crisis and the standstill agreements put great strain on the liquidity of the London accepting houses, since they were responsible for the prompt payment of the debts which the central European debtors could not meet. The Bank of England's initial

---

[3] P. 596. [4] P. 271.
[5] Readers unfamiliar with acceptance credits are recommended to consult the account in Accominotti (2012), section 2.
[6] See Forbes (1987), p. 575.
[7] See Sayers (1976), pp. 506–507.

position, before the standstill agreements had been reached, had been that bills drawn against frozen credits, once renewed, would not be eligible for rediscount, and that no loans would be made to accepting houses with large frozen positions (see Sayers 1976, p. 505), though the Bank encouraged the clearing banks to provide support to the accepting houses.[8] The Bank's attitude is not surprising, since the total debts in London covered by the standstill agreement were £66 million, compared to the Bank of England's gold reserves of £132 million at the end of July 1931. However, the standstill agreement with Germany required the debtors to provide eligible bills for acceptance. Eligibility was a matter for the Bank of England, and Sayers reports that 'the Bank [of England] leaned over backwards to ensure marketability' of standstill bills, and that 'in the first half of 1932 nearly half the bills discounted at the Bank [of England] were of German origin'.[9] It is impossible to trace through time the amounts of such bills that the Bank purchased.[10] But whatever the amounts may have been, the residual liquidity problems of the merchant banks represented a kind of contingent liability of the Bank of England, and the adequacy of the Bank's own liquidity was in any case already a source of serious doubt about the sustainability of sterling's gold parity.[11] The central European banking crisis seriously aggravated the existing lack of liquidity of the London money market.

The alternative to the standstill agreements would have been a default by the debtors, which 'threatened to bankrupt several of the merchant banks, probably some of the discount houses, and possibly to provoke

---

[8] See Diaper (1986), p. 69 and Roberts (1992), pp. 252–253. It appears that the Bank of England did in the event provide financial support to certain accepting houses: see Sayers (1976), p. 531. The position that the Bank initially took in 1931 was very different from the one it had taken in comparable circumstances in 1914: see Sayers (1976), pp. 77–78.

[9] Sayers (1976), pp. 507 and 509 footnote 1.

[10] Changes in the 'other securities' recorded in the Bank of England's weekly return are not a reliable guide, since they were the net result of several influences, not just liquidity provision to a particular group of banks.

[11] The Macmillan report, published on 13 July 1931, had disclosed that the UK's short-term external liabilities were much larger than its short-term external assets. Its estimate of short-term external liabilities as at 31 March 1931 was £407 million in deposits, bills and advances, plus £153 million in acceptances (Committee on Finance and Industry 1931, appendix I table 11). This estimate has now been superseded (it was too low). The Bank of England's gold reserves averaged £142 million in March 1931 (appendix II).

a crisis in the banking system' (Roberts 1992, p. 253). The artificial maintenance of the fiction that standstill bills were high-quality liquid assets in London was the price of avoiding that outcome. Complete bank-by-bank information about exposures to standstill bills is not yet publicly available, though Diaper (1986, p. 68) says that the merchant banks Kleinwort, Sons and Co. and J. Henry Schröder and Co. were particularly hard hit. Using such bank-by-bank data as are publicly available, Accominotti (2012) shows that the banks which were most exposed to standstill bills also experienced large deposit outflows during 1931, and thus faced a double threat to their liquidity. Nearly all of the accepting houses' deposits were of foreign origin, according to Truptil (1936, p. 314), and it is possible that those banks whose acceptances were largely central European also had a high proportion of central European deposits, which would naturally have been withdrawn during the crisis to meet the depositors' liquidity needs. Kleinworts and Schröders both survived the crisis, but at great cost to their partners, as Diaper (1986) and Roberts (1992) relate.

The British clearing banks, of course, had much larger liquid liabilities than the accepting houses,[12] but the vast majority of their liabilities were presumably of domestic origin and not very vulnerable to flight. Their demand and time deposits fell by £58 million between June and October 1931, but as Billings and Capie (2010) recount, they were able to withstand the shocks of 1931 without any special support, and to provide support themselves to accepting houses and other banks in distress.[13] Thus there was no financial crisis in Britain in 1931. This can be attributed to the fact that the gold and other reserves available to the Bank of England to defend the gold parity were smaller than the liquid assets of the clearing banks encashable at the Bank of England.[14] According to the British Government statement issued on 20 September 1931, when the gold standard was suspended, 'since the end of July funds amounting to more than £200 millions have been withdrawn from the London market'.[15] The cash and liquid

---

[12] Demand and time deposits in the ten London clearing banks were £950 million and £792 million, respectively, in June 1931. Source: Board of Governors of the Federal Reserve System (1976), section 15, table 168.

[13] See Billings and Capie (2010), table 1, for details.

[14] For the definition of financial instability on which this judgement is based, see Allen and Wood (2006).

[15] See Sayers (1976), appendix 23.

assets of the London clearing banks amounted to £586 million in June 1931, however.[16] The Bank of England ran out of money before the clearing banks did.

As a result of the turmoil in financial markets, there were large international flows of gold and foreign exchange in 1931 (see Table 10.1). Total world gold reserves actually rose somewhat, but they were also redistributed among countries and some countries lost large amounts of gold. The redistribution occurred as the natural consequence under the gold standard of international flows of funds, which in the turbulent conditions of 1931 were dominated by financial flows rather than current account flows. As Table 10.1 shows, there were large inflows of gold into France, Switzerland and the Netherlands, and outflows from Germany, Japan, the USA, Argentina and the UK.[17]

The central banks of Belgium, the Netherlands, Switzerland and above all France experienced heavy inflows of gold during 1931. In Belgium, this seems to have reflected mainly sales of foreign exchange reserves for gold; the net change in foreign exchange and gold reserves was only $28 million. The inflows into France, the Netherlands and Switzerland totalled $771 million (increase in gold reserves net of reduction in foreign exchange reserves).

There were heavy outflows of gold and foreign exchange from Germany, Austria and Hungary, where there were banking crises. The UK also experienced very heavy outflows from July onwards, and abandoned the gold standard in September to escape the risk of a banking crisis, according to James's plausible interpretation, as well as to avoid raising interest rates and thereby worsening the depression.[18] The scale of these countries' financial problems was larger than the

---

[16] Source: Board of Governors of the Federal Reserve System (1976), table 168. The figure of £586 million includes cash reserves, money at call and short notice, and bills discounted. Of course, individual banks, notably some of the accepting houses, had liquidity problems, even though the banking system as a whole had plenty of liquidity.

[17] The data in Table 10.1 are from the League of Nations *Statistical Yearbook 1936–37*. They are not in all cases consistent with the data in section 2, which are mainly from national sources. We have not explained all the differences, but they are not large enough to affect our interpretation of the data.

[18] James (2001), pp. 70–74, argues that bank liquidity was an important influence on official decision-making in the UK. This seems plausible, even though, as already noted, the London clearing banks were not short of liquid assets.

Table 10.1 *Changes in gold and foreign exchange reserves in 1931 (US dollar millions)*

Country	Change in gold reserves (valued at 1931 parity)	Change in foreign exchange reserves	Total change in gold and foreign exchange reserves
Canada	−50	+4	−46
USA	−174[a]	0	−174
Argentina	−159	0	−159
India	+34	−5	+29
Japan	−178	0	−178
USSR	+79		+79
Germany	−293	−211	−504
Austria	−3	−93	−96
Hungary	−11	−8	−19
Belgium	+163	−135	+28
Spain	−37	+2	−35
France	+584	−184	+400
Netherlands	+186	−65	+121
UK	−132	0	−132
Switzerland	+315	−65	+250
Total (incl. other countries)	+340		

Note: Countries which experienced a change of $30 million or more in their gold reserves are included in the table, along with certain countries which experienced banking crises. [a] Includes holdings of US Treasury as well as Federal Reserve.
Source: League of Nations *Statistical Yearbook* 1936–37, available at www.library. northwestern.edu/govinfo/collections/league/.

figures in Table 10.1 suggest, because they all received official loans which partly offset their gold and foreign exchange losses. The United States also lost gold, as Table 10.1 shows, but this was entirely the result of official loans from the gold-rich United States to countries in distress, which increased by $306 million during 1931 (author's calculation).

International gold flows in 1931 were extremely large by the standards of the time: the sum of the absolute values of the changes in gold reserves of the 56 countries reported in the League of Nations *Statistical Yearbooks* was $2.6 billion that year, compared with $1.1 billion in 1929 and $1.4 billion in 1930. The scale of the flows reflected the banking crises in Europe and the well-founded fear that not all countries would be able to continue on the gold standard.

2. Flight to liquidity and safety

In 1931, the dominant concerns of international investors were liquidity and safety. This meant avoiding currencies which might leave the gold standard and be either devalued or subjected to standstill agreements, exchange controls or other administrative obstructions to scheduled payments, and avoiding exposures to commercial banks whose soundness was in doubt.[19] It is interesting to consider the counterparts to the flows of gold in the countries that were most affected by the crisis.

Table 10.2 provides such information in respect of the three main gold-losing countries, namely Germany, Austria and the United Kingdom. In Germany and Austria, the central bank's loss of gold and foreign exchange reserves was more than compensated by an increase in its domestic assets, largely if not entirely accounted for by emergency assistance provided to distressed domestic commercial banks. In the United Kingdom, the central bank's balance sheet (with the Issue and Banking Departments consolidated) contracted slightly during 1931 and the increase in domestic assets was slightly smaller than the fall in gold and foreign exchange.

Central bank liabilities (notes and deposits) increased moderately in Austria and the UK, but they fell sharply in Germany, where the banknote circulation fell by 7.8 per cent. It can safely be assumed that central banks supplied banknotes on demand, and that the fall in the note circulation was driven by demand, not supply. Real GDP in Germany fell by 7.6 per cent in 1931,[20] and retail prices fell by 8.5 per cent,[21] and it is plausible that the fall in incomes caused the fall in demand for banknotes. However, the frailty of the banking system might have been expected to stimulate the demand for banknotes. It was less than

---

[19] At that time commercial banks disclosed much less about their financial condition than they do these days, so that there was plenty of scope for such doubt.

[20] Source: Maddison (2010).

[21] Source: League of Nations *Statistical Yearbook* 1932–33, table 125.

Table 10.2 *Changes in central and commercial bank balance sheets in gold-losing countries in 1931 (US dollar millions, unless otherwise specified)*

| | Change in | | | | | | |
	Gold	Foreign exchange	Domestic assets	Note issue	Deposits in central bank	*Deposits in commercial banks*	*Commercial bank assets*
Germany	–293	–77	361	–88	–61	–1,242	–1,238
Austria	–3	–93	106	13	5	N/A	N/A
UK (GBP mn)	–27	–9	31	3	–1	–171	–183

Sources: Central bank data: Board of Governors of the Federal Reserve System (1976); Commercial bank data: Deutsche Bundesbank (1976), Sheppard (1971).

a decade since Germany had experienced hyperinflation, and it is also possible that the fall in demand for banknotes reflected at least partly a loss of confidence in the Reichsmark and in Germany's ability to remain on the gold standard.

All of the gold-receiving countries listed in Table 10.3 ran down their foreign exchange reserves in 1931, but in each case total reserves, of gold and foreign exchange, rose by a large amount. In each case also there were large increases in both the banknote issue and in deposits with the central bank. The percentage increases in the banknote issue in France, the Netherlands and Switzerland were 12.2, 21.4 and 51.5 respectively, far more than could be explained by changes in domestic economic conditions.[22] It seems highly likely that French, Dutch and Swiss banknotes were among the destinations of the flight to liquidity and safety. It is also quite possible that the same can be said of deposits in the three central banks. The Banque de France dominated the French banking scene in that era: its note circulation alone was much larger than the total of commercial bank deposits. It did a great deal of what would now be regarded as commercial banking business and

---

[22] For example, the retail price index of thirty-four products sold in Paris fell by 12.8 per cent during 1931 (source: *Bulletin de Statistique Generale*, accessible on NBER historical statistics website). Williams (1963), p. 101, says that a series of bank failures in France in 1930 stimulated the demand for banknotes, but data published by the League of Nations show that the note circulation rose by FRF 9.3 billion in 1931, whereas bank deposits fell by just FRF 1.5 billion.

Table 10.3 *Changes in central and commercial bank balance sheets in gold-receiving countries in 1931 (US dollar millions)*

		Change in					
	Gold	Foreign exchange	Domestic assets	Note issue	Deposits in central bank	Deposits in commercial banks	Commercial bank assets
France	599	–199	101	364	147	–61	53
Netherlands	184	–70	15	76	54	–228	–415
Switzerland	315	–48	–23	106	139	–60	–205

Sources: France: Federal Reserve Board *Banking and Monetary Statistics 1914–1941*; Netherlands: *Nederlandse financiële instellingen in de twintigste eeuw: Balansreeksen en naamlijst van handelsbanken*. De Nederlandsche Bank Statistische Cahiers Nr 3, 2000; Switzerland: Swiss National Bank www.snb.ch/en/iabout/stat/statpub/histz/id/statpub_histz_actual.

it seems highly likely that funds seeking a safe home were attracted into deposits there.[23]

3. Central bank reserve management

As already noted, there were extensive reductions in foreign exchange reserves in 1931 (see Table 10.1), and they continued in 1932. The Genoa Conference of 1922 had recommended economising on gold in order to enable the world monetary system to adapt to the higher price levels that followed the inflation of the Great War while retaining the essential features of the gold standard.[24] One technique was for foreign exchange reserves to be used to supplement gold as backing for national currencies. Foreign exchange reserves had the incidental attraction for the holder that, unlike gold reserves, they were interest-bearing. In addition, in many countries gold coins, which had circulated freely before being withdrawn at the outbreak of war in 1914, were not returned to general circulation, so that the available gold could be concentrated on central bank reserves, as an additional

[23] For a description of the Banque de France and its activities, see Mouré (1991), ch. 4.
[24] See Brown (1940), ch. 20, and Eichengreen (1992), pp. 157–162.

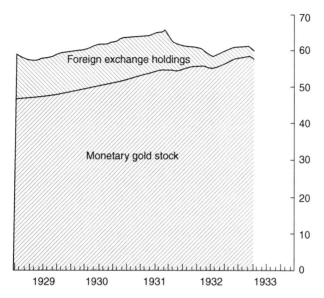

Figure 10.1 Gold stock and net holdings of foreign exchange (in European central banks, the Bank of Japan, Federal Reserve Banks and US Treasury, in billion Swiss francs).
Source: Bank for International Settlements (1933).

means of economising on gold. However, when it became clear that national currencies might depart from the gold standard, foreign exchange reserves were hastily liquidated, as is evident from Table 10.1 and Figure 10.1. By the end of 1932, foreign exchange holdings of central banks had fallen to 25 per cent of the amount before the outbreak of the crisis in spring 1931. The BIS explained that countries reduced their foreign exchange reserves by two main methods. First, the central banks of countries which had short-term international debts used foreign exchange reserves to meet foreign payments. The BIS estimates this use to have amounted to around CHF 2.5 billion. Second, central banks converted foreign exchange into gold. The BIS estimates that these conversions amounted to around CHF 5 billion (see Bank for International Settlements 1933).[25]

[25] In addition, the value in gold and gold-linked currencies (including the Swiss franc) of foreign exchange reserves held in sterling and other currencies that left the gold standard during the period will have fallen (by the end of 1932, sterling had depreciated by 32.5 per cent against its earlier gold parity).

Just as the addition of foreign exchange to gold as a medium for the holding of national reserves had enabled a larger amount of credit and bank deposits to be extended on the foundation of a limited global supply of gold during the 1920s, so the conversion of foreign exchange reserves back into gold caused a contraction in credit and bank deposits in the 1930s. Central banks themselves took part in the flight to liquidity and safety.

4. The scale of the liquidity crisis

This section attempts to measure the crisis of 1931 in the same way that Chapter 3 measured the recent crisis, by reference to changes in short-term international indebtedness, and in bank deposits. The warnings in Chapter 3 about the problems of measurement apply equally to the following analysis.

a. Short-term international credit

The scale of the withdrawal of short-term international credit during the Great Depression can be gauged by the data on short-term international indebtedness (gross liabilities) of the United States and European countries shown in Table 10.4, which decreased from CHF 70 billion at the end of 1930 to CHF 45 billion a year later.

Conolly (1936) provides rough estimates of how the fall of CHF 25 billion in short-term international debts during 1931 came about. He estimates that a fall of CHF 3.5 billion was due to depreciation of currencies; that CHF 6.5 billion were liquidated from central bank foreign exchange reserves of gold and foreign exchange; CHF 5 billion via relief credits granted by central banks and others; and the remaining CHF 10 billion in other ways, including from foreign exchange reserves of commercial banks, by sales of securities, shifts in trade financing, and losses. Excluding the decrease of CHF 3.5 billion estimated by Conolly to have been due to depreciation of currencies, as a rough valuation adjustment for exchange rate changes, international

However, the foreign exchange holdings shown in Figure 10.1 may have been valued at their pre-1931 gold parity exchange rates rather than at current exchange rates.

Table 10.4 *Gross amount of short-term international indebtedness (gross liabilities) of the United States and European countries (Swiss franc billions)*

End of	Total (1)	Total excluding central bank holdings of foreign exchange (2)	External liabilities of Germany (3)	External liabilities of the UK (4)	External liabilities reported by banks in the United States (5)
1930	70	56	20	18	12
1931	45	38		7	7
1932	39	35		8	4
1933	32	28.5		9	1

Sources and notes: (1) Bank for International Settlements (1933). (2) and (3) Conolly (1936). (4) Williams (1963), and United Kingdom (1951). The UK data include banks' net external liabilities, and British government securities held by UK banks for overseas account. (5) Board of Governors of the Federal Reserve System (1976) table 161, 'Short-term foreign assets and liabilities reported by banks in the United States'. The reported external liabilities of the UK and the USA have been valued in Swiss francs using exchange rates derived from League of Nations *Statistical Yearbook* 1936–37. The data in columns (1)–(3) are mutually consistent, but not consistent with the data in columns (4) and (5), which are of later vintages and from different sources.

short-term indebtedness of the United States and European countries decreased by CHF 21.5 billion during 1931, a decrease of 30.7 per cent within a single year.

Conolly also roughly estimates the composition of short-term international indebtedness (Table 10.5). He estimates that short-term international indebtedness related to trade financing constituted only 31 per cent of the total at the end of 1930, and that it decreased by 32 per cent in Swiss franc value during 1931. He notes that the 'Other' category includes '… such classes of funds as those of Australian and Irish banks in London, which to a certain extent supplement the sterling reserves of the Commonwealth Bank and the Irish Currency Commission, but it also comprises the abnormal short-term lending of the post-war period …'. Excluding Conolly's estimates of central bank

Table 10.5 *Gross amount of short-term international indebtedness (gross liabilities) of the United States and European countries (Swiss franc billions)*

	End of 1930	End of 1931
Trade financing	22	15
Central bank holdings of foreign exchange	14	7
Foreign debt service	4	3
Other	30	20
Total	70	45

Notes: Foreign debt service estimated by Conolly (1936) roughly at three months' interest, using special table in League of Nations memoranda on balance of payments, with estimates made for missing data.
Source: Conolly (1936).

holdings of foreign exchange (see Table 10.4), short-term international indebtedness decreased from CHF 56 billion to CHF 38 billion during 1931, a decrease of 32 per cent.

As Table 10.4 shows, the fall in short-term international indebtedness had by no means finished at the end of 1931. Deleveraging in international short-term credit markets continued into 1933, and by the end of 1933 the amount had fallen by 54 per cent in Swiss franc value from the end of 1930.

In one important respect these figures understate the fall in short-term international indebtedness during the 1930s. As Section 1 explains, the resolution of the financial problems of commercial banks included 'standstill agreements' with creditors, under which creditors agreed not to demand immediate repayment. Thus in many cases, short-term debts became, in substance if not in form, longer-term debts and were no longer liquid.

b. Bank deposits

The League of Nations *Statistical Yearbooks*[26] include reports of bank deposits, country by country. Table 10.6 shows percentage changes in total commercial bank deposits calculated in national currencies.

---

[26] Available at www.library.northwestern.edu/govinfo/collections/league/stat.html.

Table 10.6 *Commercial bank deposits, 1930–35*

	Stock of deposits at end of 1929 (US$ million)	Percentage changes in:					
		1930	1931	1932	1933	1934	1935
USA	44,441	+0.5	−8.4	−22.8	−11.8	+15.3	+11.4
Canada	2,697	−7.8	−4.7	−5.2	−0.1	+5.3	+8.4
Argentina	3,765	+1.4	−11.1	+0.2	−1.6	−1.1	+0.6
Japan	4,592	−6.0	−5.6	−0.5	+7.3	+7.2	+5.6
India	746	+3.9	−7.1	+10.3	+1.6	+2.8	
UK	10,904	+3.1	−7.5	+12.8	−1.5	+1.4	+5.6
Austria	382	+18.3	−47.3[a]		−14.3	−5.3	+0.2
France	1,862	+4.3	−3.1	−2.4	−11.8	−5.6	−10.6
Germany	4,042	−7.3	−25.6	−11.5	−5.5	+6.7	
Hungary	334	+0.3	−16.1	−7.5	+1.1	−4.7	+4.6
Italy	2,223	−2.5	−12.1	−8.3	−2.5	−2.7	−8.4
Spain	1,340	+7.6	−18.0	+5.2	+2.9	−1.2	+8.7
Poland	155	+2.2	−30.3	−7.7	−6.4	+11.9	−2.6

Note: [a] Change in 1931 and 1932. Data for end 1931 are not available.
Sources: League of Nations, *Statistical Yearbook 1933–34*, table 106 (exchange rates at the end of 1929); *Statistical Yearbook 1936–37*, table 129 (commercial bank deposits in national currencies).

Countries are included in Table 10.6 if they meet either of the following criteria:

• Their estimated real GDP in 1931, as measured in 1990 international Geary-Khamis dollars[27] by Angus Maddison for the Groningen Growth and Development Centre,[28] was among the eleven largest in the world, excluding China, the USSR and Indonesia, for which no bank deposit data are available. Those eleven countries accounted for 78.5 per cent of the aggregate GDP in 1931 of countries other than China, the USSR and Indonesia for which estimated GDP data are available.
• They experienced a serious banking crisis (Austria, Hungary).

[27] For an explanation of the Geary-Khamis method of aggregation, see http://unstats.un.org/unsd/methods/icp/ipc7_htm.htm.
[28] See www.ggdc.net/maddison/.

We have not attempted to construct any global aggregate of bank deposits. Total commercial bank deposits fell in every country included in Table 10.6 in 1931, and, not surprisingly, they fell by very large percentages in Germany, Hungary and (over 1931 and 1932) Austria, where there were very serious problems of bank solvency in 1931.

11 | *The management of the 1931 crisis*

This chapter explains how the gold standard was supposed to work in theory and how it actually worked in 1931, and describes the policy actions that were taken in 1931 to manage the crisis.

1. The gold standard in theory

The theory of the functioning of the gold standard that was widely accepted while the gold standard was in general operation was the so-called price-specie flow mechanism attributed to David Hume and developed by others.[1] According to the theory, adjustment to equilibrium would be automatic. Suppose that an initial equilibrium was disturbed by an exogenous surge in the supply of credit in country A. The credit expansion would lead to an expansion of domestic demand and a rise in the general price level in country A relative to other countries. Because of the expansion of domestic demand and because its costs of production would become relatively high by international standards, country A would develop an external trade deficit and would experience an outflow of gold to other countries as a result. The outflow of gold would lead to a contraction of money supply and credit in country A, which would lead to a contraction of domestic demand and a reversal of the initial rise in prices.

This trade balance mechanism could be augmented by capital flows. The initial expansion in the supply of credit in country A would be accompanied by a fall in interest rates in that country, at least to some borrowers, because interest rates would need to fall in order to stimulate the demand for credit to expand sufficiently to meet the additional supply. If so, interest rates would fall in country A relative to other

---

[1] Meade (1951), chs XIV and XV, provides a detailed account of the theory of the working of the gold standard. Eichengreen (1992), pp. 32–42, describes how the classical gold standard was perceived after the First World War.

countries, and capital would flow abroad, entailing an outflow of gold additional to that caused by the trade deficit. The outflow of gold would constrain the availability of credit in country A and interest rates would rise again (reversing the earlier fall) so as to ration the reduced amount of available credit. And the central bank of country A, as it lost gold, could take action by increasing its discount rate, and tightening money market conditions by selling assets, so as to accelerate the natural increase in market interest rates that the outflow of gold would cause. The 'rules of the game' included raising discount rates when gold was flowing out, and lowering them when gold was flowing in. By following the rules, central banks could reinforce the automatic functioning of the gold standard.[2]

It is now widely accepted that this account of the working of the gold standard was only loosely related to reality.[3] It is true that there were periodic banking crises in gold standard countries, sometimes caused by over-exuberant credit expansion. However, rather than leaving the price-specie flow mechanism to do its corrective work undisturbed, the local central banks typically acted as 'lender of last resort' by providing emergency liquidity assistance as required, in order to offset the outflow of gold from the banks and thereby contain the consequences of the banking crisis for the 'real economy'. There was a discretionary limit to the scope of the automatic working of the gold standard.

Of course, by providing liquidity in this way, the central banks ran the risk of violating their legal obligation under the gold standard to maintain gold backing for their liabilities. In practice, the potential conflict was made less likely to occur by an increase in the central bank discount rate,[4] consistent with the 'rules of the game'. However,

---

[2] The theory of the gold standard also drew a distinction between an external drain of gold from the central bank, caused by an adverse trade balance, which could only be cured by an adjustment of domestic demand relative to output, and an internal drain, which might be caused by rising demand for gold coins for transactions purposes as the domestic economy grew. It was thought that such an internal drain could be cured more easily, e.g. by the issue of additional paper money. See Hawtrey (1947), pp. 55–59. This aspect of the theory did not, however, discuss the consequences of a loss of confidence in the sustainability of the gold standard such as occurred in 1931.

[3] See Eichengreen (1992), ch. 2.

[4] Consistent with Bagehot's prescription that, in a crisis, a central bank should lend freely, against good security, and at a high rate of interest. See Bagehot (1892), pp. 199–200.

the residual risk, when it was significant, was removed by bending or breaking the rules in one or other of two ways:

- International borrowing to supplement temporarily the central bank's gold reserves and thereby decrease the likelihood of a conflict. Thus after its reserves had been depleted by its provision of liquidity during the Baring Crisis in 1890, the Bank of England borrowed gold from the Banque de France, and sold Exchequer bonds in Russia.[5]
- An assurance from the government that the central bank would be temporarily relieved of its gold standard obligation by law if necessary. This technique was used in the UK in 1847, 1857 and 1866.[6]

In both cases the resolution was temporary only; foreign loans had to be repaid, and if the central bank was relieved of its obligation to redeem banknotes and deposits in gold for a period, the obligation had to be re-assumed at some future date.

2. The gold standard in 1931

These devices were effective in the nineteenth century, but not in 1931. Their effectiveness depended on the belief that the crisis was temporary, so that interest rate differentials would have a reliable influence on private international capital flows, any international loans would be repaid in full and on time, and any suspension of the gold standard would be purely temporary. Obviously, emergency international lending was possible only if there were no overriding political obstacles.

Those conditions were not met in 1931. If a central bank's gold holdings were close to the legally prescribed minimum, then it could not lend to commercial banks with liquidity problems (or indeed to anyone else) without breaking the rules. In the prevailing circumstances, with large commercial banks failing in several countries where gold reserves were only modest, a suspension of the rules could not have been credibly represented as temporary. This made it impossible for many central banks to provide liquidity to domestic commercial banks while remaining on the gold standard.

---

[5] See Clapham (1966), p. 330.
[6] See Clapham (1966), pp. 208–209, 232, 266.

Table **11.1** *Central bank discount rates, 1930–31 (in per cent)*

	End-December 1930	End-July 1931
USA (New York)	2	1.5
France	2.5	2
Netherlands	3	2
Switzerland	2.5	2
Average of four gold-rich countries	2.5	1.9
UK	3	4.5
Austria	5	10
Germany	5	10
Hungary	5.5	7
Average of four gold-poor countries	4.6	8.4

Source: League of Nations *Statistical Yearbook* 1930–31 table 114 and 1931–32 table 129.

Because of this conflict, the credibility of the gold standard was undermined in many countries and central bank discount rates ceased to be effective in influencing international capital flows. Table 11.1 shows central bank discount rates as at the end of December 1930 and the end of July 1931. The average interest rate differential between four gold-rich and four gold-poor countries widened by 4.4 percentage points during the first seven months of 1931, but this widening did not succeed in averting the crisis by directing flows of gold to where they were most needed. No plausible interest rate levels could have attracted money into currencies which might go off gold, or repelled it from safe havens.

Official international liquidity provision was subject to the same gold constraint as the provision of liquidity to domestic banking systems, and it was hampered in addition by political obstacles. Austria was the first country to experience a banking crisis in 1931, with the collapse of Creditanstalt, which was the country's largest commercial bank.[7] After some delay, an international loan was extended to Austria

---

[7] For an impression of the importance of Creditanstalt to the Austrian economy, see Mosser and Teichova (1991). Gil Aguado (2001) provides evidence that the Austrian National Bank had known of Creditanstalt's difficulties for a long time and had been providing covert financial support since 1929. He

to finance liquidity support to the banking system, but it was insufficient. A second loan might have prevented further contagion, though it is also possible that Austria's financial situation was so bad that liquidity support alone would not have helped. However, as Toniolo (2005) reports, the negotiations were difficult and protracted, and the second loan was not made. Political differences between France and Austria were a major obstacle, with France demanding that Austria abandon a proposed customs union with Germany as a condition of the loan, on the grounds that the union would violate the Treaty of St Germain. France was gold-rich and her participation in the loan was very important. Other countries were reluctant to lend large amounts because they were concerned about their own financial position. And the United States, which had $4.2 billion of gold reserves at the end of 1930, or 38 per cent of the world total, provided only $356 million in official international loans during 1931.[8]

According to BIS estimates, emergency help granted during 1931 to debtor countries by central banks, the BIS, principal capital centres and by Treasuries amounted to around CHF 5 billion[9] (see Bank for International Settlements 1932), which was roughly 7 per cent of the total amount of international short-term indebtedness of the United States and European countries at the end of 1930 (see Table 10.4). The gold standard always represented a potential obstacle to liquidity provision, in both the domestic and international operations of central banks. In 1931 it represented an insuperable obstacle.

It is possible to measure the amount of liquidity that central banks supplied to their domestic economies in 1931, whether by purchases of gold, purchases of other assets, or lending. The available data are stocks of gold held by central banks at the end of each year, stocks of foreign exchange held by central banks at the end of each year,[10] and the total of discounts, loans and advances, and holdings of government securities ('domestic paper assets') held at the end of 1930

also suggests that France was involved in precipitating outflows of funds from Austria after the collapse of Creditanstalt.

[8] Author's calculation, based on Toniolo (2005) table 4.1 (loans organised through or with the participation of the BIS) and Sayers (1976) appendix 22 (loans to the UK).

[9] See Bank for International Settlements (1932). We do not know how the BIS calculated this amount.

[10] The Bank of Spain also held silver reserves. We have added them to foreign exchange.

and the end of 1931.[11] It is assumed that the amount of liquidity supplied by each central bank is equal to the change in gold and foreign exchange holdings, less any revaluation effects,[12] plus the change in the total of domestic paper assets.[13] These estimates are comparable with the estimates shown in Chapter 5 of the amount of liquidity that central banks provided in the recent crisis.

The amount of liquidity supplied by each central bank is measured in units of its domestic currency. As in Chapter 5, three different methods have been used to compare and aggregate the amounts supplied by central banks:

a. By expressing the amount of liquidity supplied by each central bank during 1931 as a percentage of the domestic currency value of that central bank's gold, foreign exchange and domestic paper assets as at the end of 1930. An aggregate indicator of central bank liquidity provision can then be constructed by calculating a weighted average of these percentages, the weights being the dollar value of each central bank's gold and paper assets as at the end of 1930.

b. By expressing the amount of liquidity supplied by each central bank during 1931 as a percentage of the domestic currency value of commercial bank deposits in its territory as at the end of 1930.[14] A second aggregate indicator of central bank liquidity provision can then be constructed by calculating a weighted average of these percentages, the weights being the dollar value of each country's commercial bank deposits as at the end of 1930.

c. By expressing the amount of liquidity supplied by each central bank during 1931 as a percentage of its country's nominal GDP in 1931. A third aggregate indicator of central bank liquidity provision could in principle then be constructed by calculating a

[11] The data were published in the League of Nations *Statistical Yearbook*, various issues.

[12] In other words, net purchases of gold, valued in domestic currency, can be measured as the difference between the domestic currency value of each central bank's gold holdings at the end of 1931 and 1930, minus the effect of any currency depreciation during 1931 on the domestic currency value of the end-1930 holding. Foreign exchange holdings will also have been subject to revaluation effects, but we cannot measure them because we do not know the currency composition of foreign exchange holdings.

[13] This assumption is discussed further in the data appendix.

[14] Data on commercial bank deposits were also published by the League of Nations.

weighted average of these percentages, the weights being the dollar value of each country's GDP in 1931. However, estimates of nominal GDP in 1931 are available for only a few countries and a weighted average of those for which the data are available would not have any useful meaning.

The amounts of funds supplied by central banks, calculated according to the methods described in the previous paragraph, are shown in Table 11.2 below.

Chapter 10 described the experiences of the countries most heavily affected by the crisis. In Austria, Germany and Hungary, banking crises made it imperative for the central bank to commit large amounts of funds to bank rescues. In each case, there were substantial outflows of gold and foreign exchange from the central bank and the country imposed exchange controls to limit the outflow. The UK abandoned the gold standard and allowed the exchange rate to float. Even so, bank deposits fell in the UK in 1931, and the central bank's assets did not grow. For countries that remained on the gold standard, the restrictions it imposed were a serious obstacle to the pursuit of financial stability in a period of turmoil.

In countries, such as France, the Netherlands and Switzerland, which gained gold reserves during 1931, the rise in gold was partly offset by a fall in foreign exchange reserves. As Table 11.2 shows, their central banks' discounts, loans, advances and holdings of government securities changed little during the year. They did not sterilise the gold inflow, but they did not significantly expand their domestic assets, though they maintained their discount rates at levels well below those prevailing in the countries which were losing gold.

The result was that the global expansion of central bank assets was only moderate during 1931. As Table 11.2 shows, using the first method of measurement described above, additional average liquidity provision amounted to 3.8 per cent of the stock of identified central bank assets (gold, foreign exchange and domestic paper assets) as at the end of 1930. Using the second method, additional average liquidity provision amounted to 1.0 per cent of the stock of commercial bank deposits as at the end of 1930. However, as Table 10.6 shows, bank deposits fell by much more than that in many countries in 1931.

Economic historians have debated extensively why the gold standard malfunctioned during the 1930s. Some cite a global supply of gold

Table 11.2 *Changes in central bank assets, 1931*[a]

Country	As % of central bank gold, foreign exchange and paper assets at end-1930			Total change in gold, foreign exchange and paper assets as % of			Status
	Gold[b]	Foreign exchange	Domestic paper assets	Gold, foreign exchange and domestic paper assets of central bank at end-1930	Commercial bank deposits at end-1930	GDP in 1931	
Canada[c]	-2.9	0	-1.1	-4.0	-3.4	-1.8	Off gold 19/10/1931
USA	-3.1	0	-8.1	+4.9	+0.6	+0.4	
Japan	-22.1	0	+15.7	-6.4	-1.4	-0.9	Off gold 13/12/1931
Germany	-21.5	-15.5	+32.3	-4.8	-3.0	-0.5	Exchange control 15/07/1931
Austria	-2.0	-52.3	+61.7	+7.4	+2.9		Exchange control 09/10/1931
France	+15.1	-4.7	+1.5	+11.9	+23.9	+3.2	
Hungary	-10.5	-7.4	+22.8	+4.9	+1.5		Exchange control 17/07/1931
Italy	+2.6	-12.1	+5.3	-4.1	-1.8	-0.6	
UK	-7.2	0	+3.0	-4.2	-1.0	-0.5	Off gold 21/09/1931
Brazil	-8.4	-4.4	+17.7	+4.9	+1.8		Devalued in 1929; exchange control 18/05/1931

Chile	+6.9	−31.3	+17.7	−6.8	−3.1		Exchange control 30/07/1931
India	+8.0	−12.4	−4.1	−8.5	−6.7		Off gold 21/09/1931
Denmark	−8.7	−19.5	+12.8	−15.5	−3.2		Exchange control 18/09/1931; off gold 29/09/1931
Spain	−4.7	+0.1	+14.4	+9.9	+12.5		Devalued in 1920; exchange control 18/05/1931
Netherlands	+55.6	−19.3	−0.5	+35.8	+20.3	+5.2	
Poland	+2.0	−11.1	+3.5	−5.6	−7.2		
Switzerland	+120.4	−25.0	−2.7	+92.7	+8.4		
Weighted average				+3.8	+1.0		

Notes: [a] For each country, the table shows, in the first column, the change in the domestic currency value of the central bank's gold reserves, in the second column, the change in its paper assets, in the third column, the change in the sum of the first two columns. In each case, the changes are shown as a percentage of total gold reserves and paper assets as at end-1930. [b] In countries whose currencies depreciated in 1931, the change in gold holdings has been adjusted so as to exclude the increase in the domestic currency value of the stock of gold held at the end of 1930. [c] The data for Canada relate to chartered banks.

Sources: Exchange rates and gold holdings: League of Nations *Statistical Yearbook* 1936–37, tables 119 and 123. Paper assets: League of Nations *Statistical Yearbook* 1931–32 table 125. Available at www.library.northwestern.edu/govinfo/collections/league/. See data appendix for further information about the derivation of the data.

which was insufficient to support economic activity after the inflation of the First World War. Thus Wood (2009) claims that the deflation of 1929–33 was inevitable because the supply of gold had not kept pace with the rise in prices. Eichengreen (2008, p. 62) points out that 'the ratio of central bank gold reserves to notes and sight (or demand) deposits dropped from 48 percent in 1913 to 40 percent in 1927'. As noted in Chapter 10, a shortage of monetary gold had been foreseen, and measures were taken in the 1920s to economise on gold so as to try to mitigate its effects, but some of the measures, such as the withdrawal of gold coins from public circulation and the use of foreign exchange as an auxiliary reserve asset, were not sufficient or did not succeed.

Some economic historians also blame the distribution of gold among central banks and the behaviour of the gold-rich countries.[15] France had 19% of world gold reserves at the end of 1930, and the United States had 38%.[16] They point out in particular that the Banque de France did not recycle the very large amount of gold that it had acquired after France had returned to the gold standard in 1926 at a depreciated parity, either by substantial expansion of its domestic assets or by international lending. Irwin (2010), in a paper entitled 'Did France cause the Great Depression?', goes as far as to conclude that the answer is 'yes', though he attaches some blame to the United States as well. He calculates that over the period 1929–32, France and the United States could have released 13.7% and 11.7%, respectively, of the world's gold stock, and still have maintained their banknote cover ratios at their 1928 levels. On our calculations, 25.4% (equal to 13.7% plus 11.7%) of the stock of monetary gold as at the end of 1928 was \$2,534 million, or 12.3% of total central bank gold, foreign exchange and domestic paper assets as at the end of 1930, so that Irwin's arithmetic implies that central banks could have provided roughly four times as much support in 1931 as they actually did, had France and the United States behaved differently. However, Bernanke and James (1991) and Eichengreen (1992) say that the Banque de France lacked the legal power to engage in expansionary open-market

---

[15] See Bordo and Eichengreen (2001). Wood (2009) dismisses this explanation, however.

[16] Source: League of Nations *Statistical Yearbook* 1936–37 table 123, author's calculations.

operations, as a result of a law adopted in 1928. Mouré (1991, p. 143) has his doubts about this point. He comments that: 'The 1928 reform had given the Bank, at its request, two means to effect open market operations. The statutes were an obstacle when the Bank wished them to be.'

Moreover, as already noted, France refused for political reasons to participate in a proposed second international loan to Austria; political tension between France on one side and Austria and Germany on the other obstructed the functioning of the international monetary system. The data in Table 11.2 suggest that, like France, the Netherlands and Switzerland did not recycle the gold that they accumulated in 1931.

The United States, too, has been widely criticised for pursuing too restrictive a monetary policy. For example, Bordo, Choudhri and Schwartz (2002) claim that the Federal Reserve could have pursued a more expansionary policy between October 1930 and February 1931, and between September 1931 and January 1932, without endangering the dollar's convertibility into gold. Their argument is based on a monetarist model which allows for expansion of the Federal Reserve balance sheet to affect international gold flows; it does not distinguish between the various ways in which the Federal Reserve balance sheet might be expanded. Warburton (1952) makes a different point, namely that the Fed aggravated the depression by its choice of assets, specifically by rejecting risky assets. He says (p. 535): 'In the early 1930s the Federal Reserve Banks virtually stopped rediscounting or otherwise acquiring "eligible" paper. This was not due to lack of eligible paper … It was due directly to a combination of lines of action which must have been deliberately pursued by the Federal Reserve authorities, for they could not have been adopted in any other way.' Warburton's point is echoed by Stella (2009, appendix I), who notes that the Federal Reserve took 'almost no risk on to the balance sheet' during the Great Depression. But Ahamed (2009) states that prime commercial bills used to finance trade, which were eligible for backing 60 per cent of the currency, were scarce in 1931 as trade stagnated, so that the Federal Reserve had to rely on gold to back its currency beyond the 40 per cent share required to be backed by gold. Wells (2004, p. 53) similarly states that since commercial paper was scarce in 1931, the additional backing had to be in gold. There therefore seems to be no consensus on whether the reason why the Federal Reserve did not expand its balance sheet in 1931 by purchasing eligible commercial bills was its risk aversion, or the scarcity of such bills. In February 1932, US government securities also became eligible assets for backing currency, which allowed the Federal Reserve to inject more liquidity at a later stage in the crisis (Wells 2004; Ahamed 2009).

Kindleberger (1987, especially pp. 295–296) claims that the gold standard malfunctioned because no country was both willing and able to play a leadership role in the crisis. The United Kingdom had acted as a leader before the First World War but was no longer able to do so because its own financial position was weak. In the United States, which did have the power to act as a leader by lending freely to other countries, isolationist attitudes prevailed. Another way of expressing the same point would be to say that the United States took an excessively narrow view of its own interests and failed to perceive that the consequences of its failure to act would do enormous damage to those interests.

Whatever the merits of the criticisms that France and the United States hoarded gold during the later 1920s and the year 1930, international flows of funds in the year 1931 were highly volatile, and the risk that they would be reversed in short order was high. It would surely have been imprudent for any central bank receiving such 'hot money' inflows to place the funds in anything but highly liquid assets, if it was committed to the gold standard. Irwin (2010) is particularly critical of the Banque de France's actions in 1931 and 1932, but in view of the volatility of capital flows in those years, this aspect of his criticism seems overstated.

In one specific way, the fragmentation of the gold standard itself paradoxically damaged the prospects for international lending. The newly established BIS refused applications for credit by central banks following sterling's departure from gold, partly since the BIS's own working resources had diminished owing to the collapse of sterling, the Hoover moratorium, and the withdrawals of deposits by central banks (see Bank for International Settlements 1932). Central banks' balances at the BIS fell from CHF 870 million on 31 August 1931 to CHF 464 million on 31 December 1931. Moreover, according to Article 21 of the BIS's statutes, the BIS could no longer use currencies which had left the gold standard. Consequently, the departure of sterling and Scandinavian currencies from the gold standard diminished the BIS's usable resources.

The reactions of central banks to the banking crisis were modest, and, in the light of the results, manifestly inadequate. In many cases, the constraints of the gold standard inhibited adequate easing of monetary policy. And the volatility of international flows of funds in 1931 itself represented an additional unfortunate influence in favour of caution in monetary policy.

12 | A comparison of 1931 and 2008

This chapter compares the crises of 1931 and 2008, by reference to both the nature and scale of the crises, and their propagation and management, and discusses the similarities and differences.

1. Nature and scale of the crises

a. Economic fundamentals

Earlier chapters have made no attempt to explore or compare the fundamental causes of the two banking crises. It is entirely plausible that the fundamental disequilibria present in 1931 were so great that no amount of liquidity provision by central banks could on its own have prevented a crisis. At that time, the international financial scene was still dominated by unsettled issues related to war reparations. Moreover the successor states of the Austro-Hungarian empire, notably Austria itself, had not fully adjusted their new situations.[1] Germany had run up large foreign debts in the latter 1920s and 1930. Nevertheless, there has for many years been a consensus that the Great Depression was not inevitable, and that more expansionary macroeconomic policies, whether fiscal or monetary, could have prevented it, or at least contained it and turned it into a much less serious recession. More generous liquidity provision by central banks would certainly have been an essential part of such a policy programme, and its absence in 1931 was therefore a matter of great importance.

Likewise, it is possible that the debt burdens built up in the years before the recent crisis by governments, companies and individuals were so great that a serious setback to economic growth could not be avoided. At the time of writing, early in 2012, it is too soon to say whether the policy measures that have been taken during the recent

[1] See Brown (1940), pp. 923–926.

crisis will prove to have been effective in enabling the world economy to return to growth rates comparable with those that prevailed before the crisis. Nevertheless, large-scale liquidity provision by central banks has been a necessary component of the policy programmes pursued to support economic activity after the recent financial crisis.

b. The scale of the liquidity problem

The measurements in Chapters 3 and 10 show clearly that the contraction of international lending and of bank deposits was considerably smaller in 2008–09 than in 1931. This does not however imply that the initial disturbance was smaller. It is possible that the initial disturbance was as large or even larger, but that the policy reaction was so much more effective that the eventual financial contraction was smaller, and that the real-economy effects of the initial disturbance were better contained.

c. Existence of deposit insurance and guarantees

Deposit insurance schemes were widespread in 2008, whereas they did not exist in 1931.[2] And several governments, e.g. in the European Union, Switzerland, Australia and New Zealand, extended the coverage of their deposit insurance during 2008, in some cases by providing complete deposit guarantees.[3] Deposit insurance was surely crucial in limiting the outflow of deposits from commercial banks and thereby containing the effects of the 2008 crisis.[4] In addition, in many countries, subordinated debt issued by banks was effectively (and controversially) protected during the recent crisis.

However, guarantees are only as good as the guarantor. Deposit guarantees issued by governments lose credibility if the financial strength of the governments is in doubt, as happened in Greece and

---

[2] Federal deposit insurance was introduced in the United States in 1933, ostensibly in order to prevent bank runs and deposit flight in future. See Calomiris (2010) for a different interpretation of federal deposit insurance.

[3] For details see, for example, Reserve Bank of Australia (2009), pp. 43–46.

[4] Tallman and Wicker (2010), writing about the United States, suggest that the analogy between the recent crisis and the Great Depression is flawed because there were no widespread depositor withdrawals in the recent crisis. We, like they, think that deposit insurance explains the relative stability of bank deposits, but we do not think that the analogy is meaningless.

Ireland during the recent crisis. In that case, guarantees cannot prevent deposit flight.

d. Size and distribution of reserves

Total gold and foreign exchange reserves at the end of 1931 were $13.4 billion, or roughly 100 per cent of total short-term international indebtedness, according to the BIS estimate. At the end of 2007 they were $6,716 billion, or about 22 per cent of total short-term international indebtedness, as estimated in Table 3.4. Therefore reserve stocks in 1931 were much larger in relation to international indebtedness than in 2008.

Even if reserve stocks in 1931 appeared substantial according to this criterion, they were in the wrong place. The countries that most needed reserves, such as Austria, Germany and the UK, did not have enough; while those that had plenty, such as France, the Netherlands, Switzerland and the United States, had more than they needed.

In 2008, official reserves were much smaller relative to short-term international indebtedness than in 1931. And, as in 1931, they were concentrated in the places where they were least needed. For example, China alone accounted for over a quarter of the world's official reserves, but China was little affected by the crisis. And some of the international banking centres which, in the event, needed international liquidity most, had only small reserves of their own. For example, the UK's foreign exchange reserves were only $46.2 billion at the end of August 2008.

The provision of swap facilities by the Federal Reserve in particular rendered reserve adequacy wholly irrelevant for countries receiving these swap lines. Countries which had swap lines were able to provide the necessary foreign currency liquidity to their banks by drawing on the swap facilities and in most cases left their own reserves entirely untouched.

e. Reserve management

In both banking crises, 1931 and 2008, central bank reserve management acted pro-cyclically, adding to the supply of credit during the boom and subtracting from it during the downturn (see Chapters 5 and 10). There had been some coordination of reserve management during the 1920s, when foreign exchange reserves were being built up, but it did not last.

2. Propagation and management of the crises

Because more data were collected in 2008 than in 1931, it is possible to trace more of the ways in which the more recent crisis was propagated. Nevertheless, it is possible to identify some common features, the most important being the flight to liquidity and safety, which was a leading characteristic of both crises. In both crises, there was a sudden wave of suspicion about the safety of assets which had hitherto been regarded as secure, and institutions which were thought to be over-exposed to such newly doubtful assets were subject to the risk of liquidity crises if they had short-maturity liabilities fixed in money value. In both crises, deposit outflows were not the only important sources of liquidity pressure on banks: in 1931, the central European acceptances of the London merchant banks were a serious problem, as, in 2008, were the liquidity commitments that commercial banks had provided to shadow banks. And in both crises, the managers of central banks' international reserves participated in the flight to liquidity and safety in the same way as other market participants.

In both crises, the behaviour of creditors towards debtors, and vice versa, and the valuation of assets by creditors, were all very important. For example, the decision of the creditors of the central European countries who were affected by the 1931 crisis to reach standstill agreements, rather than declaring loans in default, meant that higher valuations could be placed on the debts. This made a difference to the immediate outlook for financial and economic stability in both central Europe and in the creditor countries, since defaults would probably have precipitated bank failures in the latter. It gave the creditors, including some London accepting houses, time to find new capital while remaining in business. Arguably, in this episode, non-transparency in accounting helped to protect financial stability.

In 2008, the environment was very different. Gorton (2010, ch. 3) argues that wholesale financial markets dried up because it was very difficult for holders of mortgage-backed securities to know how far they were exposed to sub-prime mortgage risk, and impossible for wholesale financial market participants to know how far their trading counterparties were exposed to it. In the absence of active markets, it was impossible to mark holdings of mortgage-backed securities to market for valuation purposes, and holders were driven to value them by reference to proprietary models, which, even though approved by regulators, did not carry conviction in the market. Audited accounts showing positive net worth did not provide reassurance as to solvency. In 2008, non-transparency was seriously damaging to financial stability.

Shin (2010, ch. 1) addresses accounting issues from the viewpoint of theory. He notes that prices have a dual role, as a reflection of the underlying economic fundamentals, and as an imperative to action, and that the actions which prices cause can themselves distort those same prices, undermining their role in allocating resources. Against this background, he discusses the importance of valuation practices for financial stability and considers the merits of marking to market, and comments as follows:

The double-edged nature of market prices raises important issues for accounting, especially on the role of mark-to-market accounting rules. Some proponents of marking to market like to pose the issues in black and white terms, asking rhetorically, 'Do you want the truth, or do you want a lie?'

The unstated assumption behind this rhetorical question is that accounting is just a measurement issue, leaving what is measured completely undisturbed. The assumption is that accounting is just a veil that merely obscures the true economic fundamentals, and that the role of accounting is to shine a bright light into the dark corners of a firm's accounts to illuminate the true state of that firm. In the context of completely frictionless markets, where decision making is done without distorting constraints or inefficient spillover effects, such a world view would be entirely justified.

On the other hand, in such a perfect world, accounting would be irrelevant since reliable market prices would be readily available to all, and it would simply be a matter of reading off the available prices. Just as accounting is irrelevant in such a world, so would any talk of establishing and enforcing accounting standards.

To state the proposition the other way round, accounting is relevant only because we live in an imperfect world, where actions may reflect distorted incentives or self-defeating constraints as well as the hypothetical economic fundamentals. In such an imperfect world, transaction prices may not always be readily available. Even those prices that are available may not correspond to the hypothetical fundamental prices that would prevail in frictionless perfect markets. Therefore, when we debate issues regarding accounting, it is important to be clear on the nature and consequences of the imperfections.[5]

There was a very important difference between the crises of 1931 and 2008, in the range and nature of assets that were regarded as 'safe havens' – i.e. which were regarded as liquid and safe. Central banks provided much more liquidity in 2008 than they had done in 1931 (see below), since they were not inhibited by the constraints of the gold standard, as they had been in 1931. The gold standard set a benchmark for liquidity and safety that could be met only by assets of a certain kind, namely gold itself, or assets which could be confidently expected to be convertible into gold at the parity rate. Commercial banks had experienced financial stress in many countries, there was no deposit insurance, and commercial bank liabilities were in many cases not regarded as safe. Budget deficits were regarded as incompatible with continued adherence to the gold standard. When doubts arose about particular classes of assets, such as claims on commercial banks, there was a scramble for assets in the elite group. The group included the liabilities (notes and deposits) of central banks which were regarded as being securely attached to the gold standard, but those central banks felt unable to expand their balance sheets much, partly for fear of undermining their ability to remain on the gold standard. They could not implement Bagehot's remedy for a banking crisis, of lending freely against good collateral at a high interest rate.[6] As a result, monetary policy was very tight in gold standard countries, despite the depression, and countries abandoned the gold standard when its effects became intolerable, notably the United Kingdom in 1931 and the United States in 1933. As countries left the gold standard and their currencies depreciated, the pressures on those that remained increased. In fact, no country was still on the gold standard after 1936. The supply of liquid and safe assets was not only inelastic, but it also contracted over time, and the gold standard, being therefore incompatible with satisfactory management of the crisis, collapsed.

---

[5] Shin (2010), pp. 11–12.
[6] See Bagehot (1892), pp. 198–201. Bagehot's prescription dates from the gold standard era, but its application was likely to require temporary suspension of the gold standard.

In 2008, a much larger set of assets was regarded as liquid and safe, even though the relative prices of assets within the group could change. The set included deposits in a wide range of central banks, including those of the countries with the largest banking systems, and a wide range of government securities. Market participants were much more tolerant of budget deficits than they had been in the 1930s. Most governments accepted contingent liability for the safety of at least some bank deposits, and some of them expanded deposit insurance even though the recession induced by the financial crisis had weakened their current budget balances. Crucially, it was possible to implement Bagehot's remedy and to expand the supply of liquid and safe assets massively without undermining their credibility among market participants. Thus central banks were able in effect to take on the function of money market intermediaries, as wholesale deposits migrated onto their balance sheets, and as they on-lent the funds to relieve shortages elsewhere in the market. Large budget deficits (which would have been anathema in 1931) emerged as automatic fiscal stabilisers came into operation and as some countries additionally undertook discretionary fiscal easing; moreover the contingent liabilities arising from deposit insurance became more threatening. Nevertheless there was no serious loss of confidence in the safety of most governments' debts.

Some governments' liabilities were not considered as safe, however, and yield differences between the securities issued by different governments widened. At the extreme, the government of Iceland was forced to impose exchange controls in 2008, while the governments of Greece and Ireland sought emergency support from international financial institutions in 2010. Commercial banks whose headquarters were in Iceland and Ireland were suspected of having negative net worth of such a size as to threaten the sustainability of their governments' finances, on the assumption that the governments would guarantee the deposits and perhaps some other liabilities of the banks. This undermined the credit standing of the governments of Iceland and Ireland. Other governments, such as those of France, Italy, Spain, Portugal and the United Kingdom, tightened fiscal policy out of anxiety that their credit standing would otherwise deteriorate.

Another important difference between 1931 and 2008 was the practice of liability management, which developed in the 1970s, in which commercial banks determined the size of their balance sheets by reference to their desired asset levels, making good any shortfall in funding by borrowing in wholesale deposit markets, generally from other banks.[7] Wholesale deposits, especially inter-bank deposits, are likely to be volatile in a generalised liquidity crisis, and in this respect the financial markets of 2008 were perhaps less stable than those of 1931, when inter-bank deposits were few.

In 1931, the constraints imposed by the gold standard bore on international liquidity provision just as they did on liquidity provision to domestic borrowers. International initiatives to provide assistance to the countries worst affected by the crisis were unsuccessful. For example, the international loan to Austria arranged in 1931 was disappointing both as regards its size, which was plainly insufficient to Austria's needs, and because it took too long to arrange. Moreover a second loan, which might have helped to stabilise the situation, proved impossible to agree.[8] One of the main difficulties was that the prospective lenders, such as the United Kingdom, were concerned that large-scale lending to Austria would weaken their own defences against the financial crisis.[9]

By contrast, in the recent crisis, there was no comparable constraint on liquidity creation by central banks. This was evident in both the speed and the scale of liquidity provision. In most countries, the required funds were provided quickly, so that they contained the crisis in its early stages and provided reassurance that the authorities had no doubts about providing liquidity. Swap lines ensured that liquidity was distributed internationally, roughly according to need.[10]

---

[7] See for example Battilossi (2009).

[8] See Toniolo (2005), pp. 90–96.

[9] Was it the gold standard, or just the institution of fixed exchange rates, that created the constraint on liquidity provision? The question as put is under-specified, because the non-gold standard fixed exchange rate system of 1931 whose hypothetical existence the question assumes would have needed some means whereby monetary policies were coordinated. If it had been possible to secure a coordinated easing of monetary policies, then a fixed exchange rate system might have survived, but not otherwise.

[10] There are grounds for thinking that specifically international liquidity was provided less amply in 2008–09 than in 1931. As noted in Chapter 10, the BIS estimated in 1932 that total emergency help granted during 1931 to debtor countries by central banks, the BIS, principal capital centres and by Treasuries amounted to around CHF 5 billion, or about 7 per cent of total short-term international indebtedness as calculated by the BIS. We do not know how this figure was calculated and what 'emergency help' was included; nor do we know exactly how 'international short-term indebtedness' was defined.

Table 12.1 *Central bank liquidity provision in the two crises*

	As % of central bank assets[a]	As % of commercial bank deposits[b]	As % of GDP[c]
1931	3.8	1.0	N/A
2008–09	28.5	5.5	5.4

Notes: [a] Central bank assets as at the end of 1930 and the end of August 2008, respectively. [b] Commercial bank deposits as at the end of 1930 and the end of 2007, respectively. [c] GDP in 2008.
Sources: Table 11.2 and Table 5.2.

The amounts of liquidity provided in the two crises, measured according to the three methods described in Chapters 5 and 11, are compared in Table 12.1. The data include provision of liquidity to both domestic and external borrowers. The amount provided in 2008–09 was 5½ to 7½ times as much as in 1931, depending on the choice of scale. In the recent crisis, it was clear that more would have been provided if more had been needed. In the international field, nothing illustrates the difference between 1931 and 2008 more clearly than the fact that the swap lines extended by the Fed to the ECB, the Bank of England,

Nevertheless, in 2008, international liquidity provision through central bank swaps peaked at about 2 per cent of total international short-term indebtedness (including inter-bank debts) at the end of 2007. The probable explanation is that emergency measures in 2008–09 by governments in the form of recapitalisations of banks, guarantees of banks' debts, and asset purchases or guarantees (see Panetta *et al.* 2009), as well as the existence of and strengthening of deposit insurance schemes in a number of countries, contributed sufficiently to stabilisation that large deposit flight and capital outflows were prevented, reducing the need for international emergency help. As of early June 2009, total commitments and outlays (not including the existence and strengthening of deposit insurance) by Australia, Canada, France, Germany, Italy, Japan, the Netherlands, Spain, Switzerland, the United Kingdom and the United States amounted to around €5 trillion or 18.8 per cent of GDP, and €2 trillion or 7.6 per cent of GDP, respectively (Panetta *et al.* 2009). Total commitments and outlays (excluding deposit insurance) as of early June 2009 by these eleven countries as a percentage of banking sector assets at end-2008 were 8.3 per cent and 3.3 per cent, respectively (see Panetta *et al.* 2009, table 1.2 and figure 1.1). International liquidity provision – i.e. liquidity provision to foreign central banks or governments – is only one aspect of global liquidity provision.

the Swiss National Bank and the Bank of Japan were unlimited as to amount after 13–14 October 2008.

Chapters 2, 3 and 4 identified a number of ways in which the financial crisis of 2008 was propagated internationally. The collateral squeeze in the United States, which became intense after the failure of Lehman Brothers created doubts about the stability of other financial companies in the United States, was an important propagator. The provision of large-scale swap lines by the Federal Reserve relieved many of the financial stresses in other countries that had followed Lehman Brothers' failure. The unwinding of carry trades, particularly yen carry trades, is also likely to have transmitted market volatility to the countries that had been the destination of the carry trades when they were first put in place. It seems likely that, at the time of writing, there is still a large quantity of yen carry trades outstanding.

One crucial difference between the two crises was that the supply of assets that were regarded as liquid and safe in 1931 was inelastic and became narrower with the passage of time, whereas in 2008, it could be, and was, expanded quickly in such a way as to contain the effects of the crisis. The understanding that the role of governments and central banks in a crisis is to enable such assets to be supplied was perhaps the most important lesson of 1931, and the experience of 2008 showed that it had been learned.

Another crucial difference was in international relations. As noted in Chapter 11, Kindleberger (1987) claims that the gold standard malfunctioned in the 1930s because no country was willing and able to act as a leader. There was no contingency plan in 2008 for emergency provision of international liquidity in a financial crisis (see Chapter 5), and the decisions which led the Federal Reserve to act as the international lender of last resort were taken quickly, between the middle of September, when Lehman Brothers failed, and the end of October. The decisions represented the highly enlightened and well-informed self-interest of the United States.

In 1931, political differences, such as those between Austria and France, had set back any chances there were that official international cooperation might have contained the effects of the liquidity crisis (see Chapter 11). Moreover, as Kindleberger (1987) pointed out, isolationist attitudes prevented the United States from providing the leadership that might have resolved the crisis. By contrast there were no political obstructions to the provision of necessary swap lines in 2008.

Moreover, the United States perceived that it was in its own interest to provide liquidity freely to other countries, despite some financial risks and despite some opposition within Congress.[11] Had the political climate been less benign, or had the United States adopted an isolationist attitude, the global crisis would surely have been a great deal worse than it actually was.

Thus the international monetary system, comprising official institutions, the set of prevailing market beliefs, and the state of international political relations, was much less fragile and much more resilient in 2008 than it had been in 1931, despite the absence of a contingency plan. As a result, the near-term consequences of the recent crisis were much less severe. Early in 2012, it is too early to tell what the longer-term consequences might be.

[11] See Section 1 of Chapter 7.

13 | *International liquidity management*

Earlier chapters have been about the past. This one is about the present and the future, and how liquidity management is being affected by the recent crisis. It begins, however, with a brief review of developments in reserve holding since the Bretton Woods system collapsed in 1971.

1. Reserve-holding behaviour since the end of Bretton Woods

The collapse of the Bretton Woods system was accompanied by the abandonment of pegged exchange rates against the dollar and a general though not universal resort to floating exchange rates.[1] It was widely expected that the demand for international reserves would diminish with the advent of floating exchange rates, since countries were no longer obliged to sell foreign currencies in case of need to support their own currencies in foreign exchange markets. The expectation turned out to be seriously mistaken, however. International reserves increased in total from 3.1% of world gross product at the end of 1970 to 15.7% at the end of 2009. These figures include gold valued at current market prices; over the same period, foreign exchange reserves increased from 1.6% of gross product to 13.9% (Figure 13.1).

The purpose of this section is not to attempt a full explanation of reserve developments over the past forty years, but rather to make clear that different countries have been motivated by very different considerations in their reserve-holding behaviour. Foreign exchange reserve holdings are remarkably highly concentrated: at the end of 2009, only seventeen countries each held more than 1 per cent of the world total, and those countries between them had 81.6 per cent of the world total. They are listed in Table 13.1.

---

[1] For an account of the break-up of the Bretton Woods structure, see James (1996), chs 7, 8 and 9.

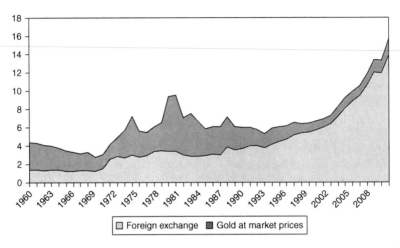

Figure 13.1 World foreign exchange and gold reserves as a percentage of world gross product.
Source: IMF International Financial Statistics.

Within this group, many countries' reserve-holding behaviour in the years preceding the recent financial crisis can most readily be explained by country-specific factors, as follows.[2]

a. Countries rich in natural resources tend to hold large foreign exchange reserves: six of the seventeen largest reserve holders listed in Table 13.1 are oil producers; and seven of the largest twenty oil producers in 2010 are among those seventeen.[3] It is understandable that they should want to save much of their income from natural resources, since those assets are depletable. Acquisition of reserves represents a diversification of wealth out of natural resources into financial assets. The correlation coefficient between year to year changes in the dollar price of crude oil and changes in total foreign exchange reserves (valued in dollars) over the period

---

[2] See also the IMF's survey of reserve behaviour in Moghadam (2010).

[3] Information about large oil producers comes from the BP *Statistical Review of World Energy 2011* (www.bp.com/sectionbodycopy.do?categoryId=7500&contentId=7068481). The thirteen of the twenty largest oil producers which are not among the seventeen large holders of foreign exchange reserves include the United Arab Emirates, Kuwait, Norway and Kazakhstan, all of which have sovereign wealth funds, as well as the United States and Iran.

Table 13.1 *Large foreign exchange reserve holdings*

Country	Foreign exchange reserves (USD bn, end-2009)	% of world total	% of domestic GDP
China	2,400	29.7	48.1
Japan	997	12.3	19.8
Russia	406	5.0	33.2
Saudi Arabia	397	4.9	105.5
Taiwan	349	4.0	92.4
Korea	265	3.3	31.9
India	259	3.2	20.4
Hong Kong	256	3.2	122.2
Brazil	232	2.9	14.5
Euro area	195	2.4	1.6
Singapore	186	2.3	101.5
Algeria	147	1.8	105.3
Thailand	134	1.7	50.7
Libya	96	1.2	159.2
Mexico	94	1.2	10.7
Malaysia	93	1.1	48.1
Switzerland	91	1.1	18.6
Others	1,490	18.4	5.4

Source: IMF.

1958–2010 was 0.28, which is statistically significant at the 97.5 per cent level (one-tailed test).

b. In some cases, notably China and Japan, very large holdings of foreign exchange reserves may be partly explained as a joint product of high domestic savings rates and economic strategies aimed at export-led economic growth, as part of which any appreciation of the nominal exchange rate is substantially restrained.[4]

c. In some countries, demographics may influence reserve-holding behaviour. For example, China's one-child policy means that the population will age over the coming decades. Japan's population is ageing too. The United Nations forecasts that the percentage

[4] For discussion of China's reserve accumulation, see Prasad and Sorkin (2009).

of the total population aged between 15 and 64 will fall between 2011 and 2050 from 71.5% to 56.7% in China and from 59.4% to 44.6% in Japan.[5] These countries will probably run current account deficits as their populations age, and building up foreign assets now can be seen as part of a strategy of smoothing consumption over time. China's official foreign assets, which amount to some $2,000 per citizen, do not seem excessive from this viewpoint, bearing in mind that China's private foreign assets are probably not large.

d. In some countries, such as Korea and Thailand, painful memories of past financial crises in which domestic banks suddenly lost access to foreign currency deposits have led to the precautionary holding of large foreign exchange reserves.

e. Other countries' behaviour is influenced by their political situation – for example Taiwan's very large reserve holdings probably partly reflect its anxiety about political isolation.

Some of these considerations are motives for holding financial wealth, but not necessarily in the form of liquid foreign exchange reserves. And indeed several countries, including many of the large reserve holders, have established sovereign wealth funds to hold less-liquid financial assets which promise a higher return over the long term, but it is not clear why they continue to hold such large liquid reserves.

After the advent of floating exchange rates, a substantial group of other countries behaved in accordance with the prior general expectation and maintained quite small foreign exchange reserves. They had no obligation to intervene in foreign exchange markets to support their currencies; and recognised that reserve holding involved some net cost, the foreign currency yield on reserve assets, minus an allowance for risk, generally being less than the cost of financing them in foreign currency; while if reserves were financed in domestic currency, they also carried a foreign exchange risk. The countries in this category include Australia, the euro area, Denmark, Sweden and the United Kingdom, all of whose reserves constituted quite a small percentage of their GDPs. Some of the countries in this group are international financial centres, which clearly did not anticipate the sudden drying-up of wholesale funding for international banks which occurred in

---

[5] See United Nations (2010).

2008. As a result, many of them had insufficient reserves to manage the crisis without help from swap lines, as Chapter 9 shows.

2. The effects of the crisis on reserve-holding behaviour

Earlier chapters have described how the demand for foreign currency liquidity increased suddenly in many countries during 2008–09 as a result of the large international flows of funds to the United States and Japan; how wholesale inter-bank markets and foreign exchange swap markets were disrupted; and how much of the demand was accommodated and the resulting disruptions eased by the provision of central bank swaps, mainly by the Federal Reserve. After the financial crisis, things cannot go back to where they were. Governments and central banks, like commercial banks and non-financial companies, want more 'liquidity assurance' – that is, assurance that they will have adequate international liquidity as protection against another financial crisis.[6] This section considers how they could obtain such assurance.

The demand for liquidity assurance depends on the extent of the liquidity risks that commercial banks are running. Regulation is being tightened in the wake of the crisis, as regards both capital and liquidity. The Basel 3 regime of bank regulation, introduced in response to the crisis and the evident failure of the previous Basel regimes to prevent it, includes the first internationally agreed minimum liquidity ratios that banks must observe.[7] The likely effects of these minimum

---

[6] By 'international liquidity' is meant access to means of international payment.

[7] In his history of the Basel Committee on Banking Supervision, Goodhart (2011), ch. 9, reports the discussions that took place in the BCBS on liquidity issues between 1975 and 1997. The BCBS achieved an accord (later known as Basel 1) on regulating the capital adequacy of banks in 1988, but, despite extensive discussion, it achieved no comparable accord on regulation of bank liquidity. In Goodhart's view, this was a serious failure, which can be attributed to three main reasons. First, the concept of liquidity was 'slippery and fluid', and there were differences of view on the extent to which liability-based management of liquidity was acceptable, and the extent to which supervisors should insist that banks held liquid assets. Second, the liquidity of particular assets depends on the willingness of central banks to purchase them, or accept them as collateral for loans, in open-market operations. Any international agreement on regulation of bank liquidity would have required central banks to harmonise the range of assets eligible for use in open-market operations. No central bank wanted to change its procedures, and in any case, the impending capital adequacy accord applied lower risk weights to liquid assets and thus was expected to encourage liquid asset holdings without the need for any

ratios are discussed in Section 4 below.[8] Despite the tightening-up of regulation, it would be foolish to assume that the risk of future crises has been eliminated.

a. Evaluating techniques for providing international liquidity assurance

Satisfactory techniques for providing international liquidity assurance should meet the following criteria:

- they should provide adequate reassurance about their international liquidity needs being met to those countries which need it;
- they should avoid excessive moral hazard, and in particular avoid giving countries in 'fundamental disequilibrium' the means to delay necessary adjustment;
- they should avoid placing unreasonable burdens on liquidity providers.

It is possible to design multilateral or bilateral structures for providing liquidity assurance that enable countries to get credit in case of need. Such structures provide, in effect, a 'lender of last resort' in international financial markets, at least up to the limit of the available credit facilities. All techniques which involve credit also involve moral hazard, however. If credit is made automatically available, then borrowers with short-term horizons have an incentive to over-borrow. In normal circumstances, the lender conducts a full credit assessment before providing funds. However, in a financial crisis, quick decisions are often essential. There may not be time for a full assessment.[9] The Fed's speed of reaction in 2008 was crucial to the effectiveness of its

---

separate accord on liquidity regulation. The third reason was simply that the time and energy of BCBS members had been largely exhausted on the capital adequacy accord, and there was none left for a negotiation about liquidity. Consequently, while the earlier downward trend in banks' capital ratios was reversed by the agreement on Basel 1 in 1988, the downward trend in liquidity ratios was not. Some issues regarding the supervision of liquidity are discussed in Allen (2010) and Davies and Green (2010), pp. 97–106.

[8] Another relevant regulatory action is the self-sufficiency rule in the new liquidity regime of the UK Financial Services Authority (see Financial Services Authority 2009).

[9] Bagehot (1892), pp. 199–200, emphasises the importance of speed in responding to panics.

swap operations. In the absence of adequate multilateral or bilateral structures, a country can get liquidity assurance by building up its own foreign exchange reserves so that it has access to the funds it thinks it might need. This is self-insurance.

This section begins by discussing possible multilateral and bilateral techniques, before discussing unilateral actions that countries can take, including self-insurance by accumulating reserves. The range of possible techniques and their principal advantages and disadvantages are summarised in Table 13.2.

b. Multilateral techniques

All multilateral techniques involve a group of countries agreeing to make funds available to each other in case of need.

In reserve pooling schemes, participating countries can draw on the pool when they need funds, and can thereby have access to more funds than if there were no pooling. It is in the nature of reserve pooling that the reserves in question are not the liability of any of the participating countries. Pooled reserves could be used in a crisis to provide foreign currencies to banks in any of the participating countries. However, the advantage of pooling might be lost in a general liquidity crisis if most or all of the participating countries wanted to draw funds at the same time.

The Chiang Mai structure is a reserve pooling scheme in East Asia. Its origins and nature were described in Chapter 6. In May 2009 the ASEAN-plus-three countries agreed to accelerate the timetable for multilateralising the Chiang Mai Initiative, which had until that time been a network of bilateral swap agreements, none of which had ever been drawn. The new multilateral facility has created a pool of $120 billion of reserves, from which each participating country can draw up to a predetermined country-specific amount.[10] With the two largest reserve-holding countries, China and Japan, among the participants, there is not much risk of all the participants wanting to draw at the same time.

The International Monetary Fund is a financial pooling scheme of a broader kind, in that member countries contribute their quota

---

[10] As noted in Chapter 6, only the first 20 per cent of the committed amount is available unless the borrowing country meets conditions specified by the IMF.

Table 13.2 *Techniques for providing liquidity assurance*

Type	Technique	Examples	Advantages	Disadvantages
Multilateral	Reserve pooling	Chiang Mai	Economy in reserve holding	Moral hazard and possible delays
				Not all participants can draw at the same time
	Pooling including own currency	IMF	Economy in reserve holding	Moral hazard and possible delays
Bilateral	Swap network managed by reserve-currency country	Fed, 1962–98	Quick access to funds assured	Moral hazard
		Fed, from December 2007	Economy in reserve holding; requires only bilateral negotiations	Choice of recipient countries
				Burden on provider of funds
	Individual country lending from own FX reserves	Denmark, Norway, Sweden lending to Iceland, 2008	Requires only bilateral negotiation	Moral hazard and possible delays
				Provision of funds may not be assured
	Central banks accept foreign currency collateral located outside home territory from commercial banks	Canada, Hong Kong, 2008	Requires no international negotiation	Not likely to be enough on its own
Unilateral	Reserve accumulation for self-insurance	East Asian countries after crisis of 1997–98	Requires no international negotiation	Diversion of resources into low-yielding assets
		Several European countries post-2008 (see text)	Quick access to funds assured	Global macroeconomic consequences of reserve accumulation

subscriptions mainly in their own currencies, but also partly in foreign exchange. Its lending is in part financed by quota subscriptions, and its resources can be augmented by borrowing, including borrowing under the General Arrangements to Borrow and the New Arrangements to Borrow. These resources can then be drawn on by member countries as foreign currency loans. In addition, Special Drawing Rights issued by the IMF enable member countries to acquire usable currencies from other member countries in exchange for SDRs. The IMF can potentially recycle very large sums from creditor to debtor countries. IMF lending has been used in the past (e.g. during the Asian crisis of 1997–98) to help countries overcome the consequences of banking crises.

The official response to a financial crisis can be accelerated if credit lines which can be drawn on in case of need have been pre-agreed. The IMF's Flexible Credit Lines were set up in March 2009, in order to provide timely lending to economies with good economic funda-mentals and policies, and without the conditionality (and associated stigma) associated with other forms of lending by the IMF. They are of finite (one-year) duration, so as to limit moral hazard. Colombia, Mexico and Poland received credit lines in 2009, 2010 and 2011, none of which had been drawn on at the time of writing in early 2012.[11]

Since the crisis of 2008–09, the resources available to the IMF have been massively increased, so as to give it the capacity to manage a future financial crisis on the scale of the recent one. Quota subscrip-tions are being doubled, and at least until the doubling of quota sub-scriptions has been completed, the amounts available under the New Arrangements to Borrow have been increased from SDR 34 billion to SDR 367 billion. And the amount of SDRs in issue has been increased from SDR 21 billion to SDR 204 billion.

c. Bilateral techniques

Bilateral techniques involve one institution accepting a commitment to provide funds on demand to foreign central banks. One conceivable bilateral solution to the problem of providing international liquidity

---

[11] See International Monetary Fund (2011) for the IMF's own assessment of the Flexible Credit Line.

assurance would be to institutionalise swap lines provided by individual central banks in their own currency.[12]

Bilateral central bank swap lines of this kind can provide adequate liquidity assurance. However, as Chapter 7 has explained, they involve financial risks to the provider of funds; and there is the problem of how the recipient countries are chosen. Clearly the provider would have to make this decision, since the provider runs the financial risks, such as exposure to sovereign risk of the recipient country. But unrelated political issues might prevent economically desirable outcomes in the choice of recipient countries.[13] More generally, the liquidity-providing central bank would need to be able to argue convincingly to its own legislature that taking on a commitment of this kind was consistent with its statutory mandate and in the national interest. While it may be possible to make a compelling case for providing swap lines in an economic emergency on national interest grounds, a permanent commitment would be harder to justify.[14]

The swap lines which the Fed provided during 2007 and 2008 were allowed to lapse in February 2010. However, some of them were reopened later in 2010 in response to the sovereign debt crisis in Europe. At the time of writing early in 2012, those swap lines are still open, though recent drawings have been much smaller than in 2008. It does not seem likely that they will be a permanent feature of the landscape.

A second bilateral technique is for an individual country to provide foreign currency liquidity to another country out of its own foreign exchange reserves. For example, as noted in Chapter 6, the central banks of Denmark, Norway and Sweden provided euros to the Central Bank of Iceland by means of swap lines. However, they had made no prior commitment to provide funds. Countries with large foreign exchange reserves could be in a position to provide foreign currencies to several countries, and might even make commitments to

---

[12] Aizenman, Jinjarak and Park (2010), p. 17, discuss many of the issues discussed in this chapter and conclude that 'there are clear limits to substitutability between swaps and reserves'.

[13] A historical example of such political difficulties is provided by the negotiations in 1931 about an international loan to Austria after the collapse of Creditanstalt. See Chapter 11.

[14] No doubt it was concerns of this kind that prevented the Basel Committee on Banking Supervision from making any cooperative contingency plans for emergency provision of international liquidity, as described in Chapter 5.

provide funds in case of future need, provided they were persuaded that such commitments were in their own interests and that the problem of moral hazard could be managed.

Cross-border collateral arrangements can also help to provide foreign currency liquidity. These involve the central bank in one jurisdiction providing domestic currency liquidity to eligible financial institutions against collateral placed by the latter's offices in another jurisdiction into the liquidity-providing central bank's account at the local central bank.[15] Strictly speaking, such arrangements do not increase the amount of foreign currency available to governments and central banks, but they do reduce the amounts of foreign currency that governments and central banks might need to provide in a crisis to banks located in their territory. Some central banks already accepted cross-border collateral in their normal operations or on an emergency-only basis before the recent crisis, including the central banks of Sweden, Switzerland, the United Kingdom and the United States (see CPSS 2006). Other central banks started accepting cross-border collateral during the crisis, as part of the widening of collateral accepted. For example, in June 2008, the Bank of Canada started accepting US Treasury securities held in the United States as collateral for its Standing Liquidity Facility; and from October 2008 until March 2009, the Hong Kong Monetary Authority expanded the range of securities eligible as collateral for its discount window lending to include US dollar assets of credit quality acceptable to the HKMA.

d. Unilateral actions

If multilateral or bilateral structures do not provide countries with as much liquidity assurance as they desire, then they are likely to resort to unilateral actions. They can hold foreign exchange reserves which they can use in a crisis to provide foreign currency liquidity to domestic banks.

In the recent crisis, Korea, among other countries, provided US dollars to domestic banks out of its foreign exchange reserves in foreign exchange swap auctions, in addition to disbursing funds drawn on the Fed's US dollar swap line (see Chapter 9). And in Brazil, the central bank provided US dollars to domestic banks

---

[15] See Committee on the Global Financial System (2010a, p. 18).

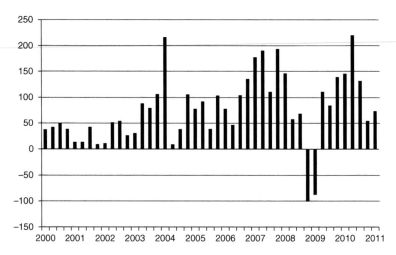

Figure 13.2 Quarterly changes in world foreign exchange reserves, 2000–11 (in US dollar billions).
Sources: IMF: Currency Composition of Foreign Exchange Reserves (www.imf.org/external/np/sta/cofer/eng/index.htm), author's calculations.

using instruments (derivatives such as foreign exchange swaps) that allowed it to limit the impact on reserves, and without drawing on its Fed swap line.[16]

Total world foreign exchange reserves fell temporarily during the crisis of 2008–09, but they have increased again since 2009 (see Figure 13.2, in which the financial crisis appears as a brief interruption in reserve growth). Some countries which had fairly small reserves before the crisis and which experienced severe shortages of foreign currency liquidity during the crisis have more recently accumulated reserves for self-insurance purposes. For example, the dollar value of foreign exchange reserves increased over 2009 and 2010 by 76.6% in Denmark, by 50.9% in Sweden, by 46.5% in Poland, by 45.5% in Brazil and by 43.1% in Korea (see Table 13.3). And the United Kingdom has announced that it intends to increase its foreign exchange reserves by £24 billion, or about 69%, over the financial years 2011–12

---

[16] See Committee on the Global Financial System (2010a, p. 9); Stone, Walker and Yasui (2009).

Table 13.3 *Large increases in foreign*
exchange reserves, end-2008 to end-2010
(US dollar billions)

Country	Increase in foreign exchange reserves	
	$ bn	%
China	901.3	46.3
Switzerland	173.2	392.3
Brazil	87.7	45.5
Korea	86.4	43.1
Hong Kong	86.2	47.2
Thailand	57.3	52.9
Singapore	50.2	28.9
Indonesia	40.6	82.4
Japan	32.6	3.2
Denmark	30.5	76.6
Poland	27.4	46.5
Israel	26.9	63.7
Russia	22.3	5.4
India	21.2	8.6
Philippines	20.9	63.4
Mexico	20.9	22.2
Qatar	20.6	215.2
Algeria	17.5	12.2
Sweden	12.8	50.9
Malaysia	11.7	12.9
Peru	11.4	37.6
Lebanon	11.0	54.4
United Arab Emirates	10.2	32.3
Other countries (net change)	47.8	
Total	1,828.7	25.4

Note: Countries are included in the table if their
foreign exchange reserves increased by $10 billion or
more between the end of 2008 and the end of 2010.
Source: IMF International Financial Statistics.

to 2014–15.[17] Some of the economies that were dependent on swap lines during the crisis, such as Australia and the euro area, have not increased their reserves materially, however.

Only a small part of the recent build-up of foreign exchange reserves has been owing to self-insurance motives. For example, China's foreign exchange reserves were already $1.9 trillion at the end of 2008, amply sufficient to provide self-insurance, and it is therefore unlikely that any of the increase of about $901.3 billion between then and December 2010 can be attributed to any desire for additional self-insurance. And the very large increase in foreign exchange reserves in Switzerland (of $173.2 billion, or $22,000 per head of population) has been the result of foreign exchange intervention by the Swiss National Bank, whose declared objective has been to prevent a further appreciation of the Swiss franc against the euro.

The advantages of self-insurance are that a country has certainty of access to foreign currency liquidity, and that there is no need for coordination. The drawbacks include the costs of holding foreign exchange reserves to the economy, as the funds held as reserves must be invested in liquid assets. Moreover, it may turn out that the amount of foreign currency liquidity provided by the foreign exchange reserves is not sufficient.

3. Post-crisis reserve accumulation

The decision that several countries have made to build up their reserves unilaterally since the financial crisis suggests that the enlargement of the resources available to the IMF has not provided complete reassurance about access to liquidity in case of need. It is worth considering why this might be.

It is probably relevant that multilateral techniques for providing international liquidity were not much used during the recent crisis. There were no known drawings on the Chiang Mai facility, and East

---

[17] The United Kingdom has explained its decision by reference to its possible need to provide increased amounts to the IMF (see HM Treasury 2011, p. 37). It would be curious for a country to incur the cost of adding to its reserves if the only purpose was to spare other countries the same cost by facilitating more reserve pooling. It is more likely that the UK's real motive is self-insurance, but that the authorities feel embarrassed about admitting it.

Asian central banks opened up new swap lines to each other during the crisis, rather than enhancing the Chiang Mai ones. The IMF's net disbursements in 2008 amounted to SDR 11.7 billion, which is roughly the equivalent of $18 billion and of a smaller order of magnitude than the $530 billion net which the Fed supplied on its swap lines in that year. The IMF's usable resources as at the end of August 2008, just before Lehmans failed, were just $257 billion.[18] The IMF created new facilities in response to the crisis, namely the Flexible Credit Line and the Precautionary Credit Line, but they were not available until March 2009.

This experience shows that multilateral organisations were not able to react to the crisis on the scale and with the speed which the situation demanded. It does not imply any failure on the part of the people responsible for managing the Chiang Mai Initiative or the IMF. International organisations necessarily make decisions by agreement, and, faced with an unexpected shock, they take time to reach the necessary shared understanding about what has changed and what needs to be done about it.[19] Crucially, a national institution like the Fed can react more quickly than an international one like the IMF. In addition, the countries which form the membership of international institutions typically endow the institutions with the resources that they appear likely to need, but not more, and providing additional resources also takes time. The IMF simply did not have enough money in 2008 to enable it to provide liquidity on the same scale as the Fed did.

In these circumstances, it is not surprising that governments attach great value to the ability to have liquid assets immediately and unconditionally available under their own control, and that the post-2009 enlargement of the IMF's financial resources has not sufficed to prevent countries from building up their own accumulations of liquid assets.

4. The global demand for liquidity and the concept of monetary policy

Against this background, partly in order to secure additional liquidity assurance, governments and central banks have accumulated

[18] Source: IMF Financial Resources and Liquidity Position, August 2008, available at www.imf.org/external/np/tre/liquid/2008/0808.htm.
[19] The prolonged inability of the euro area to agree how to deal with sovereign debt problems in 2010–11 is a case in point.

additional liquid assets since the crisis. Countries wishing to accumulate reserves may do so in any or all of the following ways:

a.   Outright purchases of foreign currency in exchange for domestic currency, which cause the exchange rate of the domestic currency to be weaker than it would otherwise have been, and switch expenditure away from foreign products towards domestic products.[20] The policy may be accompanied by measures to restrain domestic demand. In any event, it depresses demand in the rest of the world.

b.   Maintaining relatively high domestic interest rates in order to stimulate demand for the domestic currency, so that outright purchases of foreign currency can be accomplished without causing the exchange rate to depreciate.

c.   Borrowing foreign currencies at relatively long maturities in international bond markets so as to acquire short-term assets. Such borrowing is likely to crowd out borrowing to finance productive investment and, by doing so, to depress both global demand and global productive capacity. Unlike normal government bond issuance, it does not finance budget deficits which create demand and would otherwise create new liquid assets.

Thus reserve accumulation has negative effects on aggregate demand which are at least partly external to the reserve-accumulating country. A coincident effort by a substantial number of countries to build up reserves is likely to affect the global macroeconomic situation, as was the case when East Asian countries built up their foreign exchange reserves after the crisis of 1997–98. Their actions reduced aggregate demand in the rest of the world, and other countries, notably the United States, stimulated demand by easing monetary policy in the following years in order to compensate. The results included very large payments imbalances and increased demand for liquid assets, such as US government securities, from East Asian central bank reserve managers.[21]

It is likely that, since the crisis, there has been more reserve accumulation than would have been socially optimal. Unfortunately, the recent accumulation of reserves has been taking place at a time when the demand for liquid assets from other participants in the global

---

[20] See Johnson (1958).
[21] See Bernanke (2005) for an analysis of the effects.

economy has also been very strong. The coincidence of increasing demand for liquid assets from a range of sources is potentially dangerous, unless there is a matching increase in supply, because it entails the risk of depressing aggregate demand.

Banks in particular are having to increase their liquid asset holdings. After banking was deregulated in the 1970s and 1980s, banks were increasingly able to meet their needs for liquidity by borrowing in wholesale deposit markets. Banks with good names were able to borrow large amounts quickly and easily in these markets, and their holdings of liquid assets fell. The practice of liability management described in Chapter 12 meant that banks could choose within quite a wide range what quantity of assets they wanted to hold, confident that they would be able to raise the necessary liabilities.

After the financial crisis, liability management became much more difficult for most banks; and the Basel 3 liquidity requirements will make it permanently more difficult for all banks. The Liquidity Coverage Ratio, which is to become effective in 2015, will require banks to hold sufficient prescribed liquid assets to enable them to withstand a hypothetical stressed situation for a month. In the hypothetical stressed situation, it is assumed that no inter-bank deposits are rolled over; therefore banks will have to hold 100 per cent liquid assets against inter-bank deposit liabilities falling due in the next month.[22] Inter-bank borrowing with a maturity of a month or less will be pointless, and inter-bank borrowing for more than a month will not yield any usable liquidity in the last month before maturity.

Banks therefore need to acquire additional liquid assets, not just to meet the Basel 3 minimum requirements, but also to enable them to manage fluctuations in their cash flows and perhaps to provide reassurance to their own directors and shareholders. They have done so by competing aggressively for retail deposits and by issuing longer-term debt. Banks faced serious problems in acquiring such funding from commercial sources in the second half of 2011, particularly in the euro area (see for example Bank of England 2011, paragraph 3), and the ECB went to extraordinary lengths in late 2011 and early 2012 to provide banks with three-year secured funding.

Non-financial companies are also likely to need more liquid assets. The Liquidity Coverage Ratio will require banks to hold increased

---

[22] See Basel Committee on Banking Supervision (2010b).

liquid asset cover against undrawn lending commitments. This has increased the cost to non-bank companies of maintaining bank facilities as a source of liquidity, and reduced the availability of such facilities. As a result, those companies, too, need to build up larger stocks of liquid assets as an alternative means of managing their cash flows.

Thus the global demand for liquid assets has been greatly intensified as a result of the crisis, partly as a result of changes in private sector behaviour, but also partly as a result of official regulation, which affects banks directly and non-financial companies indirectly, and partly as a result of decisions by national governments and central banks to acquire additional liquid official foreign exchange reserves.

This surge in the global demand for liquidity is capable of having macroeconomic consequences. While it is in progress, the ability of banks to supply credit is inhibited by their need to build up liquid assets and repay official emergency financing provided during the crisis, as well as by their inescapable need for higher capital ratios. And demand to borrow in longer-term credit markets is amplified by banks needing to secure longer-term funding, corporates seeking alternatives to bank borrowing and governments financing the acquisition of liquid foreign exchange reserves. Low official interest rates may not offset high borrowing spreads and limited availability of credit.

Macroeconomic policy management will in the future need to take account of the supply and demand for liquid assets – a procedure that has been unfamiliar since quantitative controls on bank balance sheet growth were abandoned in many countries in the 1970s and 1980s. The objective of those controls was to restrain the growth of money and credit, as a means of containing inflation. In current circumstances, however, perhaps the principal threat to financial stability is the risk that economic growth will be insufficient to enable the overhang of excessive debts to be worked off and repaid.

Central banks need now to broaden their vision of what constitutes 'monetary policy' beyond the making of decisions about the appropriate level of short-term interest rates. Before the crisis, commercial banks were able and willing to provide liquidity at low cost and in ample quantities to their customers, financed by readily available wholesale deposits. Central banks provided liquidity through their open market operations, and government debt management operations also affected the liquidity of the economy, but in both cases the amounts involved were not significant when compared with the liquidity-providing capacity of the commercial banks.

In the post-crisis environment, the liquidity that central banks provide through open-market operations has become much more important, and their balance sheets have grown by a multiple, as Chapter 2 described; equally, the liquidity effects of government debt management operations have also become more important. The concept of 'monetary policy' needs to embrace, for example, decisions about what assets should be 'eligible', i.e. what kinds of assets central banks are willing to buy, or accept as collateral for loans.[23] Assets that are eligible are *ipso facto* more liquid, and likely to yield somewhat less in consequence; this benefits the issuers, and it may also affect the value of the underlying collateral. Central banks need to be conscious of the effects of their decisions. Moreover, central banks' decisions about eligibility influence commercial banks' decisions about their own asset choices, and eligibility is therefore also a potentially very powerful weapon of macro-prudential policy as well as monetary policy. Indeed, it is doubtful if any clear demarcation line can be drawn between macro-prudential and monetary policy.

After the crisis, monetary/macro-prudential policy needs not to restrain risk-taking but to encourage it, with the intention of ensuring that economic growth is not obstructed by the surge in demand for liquid assets.[24] The new set of macro-prudential policy weapons has not yet been precisely defined, but in addition to the controls on financial intermediaries' balance sheets that have been widely discussed, it will need to include eligibility, as mentioned above, and other policies

---

[23] Decisions about the appropriate level of short-term interest rates are logically incomplete without an accompanying decision about what assets the central bank is willing to buy, or accept as collateral for loans, at that rate. One school of thought holds that central banks should confine their purchases to government securities, on the grounds that they are supposedly free of credit risk (see e.g. Goodfriend 2011). However, they are not in fact free of credit risk, though the risk may be very small; any and all asset purchases carry financial risk, and central banks need to assess the risks very carefully when making decisions about eligibility. Neither risk management considerations nor history support the view that central banks should buy only government securities.

[24] For a review of the literature on macro-prudential policies, see Galati and Moessner (2011). For a similar view on what the current priorities for macro-prudential policy should be, see Haldane (2011).

that affect the liquidity of financial intermediaries. Thus, for example, public debt management has once more become an important instrument of national macroeconomic policies.[25]

As the crisis has shown, liquidity management needs to be conducted at an international level. The Basel Committee on the Global Financial System commented that:

> What is needed is a consistent policy framework for addressing global liquidity ... Specifically, while country-specific or regional shocks may be addressed through self-insurance and existing arrangements for the international distribution of liquidity, such as IMF programmes and similar facilities, global liquidity shocks will require interventions by institutions with the ability to supply official liquidity in an elastic manner and in potentially very sizeable amounts to break downward liquidity spirals. Only central banks have this ability.
>
> Central banks, working cooperatively through the Basel process, thus remain well placed to address future surges and shortages in global liquidity.[26]

This is a sign that central banks collectively have recognised the importance of this issue. Addressing it will be a formidable but vital task.

---

[25] 'Quantitative easing' is most naturally seen as a form of debt management, and the Federal Open Market Committee has decided to implement a new 'Operation Twist' (see Federal Open Market Committee 2011). See also Turner (2011) and Allen (2012).

[26] Committee on the Global Financial System (2011), p. 29.

Data appendix

This appendix provides detailed information about some of the data quoted in the book.

Proxy measurement of currency-specific liquidity shortages (Chapter 3)

The proxy measure of liquidity shortages used in Figure 3.3–Figure 3.7 is based on the BIS locational international banking statistics by residence of counterparty. The BIS locational international banking statistics record the aggregate international claims and liabilities of all banks resident in the BIS reporting countries, broken down by instrument, currency, sector and country of residence of counterparty, and nationality of reporting banks. Both domestic and foreign-owned banking offices in the reporting countries report their positions gross (except for derivative contracts for which a master netting agreement is in place) and on an unconsolidated basis, i.e. including banks' positions vis-à-vis their own affiliates.[1]

Another set of BIS statistics, the consolidated international banking statistics, provide information on the country risk exposures of the major banking groups of various countries vis-à-vis the rest of the world. The consolidated banking statistics report banks' on-balance sheet financial claims (i.e. contractual lending) vis-à-vis the rest of the world and provide a measure of the risk exposures of lenders' national banking systems. The data cover contractual (immediate borrower) and ultimate risk lending by the head office and all its branches and subsidiaries on a worldwide consolidated basis, net of inter-office accounts. Reporting of lending in this way allows the

---

[1] This is consistent with the principles of national accounts, money and banking, balance of payments and external debt statistics (see Bank for International Settlements 2008).

allocation of claims to the bank entity that would bear the losses in the event of default by borrowers (see Bank for International Settlements 2009).[2] However, the consolidated statistics do not measure bank liabilities.

The main reason why our particular measure of currency-specific shortages is based on the BIS locational international banking statistics by residence of counterparty is that in a financial crisis gross positions can matter, including of banks vis-à-vis their branches and subsidiaries, rather than just net positions, and they did matter in the recent crisis. Head offices may be unable or unwilling to provide their branches and subsidiaries with necessary liquidity during a crisis, either for reasons of balance sheet management or just because of time zone differences; and they may even withdraw liquidity from them.

Table 3.4

The data on bank deposits come from table 3A of the BIS international banking statistics (amounts outstanding and exchange rate-adjusted quarterly changes). The data on international debt securities with remaining maturity up to a year come from table 17B of the BIS international securities statistics (amounts outstanding only). The partly exchange rate-adjusted quarterly changes in international debt securities are calculated as the sum of:

• Net issues of international money market instruments (from table 14A of the BIS international securities statistics), which are exchange rate adjusted; and
• The differences between successive quarterly amounts outstanding of international debt securities with remaining maturity up to a year other than international money market instruments, calculated by subtracting the amounts outstanding in table 14A from those in table 17B. The estimated quarterly changes in international debt securities with remaining maturity up to a year other than international money market instruments are thus not exchange rate adjusted.

---

[2] See McGuire and von Peter (2009a, 2009b) for currency-specific net foreign positions of banks by nationality of head office based on the BIS locational international banking statistics by nationality of head office and the BIS consolidated international banking statistics.

Table 3.6

Statistical information on bank deposits is available in great detail, but the basis of compilation is not consistent across countries. Care has to be taken in determining which aggregates to analyse. It is clear that inter-bank deposit markets contracted during the crisis, but the reduction in inter-bank depositing cannot have reduced the funding resources available to the banking industry as a whole.[3] Table 3.6 therefore measures, where possible, the change in deposits from non-bank sources. Accordingly, it uses consolidated banking statistics where they are available, since, for each country, they net out deposits placed by one domestic bank with another. However, consolidated banking statistics typically do not distinguish between deposits from foreign banks and foreign non-banks, or between loans to foreign banks and foreign non-banks. Therefore, where consolidated banking statistics are used,[4] the deposit totals include deposits from foreign banks.

USA

The data are taken from Federal Reserve table H8.1.

Canada

Bank of Canada Monthly Statistical Bulletin Table C4 shows the end-month Canadian dollar deposits of the chartered banks. The data appear to include inter-bank deposits. Table C9 shows the foreign currency deposits of chartered banks, wherever booked. We assume that all foreign currency deposits are denominated in US dollars. On that assumption, we calculate the USD value of each month-end total and then convert the month-to-month changes back into CAD using monthly-average exchange rates. The changes in total deposits that we quote are the sum of the changes in Canadian dollar-denominated deposits from table C4 and the calculated changes in foreign currency-denominated deposits (from all sources) from table C9.

---

[3] However the ease with which banks could borrow funds from each other was greatly reduced, so that banks' demand for liquid assets became larger.
[4] The euro area, the UK and Denmark in Table 3.6.

Euro area

Total deposits of MFIs (monetary financial institutions) from non-MFIs are to be found in ECB table 2.2 (consolidated balance sheets of euro-area MFIs). We use the transactions data, cumulated from the end of August 2008, since these data do not include the effects of exchange rate fluctuations on the euro value of pre-existing positions. The MFI sector includes the Eurosystem (i.e. the ECB and the national central banks of the euro area). The total deposits of the Eurosystem from non-MFIs are to be found in table 2.1 (aggregated balance sheets of euro-area MFIs). There are no transactions data in table 2.1, so we simply deduct the differences between the end-month stocks from the total MFI transactions data in table 2.2 to get an estimate of the changes in deposits of MFIs outside the Eurosystem, accepting that there may be some pollution from any exchange rate and other valuation effects that are present in the data for the Eurosystem (any such pollution is likely to be very small in scale because deposits of the Eurosystem from non-MFIs are only 1.3 per cent of total MFI deposits from non-MFIs).

UK

We use essentially the same technique as in the case of the euro area. The data come from Bank of England table B 2.1 (MFIs' consolidated balance sheets). The data for the Bank of England itself (from table B 2.2) are subtracted from the data for all MFIs so as to obtain data for MFIs other than the Bank of England. The published data for changes are used, so as to exclude changes in the value of outstanding balances that result from exchange rate-induced changes in the sterling value of those balances and not from flows.

Switzerland

The basic data come from the Swiss National Bank *Monthly Bulletin of Banking Statistics* table 1B, in which the data are reported by banking group. The groups are 'all banks', 'big banks' (of which there are only two), 'cantonal banks', 'regional banks and savings banks' and 'foreign banks'. Because 'all banks' includes the Swiss National Bank, we use the sum of the data for the other four groups, unless otherwise specified. The figures quoted in the table are for the sum of 'money market instruments issued', 'liabilities to customers in the form of savings and deposits' and 'other liabilities to customers', and for 'liabilities to customers in the form of savings and deposits' and 'other liabilities to customers'. The data are quoted in table 1B as totals across all currencies, but the CHF values of the components denominated in CHF, USD and EUR, and, in some cases, precious metals, are shown separately. In order to estimate transactions flows we calculated the values of the USD and EUR components at each end-month in their respective own currencies, using end-month exchange rates, and from those data calculated the monthly changes. We then converted the monthly changes back into CHF using monthly average exchange rates. We performed analogous calculations on the precious metal amounts assuming that the precious metal accounts were in fact all gold accounts.

Denmark

The data are from Danmarks Nationalbank table DNSEKT1. http:// nationalbanken.statistikbank.dk/statbank5a/SelectTable/omrade0.asp ?SubjectCode=902&PLanguage=1&ShowNews=OFF.

Iceland

The data are from Central Bank of Iceland 'Accounts of Deposit Money Banks'. We attempt to adjust the percentage changes in the ISK value of total deposits to exclude the effects of exchange rate changes on the ISK value of the initial stock of foreign currency deposits; in doing so, we assume, lacking any better information, that all foreign currency deposits are denominated in euros.

Russia

Data from Haver Analytics; ultimate source is Central Bank of Russia *Bulletin of Banking Statistics* table 1.16 (various issues 2008–10).

China

The data are from People's Bank of China statistical table 'Depository Corporations Survey', www.pbc.gov.cn/english/diaochatongji/ tongjishuju/2008.asp.

Hong Kong

The data are from Hong Kong Monetary Authority table 3.2. www.hkma. gov.hk/eng/market-data-and-statistics/monthly-statistical-bulletin/ table.shtml#section3.

Japan

The data are from the Bank of Japan website. The relevant codes are FA'FAABK_FAAB2DBEL01 for the deposits of domestically licensed banks and FA'FAFBK_FAFB2L1 for the deposits of foreign banks. www.stat-search.boj.or.jp/ssi/cgi-bin/ famecgi2?cgi=$nme_a000_en&lstSelection=3.

Korea

The data are from the Korean Financial Supervisory Service Financial Statistics Information System, http://efisis.fss.or.kr/.

Singapore

The data are from Monetary Authority of Singapore table I.10. www.mas.gov.sg/en/Statistics/Monthly-Statistical-Bulletin/ Money-and-Banking.aspx.

India

The data are from Reserve Bank of India Data Warehouse table Commercial Bank Survey. http://dbie.rbi.org.in/DBIE/dbie.rbi? site=statistics.

Australia

The data are from Reserve Bank of Australia table B3. We attempt to adjust the percentage changes in the AUD value of total deposits to exclude the effects of exchange rate changes on the AUD value of the initial stock of foreign currency deposits; in doing so, we assume, lacking any better information, that all foreign currency deposits are denominated in US dollars. www.rba.gov.au/statistics/tables/index.html.

Brazil

The data are from the central bank's 'time series management system' (www3.bcb.gov.br/sgspub/consultarvalores/telaCvsSelecionarSeries. paint), and the series included are #1883, #1884 and #1886. They all relate to 'deposit money banks', and therefore include the deposits of the central bank. However, the central bank's balance sheet records deposits only from financial institutions and international organisations, the latter being very small. Therefore the changes in the deposits of 'deposit money banks' should be close to the changes in the deposits of commercial banks. We attempt to adjust the percentage changes in the BRL value of total deposits to exclude the effects of exchange rate changes on the BRL value of the initial stock of foreign currency deposits; in doing so, we assume, lacking any better information, that all foreign currency deposits are denominated in US dollars.

Mexico

The data are from the Banco de Mexico table 'Agregados monetarios y flujo de fondos'. We attempt to adjust the percentage changes in the MXN value of total deposits to exclude the effects of exchange rate changes on the MXN value of the initial stock of foreign currency deposits; in doing so, we assume, lacking any better information, that all foreign currency deposits are denominated in US dollars. www. banxico.org.mx/SieInternet/consultarDirectorioInternetAction.do?acc ion=consultarDirectorioCuadros&sector=3&sectorDescripcion=Agre gados monetarios y flujo de fondos&locale=es.

Table 11.2

As noted in the text, we assume that the amount of liquidity supplied by each central bank is equal to the change in gold and foreign exchange holdings, less any revaluation effects, plus the change in the total of domestic paper assets (discounts, loans and advances, and holdings of government securities), as published by the League of Nations. The League of Nations *Statistical Yearbooks* do not provide comprehensive central bank balance sheets, however. Our assumption amounts to assuming that the three classes of central bank assets for which the League did publish statistics are the only ones that mattered, i.e. that any other assets (such as land and buildings) either were small in amount or that they did not change much in 1931.

We can test this assumption for countries for which we have comprehensive central bank balance sheet data. Data appendix table 1 below contains the relevant data.

GDP data

Canada:	Thelma Liesner, *One Hundred Years of Economic Statistics*, The Economist publications, 1989, table C1
USA:	National data via BIS DBS database
Japan:	Global Financial Database
Germany:	Global Financial Database
France:	CEPII (www.cepii.fr/francgraph/bdd/villa.htm)
Italy:	Liesner table It1
UK:	Global Financial Database
Netherlands:	National data via BIS DBS database

Data appendix table 1

Central bank assets: tests of comprehensiveness of estimates based on League of Nations data

Country	Units	Date of observation	Estimate of central bank assets based on League of Nations data	Total assets reported by national source	Difference of levels end-1930 (%)	Change in total assets reported by national source (%), end-1930 to end-1931; (percentage point difference to estimate based on League of Nations data in parentheses)
USA	USD millions	End of 1930	5,570	5,201[a]	-6.6	9.1 (4.1)
France	FRF millions	End of 1930	99,958	103,886[b]	3.9	11.5 (-0.5)
Switzerland	CHF millions	End of 1930	1,338	1,392[c]	4.0	91.1 (-1.6)
Germany	RM millions (Reichsmarks)	End of 1930	5,687	6,253[d]	10.0	-6.2 (-1.4)
Austria	ATS millions	End of 1930	1,264	1,538[e]	21.7	8.5 (-2.0)
UK	GBP millions	End of 1930	546	562[f]	2.9	-0.9 (-8.7)
Japan	JPY millions	End of 1930	1,852	2,175[g]	17.5	-8.9 (-8.8)

Notes: [a] *Source:* Federal Reserve Board Banking and Monetary Statistics 1914–1941, available at http://fraser.stlouisfed.org/publications/bms/.
[b] *Source:* Banque de France: situation hebdomadaire 1898–1974, www.banque-france.fr/fr/statistiques/base/annhis/html/idx_annhis_fr.htm. Figure is for 1 January 1931.

Notes to Data appendix table 1 (*cont.*)

c *Source:* Swiss National Bank, Historical Time Series, www.snb.ch/en/iabout/stat/statpub/histz/id/statpub_histz_actual.

d *Source:* Deutsche Bundesbank, *Deutsches Geld- und Bankwesen in Zahlen 1876–1975*, table C I 1.01.

e *Source: Wirtschafts-Statistisches Jahrbuch* 1930/31, Kammer für Arbeiter und Angestellte in Wien (Herausgeber).

f *Source:* Federal Reserve Board Banking and Monetary Statistics 1914–1941, available at http://fraser.stlouisfed.org/publications/bms/, which provides the balance sheets of both the Issue and Banking departments of the Bank of England. In calculating the figure of £562 million, we have added the total assets of the two departments and subtracted from the total the amount of banknotes (Issue Department liabilities) included in the assets of the Banking Department.

g *Source:* Information provided to the author by the Bank of Japan. I am very grateful to Takamasa Hisada for translating it into English.

References

Accominotti, O. (2012), 'London merchant banks, the central European panic, and the sterling crisis of 1931', *Journal of Economic History*, vol. 72 issue 1, pp. 1–43.

Acharya, V. V., J. N. Carpenter, X. Gabaix *et al.* (2009), 'Corporate governance in the modern financial sector', in V. V. Acharya and M. Richardson, *Restoring Financial Stability*, Wiley, Hoboken, NJ.

Ahamed, L. (2009), *Lords of Finance*, Windmill Books, London.

Aiyar, S. (2011), 'How did the crisis in international funding markets affect bank lending? Balance sheet evidence from the United Kingdom', Bank of England Working Paper No. 424.

Aizenman, J. and G. Pasricha (2009), 'Selective swap arrangements and the global financial crisis: analysis and interpretation', NBER Working Paper No. 14821.

Aizenman, J., Y. Jinjarak and D. Park (2010), 'International reserves and swap lines: substitutes or complements?', NBER Working Paper No. 15804, March.

Allen, W. (2010), 'Liquidity regulation and its consequences', *Central Banking*, November.

(2012) 'Government debt management and monetary policy in Britain since 1919' in *Threat of fiscal dominance?*, Bank for International Settlements, BIS Paper no 65.

Allen, W. and R. Moessner (2010), 'Central bank co-operation and international liquidity in the financial crisis of 2008–9', Bank for International Settlements Working Paper No. 310.

(2011), 'The international liquidity crisis of 2008–2009', *World Economics*, vol. 12 no. 2, April–June.

(2012) 'The international propagation of the financial crisis of 2008 and a comparison with 1931', *Financial History Review*, vol. 19 no. 2, pp. 123–147.

Allen, W. and G. Wood (2006), 'Defining and achieving financial stability', *Journal of Financial Stability*, vol. 2, pp. 152–172.

Almunia, M., A. Bénétrix, B. Eichengreen, K. O'Rourke and G. Rua (2010), 'From Great Depression to Great Credit Crisis: similarities, differences and lessons', *Economic Policy*, vol. 62 (April), pp. 219–265.

American International Group (2008), '10-Q Quarterly report pursuant to sections 13 or 15(d)', available at www.aigcorporate.com/investors/sec_filings.html (last accessed 24 June 2012).

Auer, R. and S. Kraenzlin (2011), 'International liquidity provision during the financial crisis: a view from Switzerland', *Federal Reserve Bank of St. Louis Review*, vol. 93 no. 6, pp. 409–417.

Austrian National Bank (2008), *Financial Stability Report*, available at www.oenb.at/en/img/fsr_16_gesamt_tcm16–95413.pdf (last accessed 24 June 2012).

Baba, N. and F. Packer (2009), 'From turmoil to crisis: dislocations in the FX swap market before and after the failure of Lehman Brothers', BIS Working Paper No. 285.

Baba, N. and I. Shim (2010), 'Policy responses to dislocations in the FX swap market: the experience of Korea', BIS *Quarterly Review*, June, pp. 29–39, available at www.bis.org/publ/qtrpdf/r_qt1006e.pdf (last accessed 24 June 2012).

Baba, N., R. McCauley and S. Ramaswamy (2009), 'US dollar money market funds and non-US banks', BIS *Quarterly Review*, March, pp. 65–81, available at www.bis.org/publ/qtrpdf/r_qt0903g.htm (last accessed 24 June 2012).

Baba, N., F. Packer and T. Nagano (2008), 'The spillover of market turbulence to FX swap and cross-currency swap markets', BIS *Quarterly Review*, March, available at www.bis.org/publ/qtrpdf/r_qt0803h.pdf (last accessed 24 June 2012).

Bagehot, W. (1892), *Lombard Street: A Description of the Money Market*, tenth edition, Kegan Paul, French, Trübner and Co Ltd, London.

Banco de Mexico (2009), *Reporte sobre el Sistema Financiero*, Julio.

Bank for International Settlements (1932), *2nd Annual Report*, 1931/32.

(1933), *3rd Annual Report, 1932/33*.

(1934), *4th Annual Report, 1933/34*.

(2007), 'Triennial Central Bank Survey: foreign exchange and derivatives market activity in 2007', December.

(2008), 'Guidelines to the international locational banking statistics', available at www.bis.org/statistics/locbankstatsguide.htm (last accessed 24 June 2012).

(2009), *79th Annual Report, 2008/09*.

G10 (1964), 'Short-term credit arrangements among central banks and monetary authorities', 22 January 1964, BISA, 7.18(12), Papers Michael Dealtry, box DEA14, f02:G10.

International banking statistics, available at www.bis.org/statistics/bankstats.htm (last accessed 24 June 2012).

International securities statistics, available at www.bis.org/statistics/secstats.htm (last accessed 24 June 2012).

Bank for International Settlements Markets Committee (2008), 'Monetary policy frameworks and central bank market operations', MC compendium, available at www.bis.org/publ/mktc02.htm (last accessed 24 June 2012).

Bank of England (2007), 'Liquidity support facility for Northern Rock plc – Tripartite statement by HM Treasury, Bank of England and Financial Services Authority', 14 September, available at www.bankofengland.co.uk/publications/news/2007/090.htm (last accessed 24 June 2012).

(2009), 'Additional information provided to the Treasury Committee by the Bank of England: Tuesday 24 November 2009', available at www.bankofengland.co.uk/publications/other/treasurycommittee/financial-stability/ela091124.pdf (last accessed 24 June 2012).

(2011), Minutes of the Monetary Policy Committee, October 2011, available at www.bankofengland.co.uk/publications/minutes/mpc/pdf/2011/mpc1110.pdf (last accessed 24 June 2012).

Bank of Japan (2009), 'Financial markets report', Reports and Research Papers, March, available at www.boj.or.jp/en/type/ronbun/mkr/data/mkr0903.pdf (last accessed 24 June 2012).

Bank of Korea (2009a), *Annual Report 2008*, available at http://eng.bok.or.kr/broadcast.action?menuNaviId=740 (last accessed 24 June 2012).

(2009b), 'Policy response to the financial turmoil', available at http://eng.bok.or.kr/broadcast.action?menuNaviId=1915 (last accessed 24 June 2012).

(2009c), *Financial Stability Report*, April, available at http://eng.bok.or.kr/broadcast.action?menuNaviId=737 (last accessed 24 June 2012).

Basel Committee on Banking Supervision (2008), 'Principles for sound liquidity risk management and supervision', available at www.bis.org/publ/bcbs138.htm (last accessed 24 June 2012).

(2010a), 'Basel III: a global regulatory framework for more resilient banks and banking systems', available at www.bis.org/publ/bcbs189_dec2010.htm (last accessed 24 June 2012).

(2010b), 'Basel III: international framework for liquidity risk measurement, standards and monitoring', available at www.bis.org/publ/bcbs188.htm (last accessed 24 June 2012).

Battilossi, S. (2009), 'The eurodollar revolution in financial technology: deregulation, innovation and structural change in Western banking in the 1960s–70s', Universidad Carlos III de Madrid Working Papers in Economic History WP 09–10.

Bernanke, B. (2000), *Essays on the Great Depression*, Princeton University Press.

(2005), 'The global savings glut and the US current account deficit', Sandridge Lecture, Virginia Association of Economics.

(2009a), 'Reflections on a year of crisis', speech at the Brookings Institution's conference on 'A year of turmoil', Washington, DC, 15 September 2009.

(2009b), 'The Federal Reserve's balance sheet: an update', speech at the Federal Reserve Board's conference on 'Key developments in monetary policy', Washington, DC, 8 October 2009.

Bernanke, B. and H. James (1991), 'The gold standard, deflation and financial crisis in the Great Depression: an international comparison', reprinted in Bernanke (2000).

Bernholz, P. (2007), 'From 1945 to 1982: the transition from inward exchange controls to money supply management under floating exchange rates', in *The Swiss National Bank 1907–2007*, Neue Zürcher Zeitung Publishing, Zurich, pp. 109–199.

Bernstein, N. (2010), 'Outside the euro in the financial crisis – the Danish experience', speech at Copenhagen Business School, 22 March, available at www.nationalbanken.dk/dnuk/pressroom.nsf/side/Governor_Nils_Bernstein_Outside_the_euro_in_the_financial_crisis_-_the_Danish_experience!OpenDocument (last accessed 24 June 2012).

Bertaut, C. and L. Pounder (2009), 'The financial crisis and US cross-border financial flows', *Federal Reserve Bulletin*, vol. 95; available at www.federalreserve.gov/pubs/bulletin/2009/pdf/Crossborder09.pdf (last accessed 24 June 2012).

Bertuch-Samuels, A. and P. Ramlogan (2007), 'The euro: ever more global', *Finance and Development*, March, vol. 44 no. 1.

Billings, M. and F. Capie (2010), 'Financial crisis, contagion and the British financial system between the wars', manuscript.

Blinder, A. (1999), *Central Banking in Theory and Practice*, MIT Press, Cambridge, MA.

Board of Governors of the Federal Reserve System (1976), *Banking and Monetary Statistics 1914–1941*, available at http://fraser.stlouisfed.org/publications/bms/ (last accessed 24 June 2012).

(2005) *The Federal Reserve System: Purposes and Functions*, available at www.federalreserve.gov/pf/pf.htm (last accessed 4 August 2012).

Bordo, M. and B. Eichengreen (2001), 'The rise and fall of a barbarous relic: the role of gold in the international monetary system', in G. Calvo, R. Dornbusch and M. Obstfeld (eds), *Money, Capital Mobility and Trade: Essays in Honor of Robert A. Mundell*, MIT Press, Cambridge, MA.

Bordo, M., E. Choudhri and A. Schwartz (2002), 'Was expansionary monetary policy feasible during the Great Contraction? An examination of the gold standard constraint', *Explorations in Economic History*, vol. 39, pp. 1–28.

Borio, C. and G. Toniolo (2006), 'One hundred and thirty years of central bank cooperation: a BIS perspective', BIS Working Paper No. 197, February 2006.

Brown, W. A., Jr. (1940), *The International Gold Standard Reinterpreted 1914–1934*, National Bureau of Economic Research, New York.

Bryant, R., D. Henderson and T. Becker (2012), *Maintaining Financial Stability in an Open Economy: Sweden in the Global Crisis and Beyond*, SNS Förlag, available at www.sns.se/sites/default/files/maintaining_financial_stability_2012.pdf (last accessed 24 June 2012).

Calomiris, C. W. (2010), 'The political lessons of depression-era banking reform', *Oxford Review of Economic Policy*, vol. 26 no. 3, pp. 540–560.

Capie, F. (1998), 'Can there be an international lender-of-last-resort?', *International Finance*, vol. 1 no. 2, pp. 311–525.

Cecchetti, S. and R. Moessner (2008), 'Commodity prices and inflation dynamics', BIS *Quarterly Review*, December, pp. 55–66, available at www.bis.org/publ/qtrpdf/r_qt0812f.pdf (last accessed 24 June 2012).

Cecchetti, S., I. Fender and P. McGuire (2010), 'Toward a global risk map', BIS Working Paper No. 309.

Central Bank of Iceland statement, 10 October 2008, 'Currency swap agreements and attempts to reinforce the foreign exchange reserves', available at www.sedlabanki.is/?PageID=287&NewsID=1890 (last accessed 24 June 2012).

Cetorelli, N. and L. Goldberg (2009), 'Banking globalization and monetary transmission', Federal Reserve Bank of New York Staff Report No. 333, available at http://newyorkfed.org/research/staff_reports/sr333.pdf (last accessed 24 June 2012).

Clapham, J. (1966), *The Bank of England: Money, Power and Influence, 1694–1914*, Vol. II, Cambridge University Press.

Committee (Macmillan Committee) on Finance and Industry (1931), *Report*, Her Majesty's Stationery Office, Cmnd 3897.

Committee on the Global Financial System (CGFS, 2008), 'Central bank operations in response to the financial turmoil', CGFS Papers No. 31, available at www.bis.org/publ/cgfs31.htm (last accessed 24 June 2012).

(CGFS, 2010a), 'The functioning and resilience of cross-border funding markets', CGFS Papers No. 37, available at www.bis.org/publ/cgfs37.pdf?noframes=1 (last accessed 24 June 2012).

(CGFS, 2010b), 'Funding patterns and liquidity management of internationally active banks', CGFS Papers No. 39, available at www.bis.org/publ/cgfs39.htm (last accessed 24 June 2012).

(CGFS, 2011), 'Global liquidity – concept, measurement and policy implications', CGFS Papers No. 45, available at www.bis.org/publ/cgfs45.htm (last accessed 24 June 2012).

Committee on Payment and Settlement Systems (CPSS, 2006), 'Cross-border collateral arrangements', January.

Conolly, F. (1936), 'International short-term indebtedness', memorandum (BIS), November, Bank of England Archive BE OV50/10.

Coombs, C. (1976), *The Arena of International Finance*, Wiley, New York.

Copeland, A., A. Martin and M. Walker (2010), 'The tri-party repo market before the 2010 reforms', Federal Reserve Bank of New York Staff Report No. 477, available at http://data.newyorkfed.org/research/staff_reports/sr477.pdf (last accessed 24 June 2012).

Cottrell, P. L. (1995), 'The Bank in its international setting', in R. Roberts and D. Kynaston (eds), *The Bank of England: Money, Power and Influence, 1694–1994*, Oxford University Press.

Danmarks Nationalbank (2008), *Monetary Review*, 3rd quarter 2008.

(2009a), *Monetary Review*, 4th quarter 2008.

(2009b), *Monetary Review*, 3rd quarter 2009.

Darling, A. (2011), *Back from the Brink*, Atlantic Books, London.

Davies, H. (2010), *The Financial Crisis: Who is to Blame?*, Polity Press, Cambridge.

Davies, H. and D. Green (2010), *Banking on the Future*, Princeton University Press.

Deutsche Bundesbank (1976), *Deutsches Geld- und Bankwesen in Zahlen 1876–1975*, Verlag Fritz Knapp GmbH, Frankfurt am Main.

Diaper, S. (1986), 'Merchant banking in the inter-war period: the case of Kleinwort, Sons & Co.', *Business History*, vol. 28 no. 4, pp. 55–76.

Duisenberg, W. F. (1998), Statement to the European Banking Congress, Frankfurt am Main, 20 November, available at www.ecb.int/press/key/date/1998/html/sp981120.en.html (last accessed 24 June 2012).

Eichengreen, B. (1992), *Golden Fetters: The Gold Standard and the Great Depression 1919–1939*, Oxford University Press.

(2008), *Globalising Capital: A History of the International Monetary System*, second edition, Princeton University Press.

Ejerskov, S. (2009), 'Money market segmentation and bank retail rates during the financial crisis', Danmarks Nationalbank *Monetary Review*, first quarter 2009, pp. 45–54.

European Central Bank (2008), 'The international role of the euro', July 2008, available at www.ecb.int/pub/pdf/other/euro-international-role200807en.pdf (last accessed 24 June 2012).

(2009a), *Annual Report 2008*, available at www.ecb.int/pub/pdf/annrep/ar2008en.pdf (last accessed 24 June 2012).

(2009b), *Money Market Study 2008*, available at www.ecb.int/pub/pdf/other/euromoneymarketstudy200902en.pdf (last accessed 24 June 2012).

Federal Open Market Committee (FOMC, 1962), Transcript of the FOMC meeting of 13 February, available at www.federalreserve.gov/monetary-policy/files/fomchistmin19620213.pdf (last accessed 24 June 2012).

(FOMC, 1998), Minutes of the Federal Open Market Committee meeting of 17 November 1998, available at www.federalreserve.gov/fomc/minutes/19981117.htm (last accessed 3 August 2012).

(FOMC, 2007), Minutes of conference call on 6 December 2007, available at www.federalreserve.gov/monetarypolicy/files/fomcminutes20071211.pdf (last accessed 24 June 2012).

(FOMC, 2008a), Minutes of the Federal Open Market Committee meeting of 16 September 2008, available at www.federalreserve.gov/monetary-policy/files/fomcminutes20080916.pdf (last accessed 24 June 2012).

(FOMC, 2008b), Minutes of the Federal Open Market Committee meeting of 28–29 October 2008, available at www.federalreserve.gov/monetary-policy/files/fomcminutes20081029.pdf (last accessed 24 June 2012).

(FOMC, 2011), Minutes of the Federal Open Market Committee meeting of 20–21 September 2011, available at www.federalreserve.gov/newsevents/press/monetary/fomcminutes20110921.pdf (last accessed 24 June 2012).

Federal Reserve Bank of New York (2008), 'Treasury and Federal Reserve Foreign Exchange Operations: October-December 2007', available at www.newyorkfed.org/newsevents/news/markets/2008/fxq407.pdf (last accessed 4 August 2012).

Fender, I. and J. Gyntelberg (2008), 'Overview: global financial crisis spurs unprecedented policy action', BIS *Quarterly Review*, December, pp. 1–24, available at www.bis.org/publ/qtrpdf/r_qt0812a.pdf (last accessed 24 June 2012).

Financial Crisis Inquiry Commission (FCIC, 2011a), *Report*, US Government Printing Office, available at http://fcic.law.stanford.edu/report (last accessed 24 June 2012).

(FCIC, 2011b), Transcript of interview with Ben Bernanke, Chairman of the Federal Reserve, 17 November 2009, available at http://fcic.law.stanford.edu/resource/interviews (last accessed 24 June 2012).

Financial Services Authority (2009), 'Strengthening liquidity standards', Policy Statement 09/16, October.

Forbes, N. (1987), 'London banks, the German standstill agreements, and "economic appeasement" in the 1930s', *Economic History Review*, 2nd series, vol. XL no. 4.

Friedman, M. and A. Schwartz (1963), *A Monetary History of the United States 1867–1960*, Princeton University Press for the National Bureau of Economic Research.

Galati, G. and R. Moessner (2011), 'Macroprudential policy – a literature review', BIS Working Paper No. 337.

Galati, G. and P. Wooldridge (2006), 'The euro as a reserve currency: a challenge to the pre-eminence of the US dollar?', BIS Working Paper No. 218.

George, E. A. J. (1993), 'The pursuit of financial stability', The Second Bank of England LSE lecture, London School of Economics, 18 November 1993.

Gil Aguado, I. (2001), 'The Creditanstalt crisis of 1931 and the failure of the Austro-German customs union project', *Historical Journal*, vol. 44 no. 1, pp. 199–221.

Goodfriend, M. (2011), 'Central banking in the credit turmoil: an assessment of Federal Reserve practice', *Journal of Monetary Economics*, vol. 58 issue 1, pp. 1–12.

Goodhart, C. (2011), *The Basel Committee on Banking Supervision – A History of the Early Years 1974–1997*, Cambridge University Press.

Gorton, G. (2010), *Slapped by the Invisible Hand: The Panic of 2007*, Oxford University Press.

Gorton, G. and A. Metrick (2009), 'Securitized banking and the run on repo', NBER Working Paper No. 15223.

Haldane, A. (2011), 'Risk off', speech, 18 August 2011, available at www.bankofengland.co.uk/publications/speeches/2011/speech513.pdf (last accessed 24 June 2012).

Hawtrey, R. (1947), *The Gold Standard in Theory and Practice*, fifth edition, Longmans, London.

HM Treasury (2011), *Debt and Reserves Management Report 2011–12*, HMSO, available at www.dmo.gov.uk/documentview.aspx?docname=remit/drmr1112.pdf&page=Remit/full_details (last accessed 24 June 2012).

Hong Kong Monetary Authority (2008), *Half-yearly Monetary and Financial Stability Report*, December.

    (2009), *Half-yearly Monetary and Financial Stability Report*, June.

International Monetary Fund (2002), *World Economic Outlook*, September, available at www.imf.org/external/pubs/ft/weo/2002/02/ (last accessed 24 June 2012).

    (2007), *Global Financial Stability Report*, October, available at www.imf.org/External/Pubs/FT/GFSR/2007/02/index.htm (last accessed 24 June 2012).

    (2009), 'Mexico: staff report for the 2008 article IV consultation', available at www.imf.org/external/pubs/ft/scr/2009/cr0953.pdf (last accessed 24 June 2012).

    (2010a), *Global Financial Stability Report*, April, available at www.imf.org/external/pubs/ft/gfsr/2010/01/index.htm (last accessed 24 June 2012).

(2010b), *Global Financial Stability Report*, October, available at www. imf.org/External/Pubs/FT/GFSR/2010/02/index.htm (last accessed 24 June 2012).

(2010c), *Annual Report 2010*, available at www.imf.org/external/pubs/ft/ ar/2010/eng/pdf/a2.pdf (last accessed 24 June 2012).

(2011), 'Review of the flexible credit line and precautionary credit line', available at www.imf.org/external/np/pp/eng/2011/110111.pdf (last accessed 24 June 2012).

Irwin, D. (2010), 'Did France cause the Great Depression?', NBER Working Paper No. 16350.

James, H. (1992), 'Financial flows across frontiers during the interwar depression', *Economic History Review*, vol. XLV no. 3, pp. 594–613.

(1996), *International Monetary Co-operation since Bretton Woods*, International Monetary Fund and Oxford University Press, New York and Oxford.

(2001), *The End of Globalization*, Harvard University Press, Cambridge, MA.

(2009), *The Creation and Destruction of Value*, Harvard University Press, Cambridge, MA.

Jara, A., R. Moreno and C. E. Tovar (2009), 'The global crisis and Latin America: financial impact and policy responses', BIS *Quarterly Review*, June, pp. 53–68, available at www.bis.org/publ/qtrpdf/r_qt0906f.pdf (last accessed 24 June 2012).

Johnson, H. G. (1958), 'Towards a general theory of the balance of payments', in *International Trade and Economic Growth*, George Allen and Unwin, London, pp. 153–168.

Kawai, M. (2007), 'Evolving economic architecture in East Asia', *Kyoto Economic Review*, vol. 76 no. 1, pp. 9–52.

Kim, C. (2010), 'Time for a new central banking paradigm', lecture to 2010 Annual Bank of Korea International Conference.

Kindleberger, C. (1987), *The World in Depression 1929–1939*, Pelican Books, Harmondsworth.

King, M. A. (2007), 'Turmoil in financial markets: what can central banks do?', paper submitted to the House of Commons Treasury Committee, 12 September 2007, available at www.bankofengland.co.uk/publications/ other/treasurycommittee/other/paper070912.pdf (last accessed 24 June 2012).

Kohn, D. (2009), 'International perspective on the crisis and response', speech at the Federal Reserve Bank of Boston 54th Economic conference, Chatham, MA, 23 October 2009.

Korea Ministry of Strategy and Finance (2008), 'Proposed measures to overcome uncertainties in the international financial markets', press release, 21 October 2008.

(2009), 'FAQs on the Korean economy', press release, 28 January 2009.

Maddison, A. (2010), *Statistics on World Population, GDP and Per Capita GDP, 1–2008 AD*, available at www.ggdc.net/MADDISON/oriindex. htm (last accessed 24 June 2012).

Magyar Nemzeti Bank (2009), *Report on Financial Stability*, April, available at http://english.mnb.hu/Root/ENMNB//Kiadvanyok/mnben_ stabil (last accessed 24 June 2012).

Mak, I. and J. Pales (2009), 'The role of the FX swap market in the Hungarian financial system', *MNB Bulletin*, May, pp. 24–34.

McCauley, R. N. and J.-F. Rigaudy (2011), 'Managing foreign exchange reserves in the crisis and after', in Bank for International Settlements, *Portfolio and Risk Management for Central Banks and Sovereign Wealth Funds*, BIS Papers No. 48.

McGuire, P. and N. Tarashev (2007), 'International banking with the euro', BIS *Quarterly Review*, December, pp. 47–61, available at www.bis.org/ publ/qtrpdf/r_qt0712f.pdf (last accessed 24 June 2012).

McGuire, P. and G. von Peter (2008), 'International banking amidst the turmoil', BIS *Quarterly Review*, June, available at www.bis.org/publ/ qtrpdf/r_qt0806e.pdf (last accessed 24 June 2012).

(2009a), 'The US dollar shortage in global banking', BIS *Quarterly Review*, March, pp. 47–63, available at www.bis.org/publ/qtrpdf/r_qt0903f.pdf (last accessed 24 June 2012).

(2009b), 'The US dollar shortage in global banking and the international policy response', BIS Working Paper No. 291.

Meade, J. E. (1951), *The Balance of Payments*, Oxford University Press, issued under the auspices of the Royal Institute of International Affairs.

Meltzer, A. (2003), *A History of the Federal Reserve*, Vol. I, 1913–1951, University of Chicago Press.

Mihaljek, D. (2010), 'The spread of the financial crisis to central and eastern Europe: evidence from the BIS data', in R. Matousek (ed.), *Banking and Financial Markets in Central and Eastern Europe after 20 Years of Transition*, Palgrave Macmillan, London.

Moessner, R. and W. Allen (2010), 'Options for meeting the demand for international liquidity during financial crises', BIS *Quarterly Review*, September, pp. 51–61, available at www.bis.org/publ/qtrpdf/r_qt1009g. pdf (last accessed 24 June 2012).

(2011), 'Banking crises and the international monetary system in the Great Depression and now', *Financial History Review*, vol. 18 no. 1, pp. 1–20.

Moghadam, R. (2010), 'Reserve accumulation and international monetary stability', International Monetary Fund, available at www.imf.org/ external/np/pp/eng/2010/041310.pdf (last accessed 24 June 2012).

Morgan Stanley (2008, 2009), Annual and Quarterly Reports Pursuant to Section 13 or 15(d) of the Securities Exchange Act of 1934, available at www.morganstanley.com/about/ir/sec_filings.html (last accessed 24 June 2012).

Mosser, A. and A. Teichova (1991), 'Investment behaviour of industrial joint-stock companies and industrial shareholding by the Österreichische Credit-Anstalt: inducement or obstacle to renewal and change in industry in interwar Austria', in H. James, H. Lindgren and A. Teichova (eds), *The Role of Banks in the Interwar Economy*, Cambridge University Press.

Mouré, K. (1991), *Managing the Franc Poincaré: Economic Understanding and Political Constraint in French Monetary Policy 1928–1936*, Cambridge University Press.

Narodowy Bank Polski (2008), *Financial Stability Report*, October, available at www.nbp.pl/en/SystemFinansowy/Financial_Stability_October2008. pdf (last accessed 4 August 2012).

    (2009a), *Monetary Policy Council Report on Monetary Policy Implementation in 2008*, Warsaw, May 2009, available at www.nbp.pl/homen.aspx?f=/en/publikacje/o_polityce_pienieznej/wykonanie.html (last accessed 24 June 2012).

    (2009b), *Financial Stability Report*, June, available at www.nbp.pl/homen. aspx?f=/en/systemfinansowy/stabilnosc.html (last accessed 24 June 2012).

Norges Bank (2008) *Financial Stability* 2/08.

Padoa-Schioppa, T. (2006), 'Interdependence and cooperation: an endangered pair?' in 'Past and future of central bank cooperation: policy panel discussion', BIS Paper No. 27, February 2006.

Panetta, F., T. Faeh, G. Grande *et al.* (2009), 'An assessment of financial sector rescue programmes', BIS Paper No. 48.

Paulson, H. (2010), *On the Brink*, Headline Publishing Group, London.

Pihlmann, J. and H. van der Hoorn (2010), 'Procyclicality in central bank reserve management: evidence from the crisis', IMF Working Paper 10/150.

Pozsar, Z., T. Adrian, A. Ashcraft and H. Boesky (2010) 'Shadow banking', Federal Reserve Bank of New York Staff Report No. 458, available at www.newyorkfed.org/research/staff_reports/sr458.html (last accessed 24 June 2012).

Prasad, E. and I. Sorkin (2009), 'Sky's the limit? National and global implications of China's reserve accumulation', Brookings Institution, available at www.brookings.edu/articles/2009/0721_chinas_reserve_prasad. aspx (last accessed 24 June 2012).

Reinhart, C. and K. Rogoff (2009), *This Time is Different: Eight Centuries of Financial Folly*, Princeton University Press.

Reserve Bank of Australia (2008), Statement on Monetary Policy, reprinted in Reserve Bank of Australia *Bulletin*, November.

    (2009), *Financial Stability Review*, March, available at www.rba.gov.au/publications/fsr/2009/mar/html/contents.html (last accessed 24 June 2012).

Ritschl, A. (2009), 'War 2008 das neue 1931?', *Aus Politik und Zeitgeschichte*, 20/2009, available at www.bpb.de/files/PQYS6J.pdf (last accessed 24 June 2012).

Roberts, R. (1992), *Schroders: Bankers and Merchants*, Macmillan, Basingstoke.

———— (1995), 'The Bank and the City' in R. Roberts and D. Kynaston (eds), *The Bank of England: Money, Power and Influence, 1694–1994*, Oxford University Press.

Roth, J.-P. (2009), 'Geldpolitik ohne Grenzen. Vom Kampf gegen die Internationalisierung des Frankens zur Internationalisierung der Geldpolitik', speech at Schweizerisches Institut für Auslandsforschung, Zürich, 6 May 2009.

Sawyer, D. (2004), 'Continuous linked settlement (CLS) and foreign exchange settlement risk', Bank of England *Financial Stability Review* (December), pp. 86–92.

Sayers, R. S. (1976), *The Bank of England 1891–1944*, 2 volumes plus appendices, Cambridge University Press.

Sheppard, D. K. (1971), *The Growth and Role of UK Financial Institutions 1880–1962*, Methuen, London.

Shiller, R. (2005), *Irrational Exuberance*, second edition, Princeton University Press.

Shin, H. S. (2010), *Risk and Liquidity*, Oxford University Press.

Singh, M. and J. Aitken (2009), 'Deleveraging after Lehman – evidence from reduced rehypothecation', IMF Working Paper No. 09/42.

Stella, P. (2009), 'The Federal Reserve system balance sheet – what happened and why it matters', IMF, unpublished.

Stone, M., W. Walker and Y. Yasui (2009), 'From Lombard Street to Avenida Paulista: foreign exchange liquidity easing in Brazil in response to the global shock of 2008–09', IMF Working Paper No. 09/259.

Swiss National Bank (2009), 'Monetary policy report', *Quarterly Bulletin* 3/2009, pp. 6–43.

Tallman, E. and E. Wicker (2010), 'Banking and financial crises in United States history: what guidance can history offer policymakers?', Federal Reserve Bank of Cleveland Working Paper No. 10–09.

Toniolo, G. (2005), *Central Bank Cooperation at the Bank for International Settlements, 1930–1973*, Cambridge University Press.

Truptil, R. J. (1936), *British Banks and the London Money Market*, Jonathan Cape, London.

Turner, P. (2010), 'Central banks, liquidity and the banking crisis', in S. Griffith-Jones, J. A. Ocampo and J. Stiglitz (eds), *Time for a Visible Hand: Lessons from the 2008 World Financial Crisis*, Oxford University Press.

(2011), 'Fiscal dominance and the long-term interest rate', London School of Economics Financial Markets Group Special Paper No. 199, available at www2.lse.ac.uk/fmg/workingPapers/specialPapers/PDF/SP199.pdf (last accessed 24 June 2012).

United Kingdom (1951), *Reserves and Liabilities 1931 to 1945*, Cmd. 8354, HMSO, London.

United Nations (2010), Department of Economic and Social Affairs, 'World Population Prospects, the 2010 revision', available at http://esa.un.org/unpd/wpp/Excel-Data/population.htm (last accessed 24 June 2012).

Verbeek, M. (2004), *A Guide to Modern Econometrics*, Wiley, Chichester.

Volcker, P. (1985), Chairman of the Board of Governors of the Federal Reserve System, Statement before the Sub Committee on Domestic Monetary Policy of the Committee on Banking, Finance and Urban Affairs, US House of Representatives, 12 December. Reprinted in *Federal Reserve Bulletin*, vol. 72 no. 2.

Warburton, C. (1952), 'Monetary difficulties and the structure of the monetary system', *Journal of Finance*, vol. VII no. 4, December.

Wells, D. (2004), *The Federal Reserve System: A History*, McFarland & Company, Jefferson, NC.

Williams, D. (1963), 'The 1931 crisis', *Yorkshire Bulletin of Economic and Social Research*, vol. 15 no. 2.

Wood, J. H. (2009), 'The Great Deflation of 1929–33 (almost) had to happen', available at http://users.wfu.edu/jw/The%20Great%20Deflation%20of%201929–33%20(almost)%20had%20to%20happen.doc (last accessed 24 June 2012).

Yehoue, E. (2009), 'Emerging economy responses to the global financial crisis of 2007–09: an empirical analysis of the liquidity easing measures', IMF Working Paper No. 09/265.

Zhou, X. (2009), 'Reform the international monetary system', 23 March 2009, speech available at www.pbc.gov.cn/publish/english/956/2009/20091229104425550619706/20091229104425550619706_.html (last accessed 24 June 2012).

Index

Latvia, *see also* Bank of Latvia
  IMF standby arrangement, 101
  statement of support by ECB
    President Trichet, 101
  swap lines received, 92, 101, 140,
    142
Lebanon
  foreign exchange reserves, 209
Lehman Brothers
  consequences of bankruptcy, 4–7,
    12–31, 32–40, 53–67, 77, 78–82,
    89–90, 115–117, 125, 126, 130,
    144, 148, 149, 195
lender of last resort, 7, 11, 13, 174,
    195, 202
liability management, 192, 213
Libya
  foreign exchange reserves, 199
liquid assets
  and macroeconomic policy, 11, 214
  central banks under the gold stand-
    ard, 184
  demand for liquid assets in and after
    2007, 5, 11, 20, 212, 213–214,
    219
  in balance sheets of shadow banks,
    15, 16, 17
  in foreign exchange reserves, 210,
    211
  London clearing banks' liquid assets
    in 1931, 162
  Morgan Stanley, 24
  non-financial companies, 213
  of commercial banks, 213, 214
  official assistance to banks in acquir-
    ing liquid assets, 80
  regulation of bank liquidity, 201,
    213–214
  standstill bills treated as liquid assets
    in London in 1930s, 161
liquidity assurance, 201, 202–203
  bilateral techniques, 205–207
  multilateral techniques, 204–205,
    210–211
  unilateral actions, 207–211
Lithuania, 92
logit, ix, 106, 107

macro-prudential policy, 214–216
Magyar Nemzeti Bank

changes in assets in 1931, 180
ECB swap line, 97, 150, 152, 153
foreign exchange reserves, 152
foreign-currency swaps with commercial banks, 150, 151, 152
gold and foreign exchange reserves
  in 1931, 163
imposition of controls on outflows
  in 1931, 158
interest rates in 1930–31, 176
interest rates in 2008, 78
SNB swap line, 65, 93, 98, 100, 120,
  150, 152, 153, 156
Malaysia, 95, *see also* Bank Negara
  Malaysia
  foreign exchange reserves, 199, 209
merchant banks, 159, 160, 161, 162,
  189
Merrill Lynch, 4
  effects of Lehman failure, 21
Mexico, *see also* Banco de Mexico
  change in bank deposits in 2008–09,
    47
  flows of funds and swap drawings in
    2008, 129, 148–149
  foreign exchange reserves, 148, 199,
    209
  IMF flexible credit line, 205
  statistical sources, 223
Monetary Authority of Singapore
  changes in assets in 2008–09, 79
  Fed swap line, 90, 97, 101, 114, 137
monetary policy
  concept, 69, 214–216
  coordination, 72–73
  credit easing and quantitative easing,
    74
  demarcation with fiscal policy and
    debt management, 74–75
  Denmark, 144
  function of Bank of England, 69
  gold standard, 185, 191
  objectives, 68, 72, 74
  pegged exchange rates and falling
    reserves, 104
  relationship with financial stability,
    69
  strategies, 68
  Switzerland, 92, 122
  United States in 1930s, 183

SNB swaps with NBP, 153, 154, 156
swap network, 87, 92, 98, 153
swaps against dollars in 1959, 83
use outside home territory, 35, 126
Swiss National Bank
    acceptance of foreign currency
        collateral located outside home
        territory, 207
    attitude to internationalisation of
        the franc, 126
    balance sheet in 1931, 166
    banknote issue in 1931, 165
    changes in assets in 1931, 180
    changes in assets in 2008–09,
        79
    dollar loans to commercial banks,
        ix, 89, 130, 133, 136
    Fed swap line, 89, 90, 96, 114, 115,
        130, 132, 195
    foreign exchange reserves, 133, 136,
        199, 209, 210
    gold and foreign exchange reserves
        in 1931, 162, 163, 188
    interest rates in 1930–31, 176
    interest rates in 2008, 42, 78
    monetary policy, 92, 93
    provision of swap lines, 65, 80, 90,
        92, 97, 98, 100, 119, 120, 122,
        126, 131, 150, 151, 152, 153,
        154, 156, 157
    purchases of foreign currency, 93,
        123, 126, 210
    statistics, 220
    swap lines in 1950s and 1960s, 83,
        84
    swaps with normal counterparties,
        120
Switzerland, 38, 79, 80, 108, *see also*
        Swiss franc, Swiss National Bank
    commercial banks in 1931, 166
    deposit insurance in 2008,
        187
    fall in bank deposits in 2008–09, 45,
        46, 47
    Fed swap line, 90
    flows of funds and swap drawings in
        2008, 33, 128, 129, 130, 132
    flows of funds in second half of
        2008, 6
    foreign banks, 115

foreign exchange reserves, 132, 133,
    136, 199, 209, 210
gold and foreign exchange reserves
    in 1931, 162, 179, 183, 188
statistical sources, 220

Taiwan, 200
    foreign exchange reserves, 199
TED spread, 14
Thailand, 200
    foreign exchange reserves, 199,
        209
time zones, 91, 107, 111, 118, 135,
    218
Trichet, Jean-Claude, Governor of the
    Banque de France 1993–2003,
    President of the European Central
    Bank, 2003–2011, 101
tri-party repo, 21, 26
    clearing banks, 21
Turkey, 92
    liquidity conditions in 2008, 89

UK Financial Services Authority, 2, 71,
    202
US commercial banks
    acquisition of assets in 2008, 20
    balance sheets after Lehman failure,
        19
    cash flow in 2008, 20
    deposits in 2008, 18
    Fed financing of purchases of
        commercial paper, 5
    foreign bank affiliates in US, 30
    liquidity guarantees, 12, 18
    net debt to foreign offices, 18, 30,
        31, 115
US dollar, ix, 105, 106, 108, 109
    acceptability of dollar assets by
        foreign central banks as collateral,
        207
    carry trades, 35
    covered interest differentials,
        130
    cross-currency basis swap spreads,
        130
    emergency liquidity provision after
        9/11, 86
    exchange rates, 126
    gold convertibility, 84

CPSIA information can be obtained at www.ICGtesting.com
Printed in the USA
BVOW02s0154010915

415548BV00013B/54/P

9 781107 420328